Table of Contents

The instruction and activities in this book are organized around the Common Core State Standards for English and Language Arts.

Reading Standards for Literature   1

Reading Standards for Informational Texts   83

PEARSON
COMMON CORE
Literature

Common Core
Companion Workbook

GRADE 9

PEARSON

UPPER SADDLE RIVER, NEW JERSEY • BOSTON, MASSACHUSETTS
CHANDLER, ARIZONA • GLENVIEW, ILLINOIS

ISBN-13: 978-0-13-327110-2
ISBN-10:   0-13-327110-2
2 3 4 5 6 7 8 9 10 V039 17 16 15 14 13

Writing Standards   178

Writing 1: Write arguments to support claims in an analysis of substantive topics or texts, using valid reasoning and relevant and sufficient evidence.

a) Introduce precise claim(s), distinguish the claim(s) from alternate or opposing claims, and create an organization that establishes clear relationships among claim(s), counterclaims, reasons, and evidence.

b) Develop claim(s) and counterclaims fairly, supplying evidence for each while pointing out the strengths and limitations of both in a manner that anticipates the audience's knowledge level and concerns.

c) Use words, phrases, and clauses to link the major sections of the text, create cohesion, and clarify the relationships between claim(s) and reasons, between reasons and evidence, and between claim(s) and counterclaims.

d) Establish and maintain a formal style and objective tone while attending to the norms and conventions of the discipline in which they are writing.

e) Provide a concluding statement or section that follows from and supports the argument presented.

Writing 2: Write informative/explanatory texts to examine and convey complex ideas, concepts, and information clearly and accurately through the effective selection, organization, and analysis of content.

a) Introduce a topic; organize complex ideas, concepts, and information to make important connections and distinctions; include formatting (e.g., headings), graphics (e.g., figures, tables), and multimedia when useful to aiding comprehension.

b) Develop the topic with well-chosen, relevant, and sufficient facts, extended definitions, concrete details, quotations, or other information and examples appropriate to the audience's knowledge of the topic.

c) Use appropriate and varied transitions to link the major sections of the text, create cohesion, and clarify the relationships among complex ideas and concepts.• Establish and maintain a formal style.

d) Use precise language and domain-specific vocabulary to manage the complexity of the topic.

e) Establish and maintain a formal style and objective tone while attending to the norms and conventions of the discipline in which they are writing.

f) Provide a concluding statement or section that follows from and supports the information or explanation presented (e.g., articulating implications or the significance of the topic).

Writing 3: Write narratives to develop real or imagined experiences or events using effective technique, well-chosen details, and well-structured event sequences.

a) Engage and orient the reader by setting out a problem, situation, or observation, establishing one or multiple point(s) of view, and introducing a narrator and/or characters; create a smooth progression of experiences or events.

b) Use narrative techniques, such as dialogue, pacing, description, reflection, and multiple plot lines, to develop experiences, events, and/or characters.

c) Use a variety of techniques to sequence events so that they build on one another to create a coherent whole.

d) Use precise words and phrases, telling details, and sensory language to convey a vivid picture of the experiences, events, setting, and/or characters.

e) Provide a conclusion that follows from and reflects on what is experienced, observed, or resolved over the course of the narrative.

Writing 4: Produce clear and coherent writing in which the development, organization, and style are appropriate to task, purpose, and audience.

Writing 5: Develop and strengthen writing as needed by planning, revising, editing, rewriting, or trying a new approach, focusing on addressing what is most significant for a specific purpose and audience.

Writing 6: Use technology, including the Internet, to produce, publish, and update individual or shared writing products, taking advantage of technology's capacity to link to other information and to display information flexibly and dynamically.

Writing 7: Conduct short as well as more sustained research projects to answer a question (including a self-generated question) or solve a problem; narrow or broaden the inquiry when appropriate; synthesize multiple sources on the subject, demonstrating understanding of the subject under investigation.

Writing 8: Gather relevant information from multiple authoritative print and digital sources, using advanced searches effectively; assess the usefulness of each source in answering the research question; integrate information into the text selectively to maintain the flow of ideas, avoiding plagiarism and following a standard format for citation.

Writing 9: Draw evidence from literary or informational texts to support analysis, reflection, and research.

    a) Apply grades 9–10 Reading standards to literature (e.g., "Analyze how an author draws on and transforms source material in a specific work [e.g., how Shakespeare treats a theme or topic from Ovid or the Bible or how a later author draws on a play by Shakespeare]").

    b) Apply grades 9–10 Reading standards to literary nonfiction (e.g., "Delineate and evaluate the argument and specific claims in a text, assessing whether the reasoning is valid and the evidence is relevant and sufficient; identify false statements and fallacious reasoning").

Writing 10: Write routinely over extended time frames (time for research, reflection, and revision) and shorter time frames (a single sitting or a day or two) for a range of tasks, purposes, and audiences.

Speaking and Listening Standards   273

Speaking and Listening 1: Initiate and participate effectively in a range of collaborative discussions (one-on-one, in groups, and teacher-led) with diverse partners on grades 9–10 topics, texts, and issues, building on others' ideas and expressing their own clearly and persuasively.

    a) Come to discussions prepared, having read and researched material under study; explicitly draw on that preparation by referring to evidence from texts and other research on the topic or issue to stimulate a thoughtful, well-reasoned exchange of ideas.

    b) Work with peers to set rules for collegial discussions and decision-making (e.g., informal consensus, taking votes on key issues, presentation of alternate views), clear goals and deadlines, and individual roles as needed.

c) Propel conversations by posing and responding to questions that relate the current discussion to broader themes or larger ideas; actively incorporate others into the discussion; and clarify, verify, or challenge ideas and conclusions.

d) Respond thoughtfully to diverse perspectives, summarize points of agreement and disagreement, and, when warranted, qualify or justify their own views and understanding and make new connections in light of the evidence and reasoning presented.

Speaking and Listening 2: Integrate multiple sources of information presented in diverse media or formats (e.g., visually, quantitatively, orally) evaluating the credibility and accuracy of each source.

Speaking and Listening 3: Evaluate a speaker's point of view, reasoning, and use of evidence and rhetoric, identifying any fallacious reasoning or exaggerated or distorted evidence.

Speaking and Listening 4: Present information, findings, and supporting evidence clearly, concisely, and logically such that listeners can follow the line of reasoning and the organization, development, substance, and style are appropriate to purpose, audience, and task.

Speaking and Listening 5: Make strategic use of digital media (e.g., textual, graphical, audio, visual, and interactive elements) in presentations to enhance understanding of findings, reasoning, and evidence and to add interest.

Speaking and Listening 6: Adapt speech to a variety of contexts and tasks, demonstrating command of formal English when indicated or appropriate.

Language Standards   309

Language 1: Demonstrate command of the conventions of standard English grammar and usage when writing or speaking.

   a) Use parallel structure.

   b) Use various types of phrases (noun, verb, adjectival, adverbial, participial, prepositional, absolute) and clauses (independent, dependent; noun, relative, adverbial) to convey specific meanings and add variety and interest to writing or presentations.

Language 2: Demonstrate command of the conventions of standard English capitalization, punctuation, and spelling when writing.

   a) Use a semicolon (and perhaps a conjunctive adverb) to link two or more closely related independent clauses.

   b) Use a colon to introduce a list or quotation.

   c) Spell correctly.

Language 3: Apply knowledge of language to understand how language functions in different contexts, to make effective choices for meaning or style, and to comprehend more fully when reading or listening.

   a) Write and edit work so that it conforms to the guidelines in a style manual (e.g., MLA Handbook, Turabian's Manual for Writers) appropriate for the discipline and writing type.

Language 4: Determine or clarify the meaning of unknown and multiple-meaning words and phrases based on grades 9–10 reading and content, choosing flexibly from a range of strategies.

   a) Use context (e.g., the overall meaning of a sentence, paragraph, or text; a word's position or function in a sentence) as a clue to the meaning of a word or phrase.

   b) Identify and correctly use patterns of word changes that indicate different meanings or parts of speech (e.g., analyze, analysis, analytical; advocate, advocacy).

c) Consult general and specialized reference materials (e.g., dictionaries, glossaries, thesauruses), both print and digital, to find the pronunciation of a word or determine or clarify its precise meaning, its part of speech, or its etymology.

d) Verify the preliminary determination of the meaning of a word or phrase (e.g., by checking the inferred meaning in context or in a dictionary).

Language 5: Demonstrate understanding of figurative language, word relationships, and nuances in word meanings.

a) Interpret figures of speech (e.g., euphemism, oxymoron) in context and analyze their role in the text.

b) Analyze nuances in the meaning of words with similar denotations.

Language 6: Acquire and use accurately general academic and domain-specific words and phrases, sufficient for reading, writing, speaking, and listening at the college and career readiness level; demonstrate independence in gathering vocabulary knowledge when considering a word or phrase important to comprehension or expression.

Performance Tasks   336

* Literature 8 is not applicable.

About the *Common Core Companion*

The Common Core Companion student workbook provides instruction and practice in the Common Core State Standards. The standards are designed to help all students become college and career ready by the end of grade 12. Here is a closer look at this workbook:

Reading Standards

Reading Standards for Literature and Informational Texts are supported with instruction, examples, and multiple copies of worksheets that you can use over the course of the year. These key standards are revisited in the Performance Tasks section of your workbook.

Writing Standards

Full writing workshops are provided for Writing standards 1, 2, 3, and 8. Writing standards 4, 5, 6, 8, 9, and 10 are supported with direct instruction and worksheets that provide targeted practice. In addition, writing standards are revisited in Speaking and Listening activities and in Performance Tasks.

Speaking and Listening Standards

Detailed instruction and practice are provided for each Speaking and Listening standard. Additional opportunities to master these standards are provided in the Performance Tasks.

Language Standards

Explicit instruction and detailed examples support each Language standard. In addition, practice worksheets and graphic organizers provide additional opportunities for students to master these standards.

Performance Tasks

Using the examples in the Common Core framework as a guide, we provide opportunities for you to test your ability to master each reading standard, along with tips for success and rubrics to help you evaluate your work.

Reading Standards for Literature

Literature 1

> 1. **Cite strong and thorough textual evidence to support analysis of what the text says explicitly as well as inferences drawn from the text.**

Explanation

In a literary work, authors provide many **explicit details,** direct statements about the characters, settings, and conflicts. In addition, authors suggest certain details, rather than expressing them directly. In order to understand this hinted-at information, readers must **draw inferences** from the text, making educated guesses based on what the text says explicitly and their own experience.

In summarizing what a text says, you have to analyze its explicit details to determine which are the most important. Then, you might have to cite **textual evidence** to show that you have chosen the most important details. Similarly, you should be able to cite strong and thorough evidence from the text to support the inferences about it that you make.

Examples

- "The black door opened slowly," "Mina lives in Japan," and "Nate is happy but nervous" are examples of explicit details from a story. In a summary, however, you cannot include every explicit detail. Instead, you must analyze which details are most important and then support your analysis with strong evidence from the text. For instance, you can prove that Nate's nervousness is an important detail by citing evidence to show that it brings about a key event in the story.

- When you draw an inference about a text, you make an educated guess based on what the author tells you and what you already know about life. For example, if you read a story in which a boy bursts through the front door of a house, runs to his room, slams the door, and refuses to come out, you can infer that he is angry or upset. All these details, which usually mean someone is upset, constitute strong evidence for your inference.

- Your evidence for an analysis or inference is strong and thorough if it relates to the point you are making and is sufficient in itself to prove that point. In the example about the boy running into his room, the fact that he was wearing glasses would probably not be relevant to his state of mind. Also, the fact that he played loud music, taken by itself, would not be enough to prove he is upset.

Academic Vocabulary

inference educated guess based on evidence, reasoning, and experience

textual evidence details in the text that support an analysis or inference

Apply the Standard

Use the worksheets that follow to help you apply the standard as you read. Several copies of each worksheet have been provided for you to use with a number of different selections.

- Using Evidence to Support an Analysis of What a Text Says Explicitly

- Using Evidence to Support Inferences About a Text

Name _____ Date _____ Selection _____

Using Evidence to Support an Analysis of What a Text Says Explicitly

In the left column, identify the most important details in a work or passage. Then, in the right column, support your analysis of explicit details with strong and thorough evidence from the text.

Title of Work: ....   **Author:** ....

Important Detail About Character, Setting, or Conflict	Textual Evidence Supporting Why It Is Important
1.	
2.	
3.	
4.	
5.	

A

Name _____ Date _____ Selection _____

Using Evidence to Support an Analysis of What a Text Says Explicitly

In the left column, identify the most important details in a work or passage. Then, in the right column, support your analysis of explicit details with strong and thorough evidence from the text.

Title of Work: ....   **Author:** ....

Important Detail About Character, Setting, or Conflict	Textual Evidence Supporting Why It Is Important
1.	
2.	
3.	
4.	
5.	

Name _____ Date _____ Selection _____

Using Evidence to Support an Analysis of What a Text Says Explicitly

In the left column, identify the most important details in a work or passage. Then, in the right column, support your analysis of explicit details with strong and thorough evidence from the text.

Title of Work: .... **Author:** ....

Important Detail About Character, Setting, or Conflict	Textual Evidence Supporting Why It Is Important
1.	
2.	
3.	
4.	
5.	

C

For use with Literature 1

Name _____ Date _____ Selection _____

Using Evidence to Support an Analysis of What a Text Says Explicitly

In the left column, identify the most important details in a work or passage. Then, in the right column, support your analysis of explicit details with strong and thorough evidence from the text.

Title of Work: .... **Author:** ....

Important Detail About Character, Setting, or Conflict	Textual Evidence Supporting Why It Is Important
1.	
2.	
3.	
4.	
5.	

Name _____ Date _____ Selection _____

Using Evidence to Support an Analysis of What a Text Says Explicitly

In the left column, identify the most important details in a work or passage. Then, in the right column, support your analysis of explicit details with strong and thorough evidence from the text.

Title of Work: ....   **Author:** ....

Important Detail About Character, Setting, or Conflict	Textual Evidence Supporting Why It Is Important
1.	
2.	
3.	
4.	
5.	

Name _____ Date _____ Selection _____

Using Evidence to Support an Analysis of What a Text Says Explicitly

In the left column, identify the most important details in a work or passage. Then, in the right column, support your analysis of explicit details with strong and thorough evidence from the text.

Title of Work: .... **Author:** ....

Important Detail About Character, Setting, or Conflict	Textual Evidence Supporting Why It Is Important
1.	
2.	
3.	
4.	
5.	

Name _____ Date _____ Selection _____

Using Evidence to Support Inferences About a Text

Use the organizer, below, to make inferences about the characters and conflicts in a poem, story, or drama. Next to each inference, write details from the text that support your inference and explain why they do.

Title:..   **Author:**..

My Inferences	Textual Evidence (Supporting Details)
1.	
2.	
3.	
4.	
5.	

A

Name _____ Date _____ Selection _____

Using Evidence to Support Inferences About a Text

Use the organizer, below, to make inferences about the characters and conflicts in a poem, story, or drama. Next to each inference, write details from the text that support your inference and explain why they do.

Title: ....   **Author:** ....

My Inferences	Textual Evidence (Supporting Details)
1.	
2.	
3.	
4.	
5.	

B

For use with Literature 1

Name _____ Date _____ Selection _____

Using Evidence to Support Inferences About a Text

Use the organizer, below, to make inferences about the characters and conflicts in a poem, story, or drama. Next to each inference, write details from the text that support your inference and explain why they do.

Title: ....   **Author:** ....

My Inferences	Textual Evidence (Supporting Details)
1.	
2.	
3.	
4.	
5.	

Name _____ Date _____ Selection _____

Using Evidence to Support Inferences About a Text

Use the organizer, below, to make inferences about the characters and conflicts in a poem, story, or drama. Next to each inference, write details from the text that support your inference and explain why they do.

Title: ....   **Author:** ....

My Inferences	Textual Evidence (Supporting Details)
1.	
2.	
3.	
4.	
5.	

D

For use with Literature 1

Name _____ Date _____ Selection _____

Using Evidence to Support Inferences About a Text

Use the organizer, below, to make inferences about the characters and conflicts in a poem, story, or drama. Next to each inference, write details from the text that support your inference and explain why they do.

Title: ....   **Author:** ....

My Inferences	Textual Evidence (Supporting Details)
1.	
2.	
3.	
4.	
5.	

E

Name _____ Date _____ Selection _____

Using Evidence to Support Inferences About a Text

Use the organizer, below, to make inferences about the characters and conflicts in a poem, story, or drama. Next to each inference, write details from the text that support your inference and explain why they do.

Title: ....   **Author:** ....

My Inferences	Textual Evidence (Supporting Details)
1.	
2.	
3.	
4.	
5.	

F

Literature 2

> 2. **Determine a theme or central idea of a text and analyze in detail its development over the course of the text, including how it emerges and is shaped and refined by specific details; provide an objective summary of the text.**

Explanation

Love conquers all. It is hard to forgive a friend's betrayal. In a dangerous situation, ordinary people can show unexpected courage. You can probably think of several books or movies that convey these messages about life. A literary work's central idea or message about life is called its **theme.** An author does not necessarily state the theme of a work directly. Often, the reader has to figure it out by studying the story details that develop and refine the theme. You can begin to analyze how an author develops a theme by making an objective **summary**, a brief restatement of the important details in a work.

Examples

- To write an objective **summary**, you briefly restate the important details in a work — without including your own opinions. For example, when summarizing the fairy tale "Cinderella," you might say, "Cinderella is treated cruelly by her stepsisters. A fairy godmother dresses Cinderella for a prince's party, but tells Cinderella to be home by midnight. Later, as Cinderella rushes home from the ball, she loses her glass slipper. The prince searches for the girl who lost the glass slipper. The glass slipper fits Cinderella. She marries the prince and lives happily ever after."

- To determine a story's **theme**, or central idea, analyze details in the text for clues about the message the writer is trying to convey. These details might relate to the main characters, the setting, the central conflict, or even the title. If the text is a story, pay special attention to whether or how the characters develop, their conflicts, and what happens to them over the course of the story. As you observe and study such details, ask yourself if you detect an emerging theme. For example, as you study the details of the story of Cinderella, you may note that a theme is being developed: With a little help, a good person can overcome hardship and difficult circumstances and find happiness.

Academic Vocabulary

summary a brief restatement of the important details in a work

theme a story's central idea or message about life

Apply the Standard

Use the worksheets that follow to help you apply the standard as you read. Several copies of each worksheet have been provided for you to use with a number of different selections.

- Summarizing a Text

- Analyzing a Central Idea or Theme

Name _____ Date _____ Selection _____

Summarizing a Text

Use this organizer to identify the most important events or ideas in the text. Then, use them to write a brief objective summary. Remember to leave your own opinions out of the summary.

Event or Idea

↓

Event or Idea

↓

Event or Idea

↓

Final Outcome

Summary:

....

....

....

....

....

....

Name _____ Date _____ Selection _____

Summarizing a Text

Use this organizer to identify the most important events or ideas in the text. Then, use them to write a brief objective summary. Remember to leave your own opinions out of the summary.

Event or Idea

↓

Event or Idea

↓

Event or Idea

↓

Final Outcome

Summary:

....

....

....

....

....

B

Name _____ Date _____ Selection _____

Summarizing a Text

Use this organizer to identify the most important events or ideas in the text. Then, use them to write a brief objective summary. Remember to leave your own opinions out of the summary.

Event or Idea

↓

Event or Idea

↓

Event or Idea

↓

Final Outcome

Summary:

....

....

....

....

....

....

Name _____ Date _____ Selection _____

Summarizing a Text

Use this organizer to identify the most important events or ideas in the text. Then, use them to write a brief objective summary. Remember to leave your own opinions out of the summary.

Event or Idea

↓

Event or Idea

↓

Event or Idea

↓

Final Outcome

Summary:

....

....

....

....

....

....

D

Name _____ Date _____ Selection _____

Summarizing a Text

Use this organizer to identify the most important events or ideas in the text. Then, use them to write a brief objective summary. Remember to leave your own opinions out of the summary.

Event or Idea

↓

Event or Idea

↓

Event or Idea

↓

Final Outcome

Summary:

....

....

....

....

....

....

E

For use with Literature 2

Name _____ Date _____ Selection _____

Summarizing a Text

Use this organizer to identify the most important events or ideas in the text. Then, use them to write a brief objective summary. Remember to leave your own opinions out of the summary.

Event or Idea

↓

Event or Idea

↓

Event or Idea

↓

Final Outcome

Summary:

....

....

....

....

....

....

F

Name _____ Date _____ Selection _____

Analyzing a Central Idea or Theme

Choose three important details from different parts of the text. Remember that these details might relate to the main characters, the setting, the central conflict, or even the title. Then, use the following organizer to analyze how the author uses these details to develop the text's theme, or central message.

Analyzing Theme Development

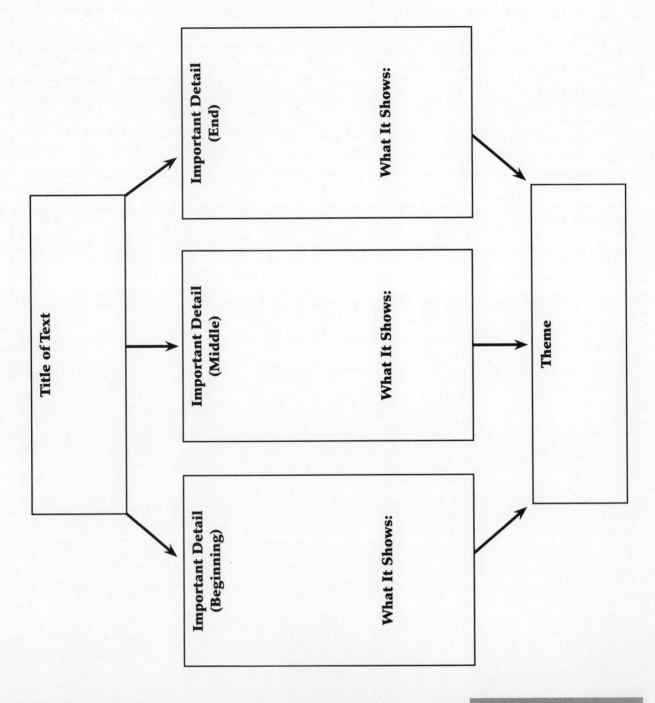

A

Name _____ Date _____ Selection _____

Analyzing a Central Idea or Theme

Choose three important details from different parts of the text. Remember that these details might relate to the main characters, the setting, the central conflict, or even the title. Then, use the following organizer to analyze how the author uses these details to develop the text's theme, or central message.

Analyzing Theme Development

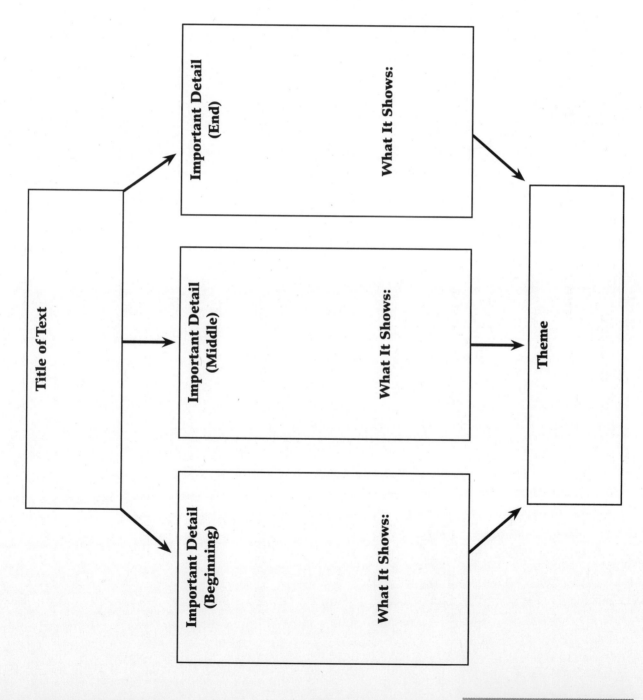

For use with Literature 2

Name _____ Date _____ Selection _____

Analyzing a Central Idea or Theme

Choose three important details from different parts of the text. Remember that these details might relate to the main characters, the setting, the central conflict, or even the title. Then, use the following organizer to analyze how the author uses these details to develop the text's theme, or central message.

Analyzing Theme Development

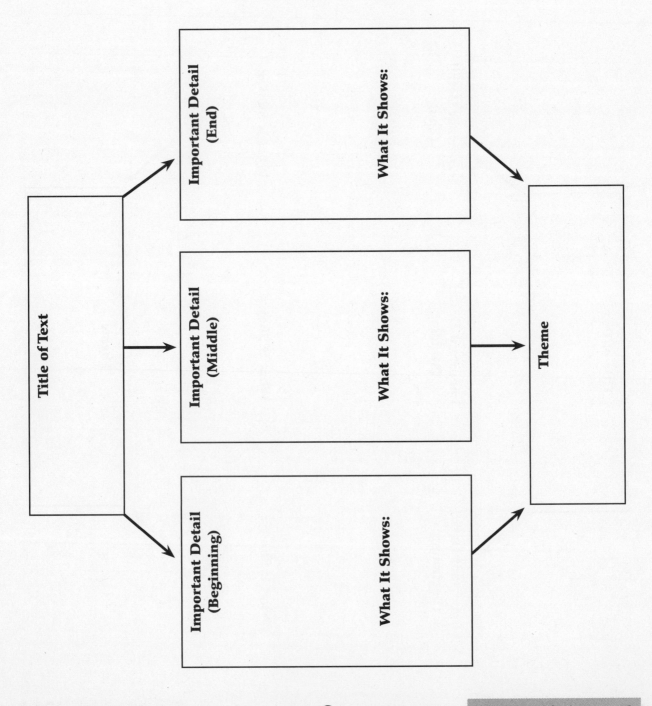

Name _____ Date _____ Selection _____

Analyzing a Central Idea or Theme

Choose three important details from different parts of the text. Remember that these details might relate to the main characters, the setting, the central conflict, or even the title. Then, use the following organizer to analyze how the author uses these details to develop the text's theme, or central message.

Analyzing Theme Development

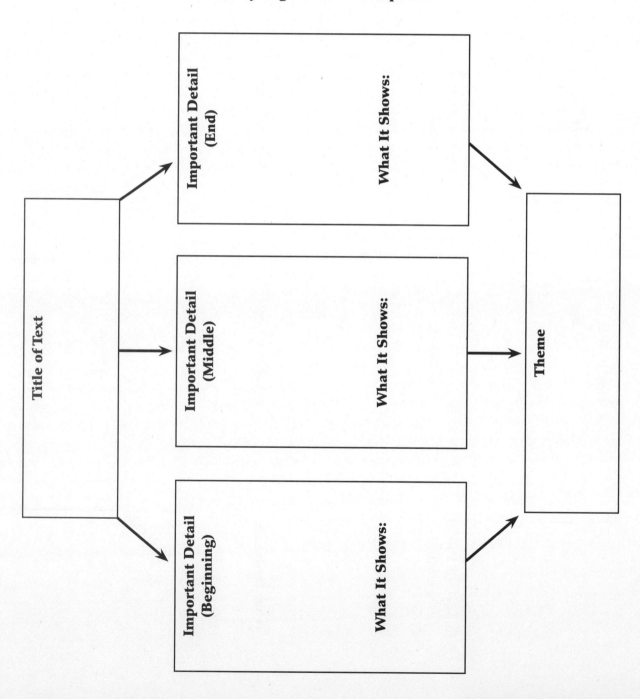

D

Name _____ Date _____ Selection _____

Analyzing a Central Idea or Theme

Choose three important details from different parts of the text. Remember that these details might relate to the main characters, the setting, the central conflict, or even the title. Then, use the following organizer to analyze how the author uses these details to develop the text's theme, or central message.

Analyzing Theme Development

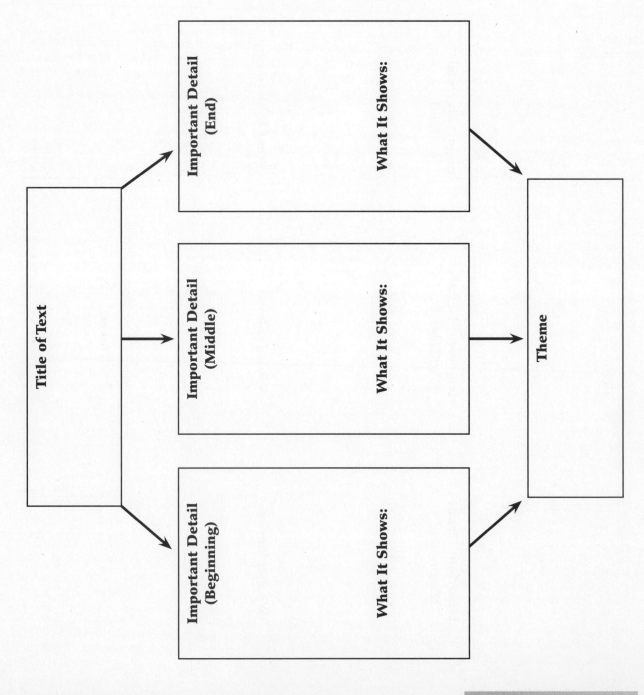

E

Name _____ Date _____ Selection _____

Analyzing a Central Idea or Theme

Choose three important details from different parts of the text. Remember that these details might relate to the main characters, the setting, the central conflict, or even the title. Then, use the following organizer to analyze how the author uses these details to develop the text's theme, or central message.

Analyzing Theme Development

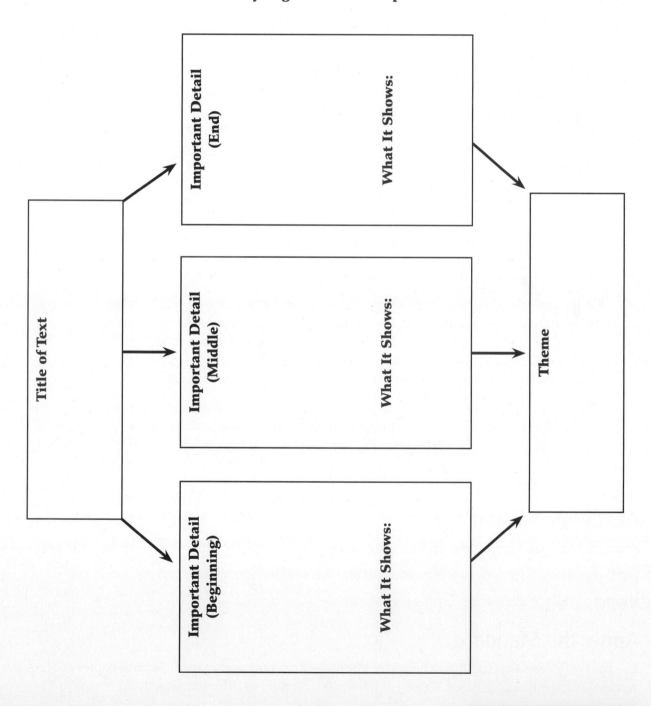

Literature 3

> 3. **Analyze how complex characters (e.g., those with multiple or conflicting motivations) develop over the course of a text, interact with other characters, and advance the plot or develop the theme.**

Explanation

Complex characters—those with several **motivations**, or reasons, for what they do—are at the heart of good stories. Like real people, complex characters have both strengths and weaknesses. They also change and develop over the course of a story. Sometimes their motivations cause internal **conflict,** as the characters struggle with their feelings or try to determine what action to take. A main character's conflicting motivations can advance the story's **plot,** the series of events that occur in a story. Noticing how a complex character changes and thinking about what he or she learns will help you analyze how the author explores and develops the story's **theme,** or message about life.

Examples

- **Complex characters** often have several, sometimes conflicting, **motivations**. Suppose, for example, you read a story about a boy who wants to be on his school's basketball team, which requires several hours of practice after school each day. However, he also wants to get a part-time job after school so that he can help his parents pay the family's bills. This character has conflicting motivations. He cannot easily achieve both of the things he wants.

- A character's conflicting motivations can serve as the engine that sets in motion a story's **plot,** or related series of events. For example, the boy trying to decide between the basketball team or a part-time job might be motivated to ask his friends or the basketball coach for advice. That action might result in a series of events; for example, the coach might then ask the boy's parents to allow their son to practice, and so forth.

- The way a complex character changes during a story can help develop the story's **theme.** For example, if the boy chooses the basketball team over the job, the writer can explore the importance of young people being part of a team. If the boy chooses the part-time job, the writer can explore the importance of young people learning to sacrifice and taking responsibility.

Academic Vocabulary

motivation a character's reason for doing things

plot the series of story events that establish and resolve the character's conflicts

theme a story's central idea or message about life

Apply the Standard

Use the worksheet that follows to help you apply the standard as you read. Several copies of the worksheet have been provided for you to use with a number of different selections.

- Analyzing Characters

Name _____ Date _____ Selection _____

Analyzing Characters

Use this organizer to analyze a complex character whose conflicting motivations advance a story's plot and help develop the story's theme.

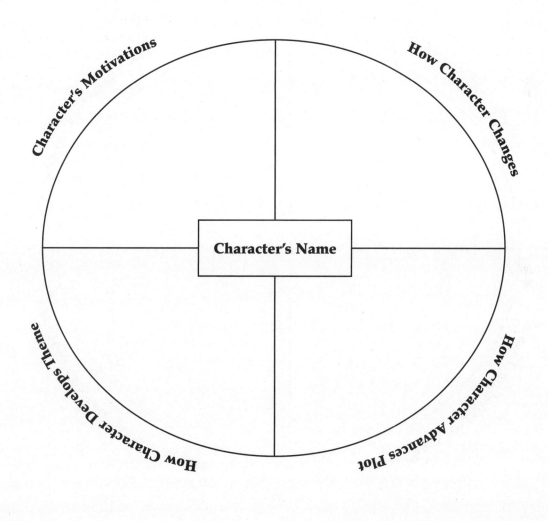

A

For use with Literature 3

Name _____ Date _____ Selection _____

Analyzing Characters

Use this organizer to analyze a complex character whose conflicting motivations advance a story's plot and help develop the story's theme.

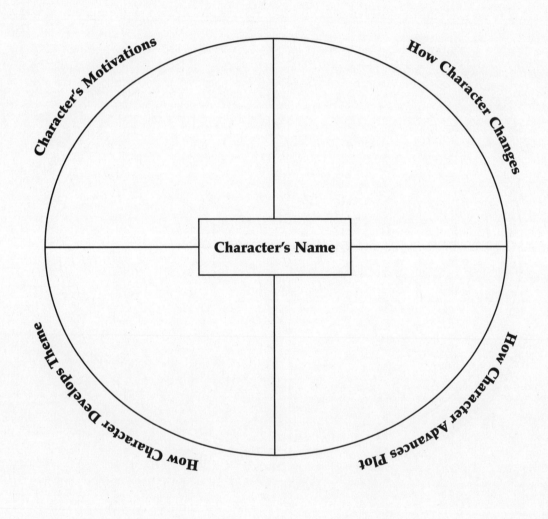

Name _____ Date _____ Selection _____

Analyzing Characters

Use this organizer to analyze a complex character whose conflicting motivations advance a story's plot and help develop the story's theme.

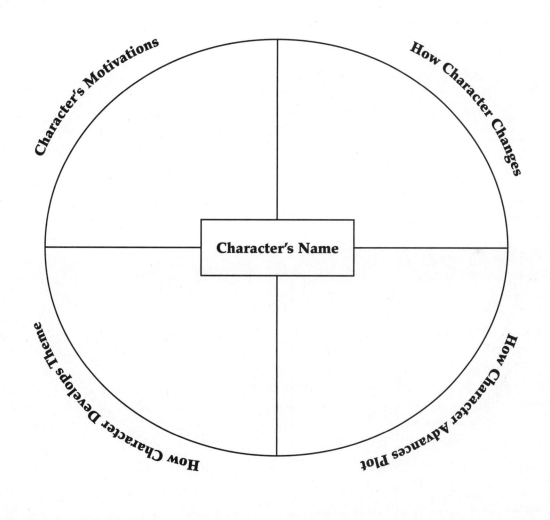

For use with Literature 3

Name _____ Date _____ Selection _____

Analyzing Characters

Use this organizer to analyze a complex character whose conflicting motivations advance a story's plot and help develop the story's theme.

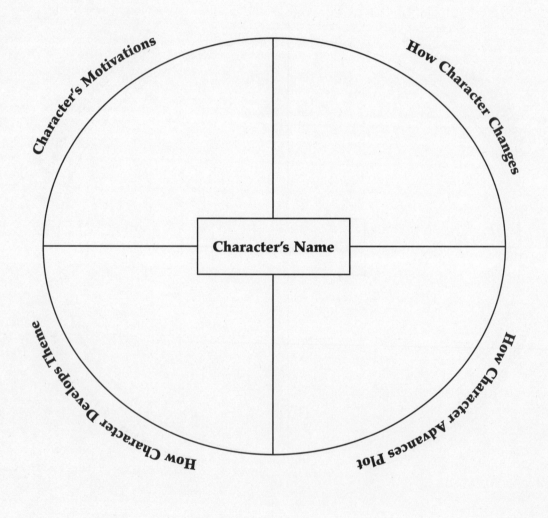

Name _____ Date _____ Selection _____

Analyzing Characters

Use this organizer to analyze a complex character whose conflicting motivations advance a story's plot and help develop the story's theme.

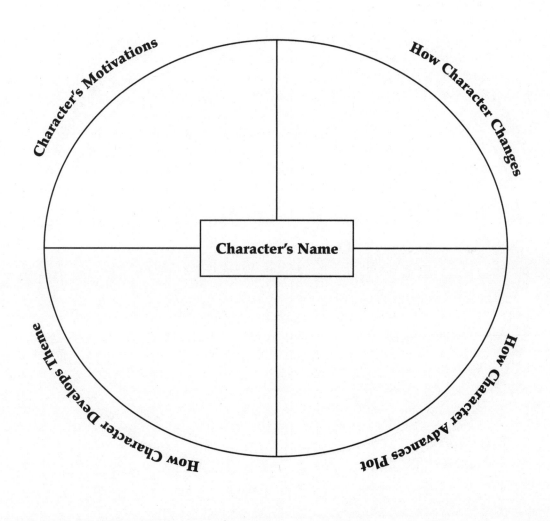

E

For use with Literature 3

Name _____ Date _____ Selection _____

Analyzing Characters

Use this organizer to analyze a complex character whose conflicting motivations advance a story's plot and help develop the story's theme.

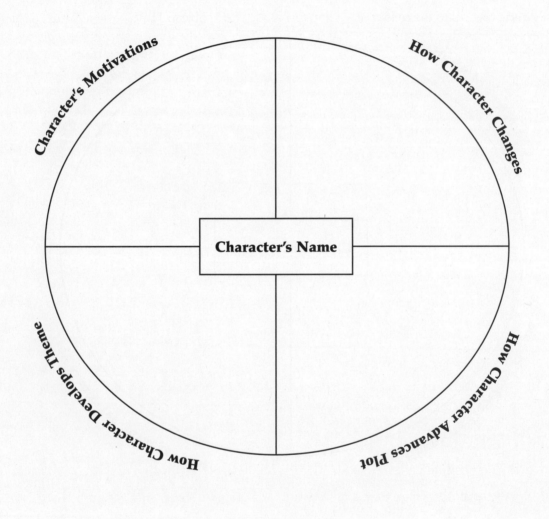

For use with Literature 3

Literature 4

> 4. **Determine the meaning of words and phrases as they are used in the text, including figurative and connotative meanings; analyze the cumulative impact of specific word choices on meaning and tone (e.g., how the language evokes a sense of time and place; how it sets a formal or informal tone).**

Explanation

Good writers choose their words carefully. They choose language that expresses exactly what they want to say and conveys to the reader how they feel about their subject. The overall attitude, or feeling, that a writer expresses about a subject is called **tone**. For example, the tone of a text might be described as *formal* or *informal*, *serious* or *playful*, or *admiring* or *harsh*. To determine the meaning and tone of a literary text, you need to analyze the words and phrases the author uses, paying special attention to connotations and figurative language. **Connotations** are the negative or positive ideas associated with a word. **Figurative language** is language that is used imaginatively, rather than literally. It includes figures of speech that make unexpected comparisons, such as similes and metaphors.

Examples

- Some words share similar dictionary meanings but have different **connotations**—that is, different positive or negative associations. Understanding connotations can help you figure out how a writer feels about a person, a place, or an idea. For instance, if a writer admires someone who refuses to give up, he or she might describe that person as *determined* or *tenacious* to convey a positive **tone**.

- **Figurative language** can evoke a clear sense of time and place and convey a writer's **tone**. For example, using the simile that a silent forest is "as hushed as a lullaby" brings to mind the image of still branches on a windless day and conveys a tone of peacefulness.

- Once you have analyzed the most important words and phrases in a text, you are ready to figure out the cumulative effect of the author's word choices: the pattern of word choices that influences the text's overall **meaning** and **tone**.

Academic Vocabulary

connotations the positive or negative feelings associated with a word

figurative language language that is not meant to be taken literally, such as similes

tone the author's overall attitude, or feeling, toward the subject of a literary work

Apply the Standard

Use the worksheets that follow to help you apply the standard as you read. Several copies of each worksheet have been provided for you to use with a number of different selections.

- Understanding Connotations and Figurative Language

- Analyzing Word Choices: Meaning and Tone

Name _____ Date _____ Selection _____

Understanding Connotations and Figurative Language

Use this organizer to analyze the meaning of important words and phrases in a text, particularly the author's use of figurative language and words with positive or negative connotations.

Word or Phrase	Connotation	Feeling It Expresses

+

Figurative Language	What It Means	Feeling It Expresses

A

For use with Literature 4

Name _____ Date _____ Selection _____

Understanding Connotations and Figurative Language

Use this organizer to analyze the meaning of important words and phrases in a text, particularly the author's use of figurative language and words with positive or negative connotations.

Word or Phrase	Connotation	Feeling It Expresses

+

Figurative Language	What It Means	Feeling It Expresses

B

Name _____ Date _____ Selection _____

Understanding Connotations and Figurative Language

Use this organizer to analyze the meaning of important words and phrases in a text, particularly the author's use of figurative language and words with positive or negative connotations.

Word or Phrase	Connotation	Feeling It Expresses

+

Figurative Language	What It Means	Feeling It Expresses

C

Name _____ Date _____ Selection _____

Understanding Connotations and Figurative Language

Use this organizer to analyze the meaning of important words and phrases in a text, particularly the author's use of figurative language and words with positive or negative connotations.

Word or Phrase	Connotation	Feeling It Expresses

Figurative Language	What It Means	Feeling It Expresses

D

Name _____ Date _____ Selection _____

Understanding Connotations and Figurative Language

Use this organizer to analyze the meaning of important words and phrases in a text, particularly the author's use of figurative language and words with positive or negative connotations.

Word or Phrase	Connotation	Feeling It Expresses

Figurative Language	What It Means	Feeling It Expresses

E

Name _____ Date _____ Selection _____

Understanding Connotations and Figurative Language

Use this organizer to analyze the meaning of important words and phrases in a text, particularly the author's use of figurative language and words with positive or negative connotations.

Word or Phrase	Connotation	Feeling It Expresses

Figurative Language	What It Means	Feeling It Expresses

F

For use with Literature 4

Name _____ Date _____ Selection _____

Analyzing Word Choices: Meaning and Tone

Use this organizer to analyze the overall impact that specific word choices have on meaning and tone in a text.

Words and Phrases with Connotations

Figurative Language

Meaning and Tone

A

For use with Literature 4

Analyzing Word Choices: Meaning and Tone

Use this organizer to analyze the overall impact that specific word choices have on meaning and tone in a text.

Words and Phrases with Connotations

Figurative Language

Meaning and Tone

Name _____ Date _____ Selection _____

Analyzing Word Choices: Meaning and Tone

Use this organizer to analyze the overall impact that specific word choices have on meaning and tone in a text.

Words and Phrases with Connotations

Figurative Language

Meaning and Tone

Name _____ Date _____ Selection _____

Analyzing Word Choices: Meaning and Tone

Use this organizer to analyze the overall impact that specific word choices have on meaning and tone in a text.

```
┌─────────────────────────────┐        ┌─────────────────────────────┐
│  ┌───────────────────────┐  │        │  ┌───────────────────────┐  │
│  │  Words and Phrases with│ │        │  │   Figurative Language  │  │
│  │      Connotations      │ │        │  └───────────────────────┘  │
│  └───────────────────────┘  │        │                             │
│                             │        │                             │
│                             │        │                             │
└─────────────────────────────┘        └─────────────────────────────┘
                    \                    /
                     \                  /
                      ↘                ↙
              ┌─────────────────────────────┐
              │  ┌───────────────────────┐  │
              │  │    Meaning and Tone    │  │
              │  └───────────────────────┘  │
              │                             │
              │                             │
              └─────────────────────────────┘
```

Name _____ Date _____ Selection _____

Analyzing Word Choices: Meaning and Tone

Use this organizer to analyze the overall impact that specific word choices have on meaning and tone in a text.

Words and Phrases with Connotations

Figurative Language

Meaning and Tone

Name _____ Date _____ Selection _____

Analyzing Word Choices: Meaning and Tone

Use this organizer to analyze the overall impact that specific word choices have on meaning and tone in a text.

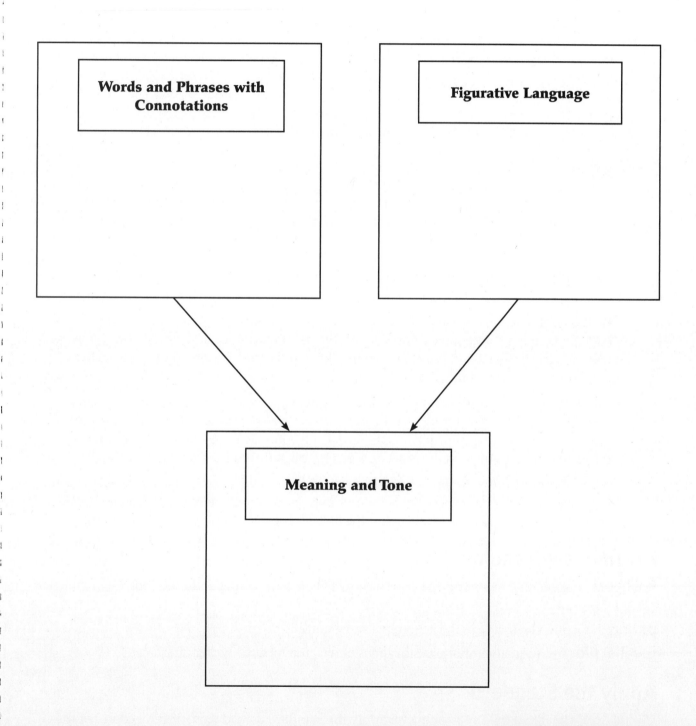

Words and Phrases with Connotations

Figurative Language

Meaning and Tone

F

For use with Literature 4

Literature 5

> 5. **Analyze how an author's choices concerning how to structure a text, order events within it (e.g., parallel plots), and manipulate time (e.g., pacing, flashbacks) create such effects as mystery, tension, or surprise.**

Explanation

When you read a story, notice how different effects result from choices authors make about the structure of their work. Authors can move back and forth between **parallel plots**, two different but related storylines, encouraging readers to consider the possibly mysterious connections between them. Authors can also manipulate time in stories by introducing **flashbacks**, events that occurred before the earliest event in the story. Finally, they can vary the **pacing** of a story, or the speed at which events occur.

Examples

- Authors **structure** stories in ways that will keep readers interested, organizing events in the plot to keep readers wondering what will happen next. In Edgar Allan Poe's story "The Pit and the Pendulum," for example, the main character is saved from falling into a deep pit below his dungeon—only to discover a razor-sharp pendulum descending toward him from above. Drawn in by the mystery, readers turn the pages wondering what will happen next.

- Sometimes authors manipulate time by interrupting the sequence of events with a **flashback** that reveals what happened in the past. In "The Pit and the Pendulum," the narrator conveys a dreamlike impression of the court that condemned him. Then, he wakes up in a dark dungeon and tries to remember how and why he ended up there. His hazy memories are a kind of flashback.

- Authors also manipulate time by varying the **pacing** of a story, speeding up or slowing down time. In "The Pit and the Pendulum," for example, tension builds as the narrator slowly and carefully explores his pitch-black dungeon. The pace suddenly quickens as he falls and discovers he is on the brink of a deadly pit, a thrilling surprise for the reader.

- A **parallel plot**— two different but related storylines— is generally just as important as the main plot. Authors of longer fictional pieces may introduce parallel plots, moving back and forth from one to the other. In this way, the two plots can reflect similar or related themes.

Academic Vocabulary

flashback a scene that interrupts the plot to show events that happened in the past, before the first event in the story

pacing how quickly or slowly the action in a story unfolds

parallel plot two equally important storylines between which the writer alternates

Apply the Standard

Use the worksheet that follows to help you apply the standard as you read. Several copies of the worksheet have been provided for you to use with a number of different selections.

- Analyze Author's Structural Choices

Name _____ Date _____ Selection _____

Analyze Author's Structural Choices

Use this organizer to analyze the author's choices in constructing a story. On the left, write the events that happen in each part of the story and describe any flashbacks. On the right, describe the pacing in each part of the story. At the bottom, describe how the author's choices create effects, such as mystery, tension, or surprise.

Beginning

Events:	Describe the Pacing:
Flashback?	

Middle

Events:	Describe the Pacing:
Flashback?	

Ending

Events:	Describe the Pacing:
Flashback?	

Describe the effects—such as mystery, tension, or surprise—that the author's choices create.

....

....

A

Name _____ Date _____ Selection _____

Analyze Author's Structural Choices

Use this organizer to analyze the author's choices in constructing a story. On the left, write the events that happen in each part of the story and describe any flashbacks. On the right, describe the pacing in each part of the story. At the bottom, describe how the author's choices create effects, such as mystery, tension, or surprise.

Beginning

Events:

Flashback?

Describe the Pacing:

⇩

Middle

Events:

Flashback?

Describe the Pacing:

⇩

Ending

Events:

Flashback?

Describe the Pacing:

Describe the effects—such as mystery, tension, or surprise—that the author's choices create.

....

....

B

For use with Literature 5

Name _____ Date _____ Selection _____

Analyze Author's Structural Choices

Use this organizer to analyze the author's choices in constructing a story. On the left, write the events that happen in each part of the story and describe any flashbacks. On the right, describe the pacing in each part of the story. At the bottom, describe how the author's choices create effects, such as mystery, tension, or surprise.

Beginning

Events:	Describe the Pacing:
Flashback?	

Middle

Events:	Describe the Pacing:
Flashback?	

Ending

Events:	Describe the Pacing:
Flashback?	

Describe the effects—such as mystery, tension, or surprise—that the author's choices create.

....

....

C

Name _____ Date _____ Selection _____

Analyze Author's Structural Choices

Use this organizer to analyze the author's choices in constructing a story. On the left, write the events that happen in each part of the story and describe any flashbacks. On the right, describe the pacing in each part of the story. At the bottom, describe how the author's choices create effects, such as mystery, tension, or surprise.

Beginning

Events:	Describe the Pacing:
Flashback?	

Middle

⇩

Events:	Describe the Pacing:
Flashback?	

Ending

⇩

Events:	Describe the Pacing:
Flashback?	

Describe the effects—such as mystery, tension, or surprise—that the author's choices create.

....

....

For use with Literature 5

Name _____ Date _____ Selection _____

Analyze Author's Structural Choices

Use this organizer to analyze the author's choices in constructing a story. On the left, write the events that happen in each part of the story and describe any flashbacks. On the right, describe the pacing in each part of the story. At the bottom, describe how the author's choices create effects, such as mystery, tension, or surprise.

Beginning

Events:	Describe the Pacing:
Flashback?	

Middle

⇩

Events:	Describe the Pacing:
Flashback?	

Ending

⇩

Events:	Describe the Pacing:
Flashback?	

Describe the effects—such as mystery, tension, or surprise—that the author's choices create.

....

....

E

For use with Literature 5

Name _____ Date _____ Selection _____

Analyze Author's Structural Choices

Use this organizer to analyze the author's choices in constructing a story. On the left, write the events that happen in each part of the story and describe any flashbacks. On the right, describe the pacing in each part of the story. At the bottom, describe how the author's choices create effects, such as mystery, tension, or surprise.

Beginning

Events:	**Describe the Pacing:**
Flashback?	

Middle

⇩

Events:	**Describe the Pacing:**
Flashback?	

Ending

⇩

Events:	**Describe the Pacing:**
Flashback?	

Describe the effects—such as mystery, tension, or surprise—that the author's choices create.

....

....

Literature 6

> 6. **Analyze a particular point of view or cultural experience reflected in a work of literature from outside the United States, drawing on a wide reading of world literature.**

Explanation

If you met someone from another country, you might discover that you have things in common, such as a love of video games and the Internet. You might also discover, however, that you have different beliefs, values, and customs. These differences reflect your **culture**, the way of life shared by the society in which you live. People are shaped by their **cultural experience**, the customs and expectations of their societies.

Works of literature are also shaped by culture. For example, an author's cultural experience can determine how the characters in a story act, what their motivations are, and how they respond to conflicts. Stories often reflect the **cultural point of view**, or way of seeing the world, of the society from which they arise. (This meaning of "point of view" should not be confused with the domain-specific definition of the phrase as the vantage point from which a story is told: first, second, or third person.) The more literature from around the world that you read, the better you will understand different cultural experiences and points of view.

Examples

- Works of literature from different cultures reflect different cultural experiences or points of view. For example, the hero of an American folk tale may have different values and beliefs than the hero of a Chinese folk tale. The American hero may be motivated by a desire for independence and success, two important values in American culture. A Chinese folk hero's actions may be motivated by a desire to honor his parents and ancestors, an important value in traditional Chinese culture.

- To analyze the point of view of a work from another country, ask yourself questions like these: *What does the main character do or feel? What values and beliefs motivate the main character's behavior? What customs and expectations in the character's world are different from those in my world?*

Academic Vocabulary

culture way of life shared by the people living in a particular society

cultural experience customs, beliefs, and expectations of a society

cultural point of view way of seeing the world that is influenced by a particular culture

Apply the Standard

Use the worksheet that follows to help you apply the standard as you read. Several copies of the worksheet have been provided for you to use with different literature selections.

- Analyzing Point of View in World Literature

Name _____ Date _____ Selection _____

Analyzing Point of View in World Literature

Use the organizer, below, to analyze the cultural point of view of the main character in a literary work from outside the United States.

Author and Title of work: ....

Culture in which the work was written: ....

What the main character does and feels:

....

....

....

↓

Values and beliefs that motivate the main character:

....

....

....

↓

Customs and expectations in the main character's world (different from character's values?):

....

....

....

↓

How these customs and expectations differ from those in my world:

....

....

....

A

Name _____ Date _____ Selection _____

Analyzing Point of View in World Literature

Use the organizer, below, to analyze the cultural point of view of the main character in a literary work from outside the United States.

Author and Title of work: ....

Culture in which the work was written: ....

What the main character does and feels:

....

....

....

↓

Values and beliefs that motivate the main character:

....

....

....

↓

Customs and expectations in the main character's world (different from character's values?):

....

....

....

↓

How these customs and expectations differ from those in my world:

....

....

....

B

For use with Literature 6

Name _____ Date _____ Selection _____

Analyzing Point of View in World Literature

Use the organizer, below, to analyze the cultural point of view of the main character in a literary work from outside the United States.

Author and Title of work: ....

Culture in which the work was written: ....

What the main character does and feels:

....

....

....

↓

Values and beliefs that motivate the main character:

....

....

....

↓

Customs and expectations in the main character's world (different from character's values?):

....

....

....

↓

How these customs and expectations differ from those in my world:

....

....

....

C

Name _____ Date _____ Selection _____

Analyzing Point of View in World Literature

Use the organizer, below, to analyze the cultural point of view of the main character in a literary work from outside the United States.

Author and Title of work: ....

Culture in which the work was written: ....

What the main character does and feels:

....

....

....

↓

Values and beliefs that motivate the main character:

....

....

....

↓

Customs and expectations in the main character's world (different from character's values?):

....

....

....

↓

How these customs and expectations differ from those in my world:

....

....

....

Name _____ Date _____ Selection _____

Analyzing Point of View in World Literature

Use the organizer, below, to analyze the cultural point of view of the main character in a literary work from outside the United States.

Author and Title of work: ....

Culture in which the work was written: ....

What the main character does and feels:

....

....

....

↓

Values and beliefs that motivate the main character:

....

....

....

↓

Customs and expectations in the main character's world (different from character's values?):

....

....

....

↓

How these customs and expectations differ from those in my world:

....

....

....

E

Name _____ Date _____ Selection _____

Analyzing Point of View in World Literature

Use the organizer, below, to analyze the cultural point of view of the main character in a literary work from outside the United States.

Author and Title of work: ....

Culture in which the work was written: ....

What the main character does and feels:

....

....

....

↓

Values and beliefs that motivate the main character:

....

....

....

↓

Customs and expectations in the main character's world (different from character's values?):

....

....

....

↓

How these customs and expectations differ from those in my world:

....

....

....

F

For use with Literature 6

Literature 7

> 7. **Analyze the representation of a subject or a key scene in two different artistic mediums, including what is emphasized or absent in each treatment (e.g., Auden's "Musée des Beaux Arts" and Brueghel's *Landscape with the Fall of Icarus*).**

Explanation

Some subjects inspire not only authors, but also painters, musicians, and other artists. For example, a character or a scene might appear in a play and also in a work in a different **medium,** or art form. Just as an author uses words to describe characters, settings, and events, other types of artist use different resources to create their own **representation,** or depiction, of a subject. By comparing an author's **treatment,** or way of presenting, a subject or key scene with that of an artist's treatment in a different medium, you can gain insights into the subject or scene itself.

Examples

- Authors use words to depict a subject or scene. They can describe people and places, express what characters say and do, and narrate events. For example, the *Odyssey*, an epic poem about the ancient Greek hero Odysseus tells the story of his long journey home from the Trojan War. The poem describes episodes in that journey, conveying Odysseus' cleverness and courage.

- Artists in visual media generally do not use words in their work. Instead, they use elements such as color, line, shape, shadow, perspective, and texture to depict subjects and scenes. For example, an illustrator might use strong lines and blocks of color to convey the strength of Odysseus.

- You can analyze the treatment of a subject or key scene in two different media by carefully studying both works. Look for important details, especially details emphasized in one work and not in the other or details absent in one but present in the other. For example, a visual depiction of a particular scene from the *Odyssey* might emphasize the physical power of Odysseus, while a passage from the poem describing the same scene might stress the hero's cleverness.

Academic Vocabulary

medium particular form of art, such as literature, painting, sculpture, film, or music

representation portrayal or depiction of a subject in a given artistic medium

treatment way of presenting a given subject

Apply the Standard

Use the worksheet that follows to help you apply the standard as you read. Several copies of the worksheet have been provided for you to use with different literature selections.

- Analyzing Representations in Different Mediums

Name _____ Date _____ Selection _____

Analyzing Representations in Different Mediums

Use this organizer to analyze and compare the treatment of a literary character or scene in two different mediums. At the top, indicate the character or scene. Below that, enter the title and medium of each work and list the details emphasized in each work. Finally, record your comparative analysis on the lines provided.

Literary Character or Scene:

....

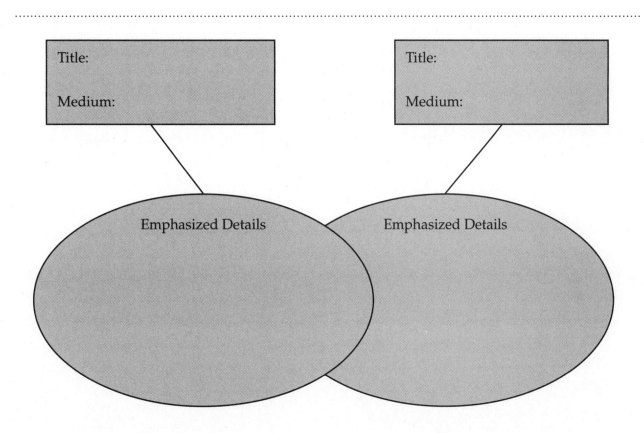

Title:

Medium:

Emphasized Details

Title:

Medium:

Emphasized Details

What key ideas, emotions, and themes are expressed or omitted in each treatment?

....

....

....

....

....

....

For use with Literature 7

Name _____ Date _____ Selection _____

Analyzing Representations in Different Mediums

Use this organizer to analyze and compare the treatment of a literary character or scene in two different mediums. At the top, indicate the character or scene. Below that, enter the title and medium of each work and list the details emphasized in each work. Finally, record your comparative analysis on the lines provided.

Literary Character or Scene:

....

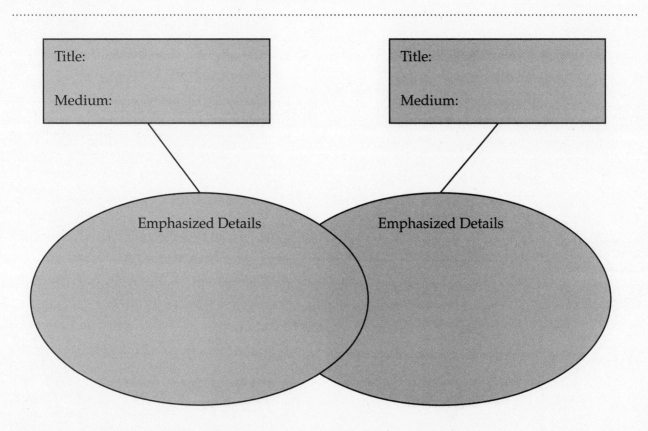

Title:

Medium:

Title:

Medium:

Emphasized Details

Emphasized Details

What key ideas, emotions, and themes are expressed or omitted in each treatment?

....

....

....

....

....

....

Name _____ Date _____ Selection _____

Analyzing Representations in Different Mediums

Use this organizer to analyze and compare the treatment of a literary character or scene in two different mediums. At the top, indicate the character or scene. Below that, enter the title and medium of each work and list the details emphasized in each work. Finally, record your comparative analysis on the lines provided.

Literary Character or Scene:

....

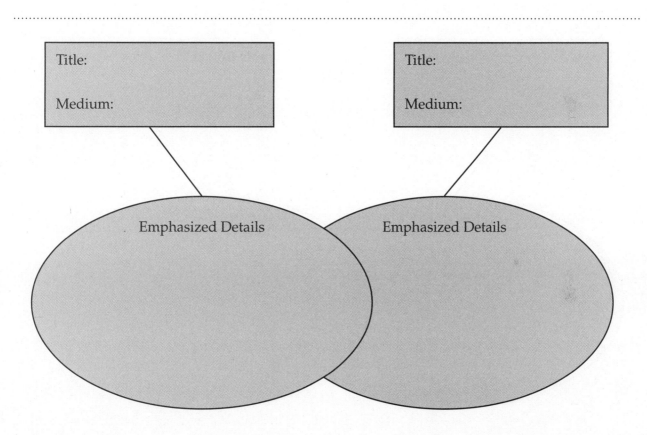

Title:

Medium:

Emphasized Details

Title:

Medium:

Emphasized Details

What key ideas, emotions, and themes are expressed or omitted in each treatment?

....

....

....

....

....

....

Name _____ Date _____ Selection _____

Analyzing Representations in Different Mediums

Use this organizer to analyze and compare the treatment of a literary character or scene in two different mediums. At the top, indicate the character or scene. Below that, enter the title and medium of each work and list the details emphasized in each work. Finally, record your comparative analysis on the lines provided.

Literary Character or Scene:

....

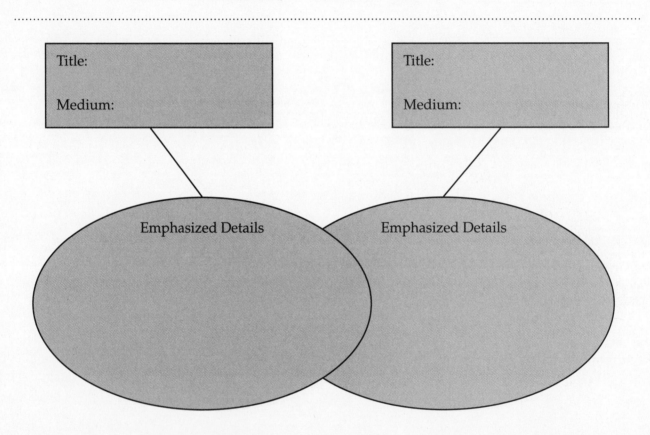

Title:

Medium:

Emphasized Details

Title:

Medium:

Emphasized Details

What key ideas, emotions, and themes are expressed or omitted in each treatment?

....

....

....

....

....

....

Name _____ Date _____ Selection _____

Analyzing Representations in Different Mediums

Use this organizer to analyze and compare the treatment of a literary character or scene in two different mediums. At the top, indicate the character or scene. Below that, enter the title and medium of each work and list the details emphasized in each work. Finally, record your comparative analysis on the lines provided.

Literary Character or Scene:

....

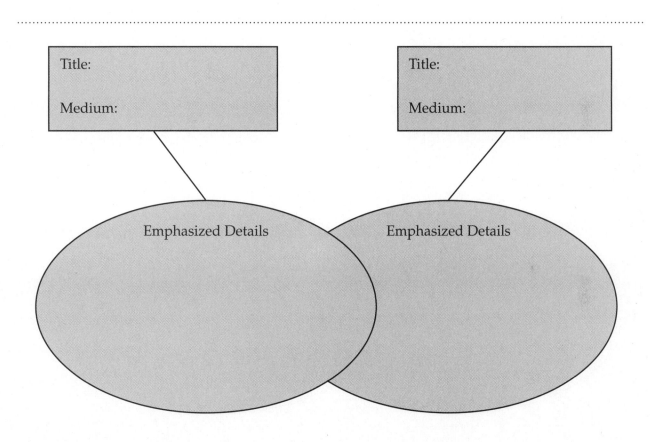

Title:

Medium:

Title:

Medium:

Emphasized Details

Emphasized Details

What key ideas, emotions, and themes are expressed or omitted in each treatment?

....

....

....

....

....

E

Name _____ Date _____ Selection _____

Analyzing Representations in Different Mediums

Use this organizer to analyze and compare the treatment of a literary character or scene in two different mediums. At the top, indicate the character or scene. Below that, enter the title and medium of each work and list the details emphasized in each work. Finally, record your comparative analysis on the lines provided.

Literary Character or Scene:

....

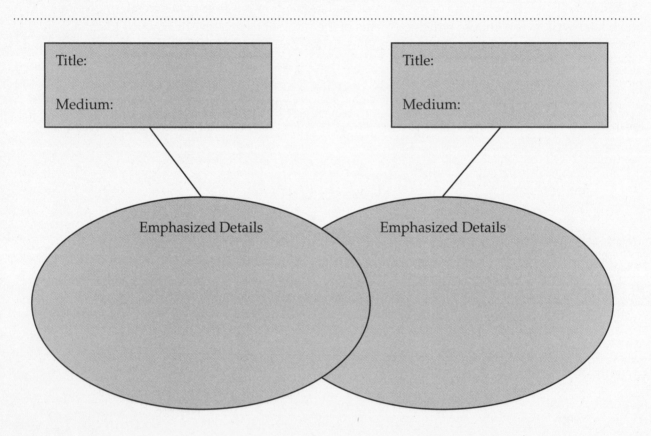

Title:

Medium:

Emphasized Details

Title:

Medium:

Emphasized Details

What key ideas, emotions, and themes are expressed or omitted in each treatment?

....

....

....

....

....

....

F

Literature 9

> **9. Analyze how an author draws on and transforms source material in a specific work (e.g., how Shakespeare treats a theme or topic from Ovid or the Bible or how a later author draws on a play by Shakespeare).**

Explanation

Characters from great literature can amuse and inspire many generations of readers. Great literary works can also inspire writers of later centuries. Drawing on the **source material,** or original text, later writers can choose which elements of the original to preserve and which to change or transform. By doing so, they challenge readers to see famous characters or plots in a new light and to broaden or question their understanding of the source material's original themes by framing them in a different context.

Examples

- Shakespeare based his play *Romeo and Juliet* on ill-fated lovers in *Metamorphoses* ("Transformations"), an epic by the Roman poet Ovid. Shakespeare borrowed the plot of one of this epic's poetic tales for his play *Romeo and Juliet* but re-imagined the two main characters as tragic figures cursed by their family's feud, rather than as disobedient children. In turn, many writers have drawn on Shakespeare's play as source material.

- Sometimes writers transform their source material so that the new work explores dimensions not present in the original. For example, the contemporary West Indian poet Derek Walcott was inspired by the ancient Greek epic the *Odyssey* to write his own long narrative poem called *Omeros* (named after Homer, the legendary author of the ancient epic). However, while Homer focused on the adventures of a warrior king, Walcott's characters are poor West Indian fishermen.

- The American short story writer O. Henry was inspired by the biblical story of the magi, or wise men, who visited the baby Jesus and brought him gifts. In his story "The Gift of the Magi," he explores the themes of gift-giving and generosity in a twentieth-century setting.

Academic Vocabulary

source material original text from which later writers draw inspiration

Apply the Standard

Use the worksheet that follows to help you apply the standard as you read. Several copies of the worksheet have been provided for you to use with different literature selections.

- Analyzing How an Author Transforms Source Material

Name _____ Date _____ Selection _____

Analyzing How an Author Transforms Source Material

Use the chart, below, to identify elements of a source that a later literary work drew upon. In the second column, explain how the later author transforms those elements.

Title and author of source: ....

Title and author of later work: ....

	Source Material Elements	How Transformed in Later Work:
Literary Form		
Main Characters		
Setting		
Conflict		
Tone		
Language		
Theme		

A

For use with Literature 9

Name _____ Date _____ Selection _____

Analyzing How an Author Transforms Source Material

Use the chart, below, to identify elements of a source that a later literary work drew upon. In the second column, explain how the later author transforms those elements.

Title and author of source: ....

Title and author of later work: ....

	Source Material Elements	How Transformed in Later Work:
Literary Form		
Main Characters		
Setting		
Conflict		
Tone		
Language		
Theme		

For use with Literature 9

Name _____ Date _____ Selection _____

Analyzing How an Author Transforms Source Material

Use the chart, below, to identify elements of a source that a later literary work drew upon. In the second column, explain how the later author transforms those elements.

Title and author of source: ....

Title and author of later work: ....

	Source Material Elements	How Transformed in Later Work:
Literary Form		
Main Characters		
Setting		
Conflict		
Tone		
Language		
Theme		

C

For use with Literature 9

Name _____ Date _____ Selection _____

Analyzing How an Author Transforms Source Material

Use the chart, below, to identify elements of a source that a later literary work drew upon. In the second column, explain how the later author transforms those elements.

Title and author of source: ....

Title and author of later work: ....

	Source Material Elements	How Transformed in Later Work:
Literary Form		
Main Characters		
Setting		
Conflict		
Tone		
Language		
Theme		

D

Name _____ Date _____ Selection _____

Analyzing How an Author Transforms Source Material

Use the chart, below, to identify elements of a source that a later literary work drew upon. In the second column, explain how the later author transforms those elements.

Title and author of source: ....

Title and author of later work: ....

	Source Material Elements	How Transformed in Later Work:
Literary Form		
Main Characters		
Setting		
Conflict		
Tone		
Language		
Theme		

E

For use with Literature 9

Name _____ Date _____ Selection _____

Analyzing How an Author Transforms Source Material

Use the chart, below, to identify elements of a source that a later literary work drew upon. In the second column, explain how the later author transforms those elements.

Title and author of source: ....

Title and author of later work: ....

	Source Material Elements	How Transformed in Later Work:
Literary Form		
Main Characters		
Setting		
Conflict		
Tone		
Language		
Theme		

F

Literature 10

> **10. By the end of grade 9, read and comprehend literature, including stories, dramas, and poems, in the grades 9–10 text complexity band proficiently, with scaffolding as needed at the high end of the range.**

Explanation

Works of literature vary in their **complexity,** or in how difficult they are to understand and analyze. Some stories, dramas, and poems have familiar subjects and include explicitly stated ideas and themes. Other stories, poems, and dramas introduce unfamiliar concepts, have implied ideas and themes, and include vocabulary, figurative language, and long sentences.

In grade 9, you will read literary works in different genres, including stories, dramas, and poems. You will also be expected to **comprehend**, or understand the meaning and importance of, texts that are more complex than those you have read before. To comprehend complex texts, use reading strategies such as monitoring comprehension, connecting, visualizing, and paraphrasing.

Examples

- To monitor your comprehension as you read, stop periodically to ask yourself questions about what you have read. For example, as you read Guy de Maupassant's short story "The Necklace," ask yourself what the necklace in the title comes to stand for. Then reread, read ahead, or use context clues to answer your questions.

- To connect with a literary work, engage with the characters. Decide whether they remind you of people you know. Think about their goals and motivations and whether or not they change. For example, in reading Saki's "The Interlopers," consider the changes that both main characters experience at the end of the story and what makes these changes ironic.

- To make a story, poem, or drama come alive, visualize, or picture, what the author describes and then relate it to your own experiences. For example, as you read Walt Whitman's poem "I Hear America Singing," picture the scenes that the speaker describes and compare them with your own impressions of life in the United States.

- To paraphrase challenging sections of a story, poem, or drama, restate the author's words and ideas in your own words. For example, as you read William Shakespeare's drama *The Tragedy of Romeo and Juliet*, paraphrase language that is difficult for you to comprehend.

Academic Vocabulary

complexity degree to which a story, poem, drama, or other work is difficult to understand

comprehend understand the meaning and importance of something

Apply the Standard

Use the worksheet that follows to help you apply the standard as you read. Several copies of the worksheet have been provided for you to use with different literature selections.

- Comprehending Complex Texts

Name _____ Date _____ Selection _____

Comprehending Complex Texts

Explain what makes the story, poem, or drama you are reading complex. Then, use the chart to explain how reading strategies help you comprehend the work.

What makes this work challenging?

....

....

Strategy	How I Used It	How It Helped
monitoring comprehension		
visualizing		
connecting		
paraphrasing		

For use with Literature 10

Name _____ Date _____ Selection _____

Comprehending Complex Texts

Explain what makes the story, poem, or drama you are reading complex. Then, use the chart to explain how reading strategies help you comprehend the work.

What makes this work challenging?

....

....

Strategy	How I Used It	How It Helped
monitoring comprehension		
visualizing		
connecting		
paraphrasing		

B

Name _____ Date _____ Selection _____

Comprehending Complex Texts

Explain what makes the story, poem, or drama you are reading complex. Then, use the chart to explain how reading strategies help you comprehend the work.

What makes this work challenging?

....

....

Strategy	How I Used It	How It Helped
monitoring comprehension		
visualizing		
connecting		
paraphrasing		

C

79

Name _____ Date _____ Selection _____

Comprehending Complex Texts

Explain what makes the story, poem, or drama you are reading complex. Then, use the chart to explain how reading strategies help you comprehend the work.

What makes this work challenging?

....

....

Strategy	How I Used It	How It Helped
monitoring comprehension		
visualizing		
connecting		
paraphrasing		

D

Name _____ Date _____ Selection _____

Comprehending Complex Texts

Explain what makes the story, poem, or drama you are reading complex. Then, use the chart to explain how reading strategies help you comprehend the work.

What makes this work challenging?

....

....

Strategy	How I Used It	How It Helped
monitoring comprehension		
visualizing		
connecting		
paraphrasing		

E

Name _____ Date _____ Selection _____

Comprehending Complex Texts

Explain what makes the story, poem, or drama you are reading complex. Then, use the chart to explain how reading strategies help you comprehend the work.

What makes this work challenging?

....

....

Strategy	How I Used It	How It Helped
monitoring comprehension		
visualizing		
connecting		
paraphrasing		

F

Reading Standards for Informational Texts

Informational Text 1

> 1. **Cite strong and thorough textual evidence to support analysis of what the text says explicitly as well as inferences drawn from the text.**

Explanation

When you **analyze** an informational text, you examine it closely and draw conclusions about it. You should take note of and analyze **explicit** details (those that are directly stated and provide basic information) to determine which are significant. By summarizing important explicit details, you can get an overall sense of what the text says.

Other story details are not stated directly and are only understood through making **inferences,** or conclusions based on evidence and reasoning. To get an overall sense of what a text says, you must combine the significant explicit details you noted with the inferences you made. These details and inferences help you form your overall understanding.

In your analysis of a text, you should cite the most important details, or **textual evidence,** to support your points. Think of the process as describing to your reader how the important explicit details and inferences you made support your overall understanding of what the text says.

Examples

- Your analysis of a text should examine what it says **explicitly**. For example, an informational article about tornadoes may include the following statement: "Tornadoes are among the most violent storms known." In your analysis, you can cite **textual evidence** that provides strong, specific support for this statement. These details might include facts about the wind speed of tornadoes and the number of people killed or injured each year.

- When analyzing a text, you also need to support any **inferences** you make with strong, thorough **textual evidence**. For example, after reading a text, you might make the following inference: "Tornadoes are very dangerous, so you need to know the signs that one is approaching." Although the article does not make this point explicitly, it does give you a basis for making the inference: It describes how tornadoes look and sound and tells the speed of tornado winds. It also explains that tornadoes can destroy homes.

Academic Vocabulary

analysis a close examination of a text, including what the text states explicitly and what is implied

inferences conclusions reached from evidence and reasoning

Apply the Standard

Use the worksheets that follow to help you apply the standard as you read. Several copies of each worksheet have been provided for you to use with different informational texts.

- Identifying Strong Textual Evidence

- Making Inferences

Name _____ Date _____ Assignment _____

Identifying Strong Textual Evidence

Use this organizer to identify textual evidence that supports an important statement made by the author. In the top box, write the author's statement. Then, complete the chart with strong specific textual evidence that serves as support for the statement.

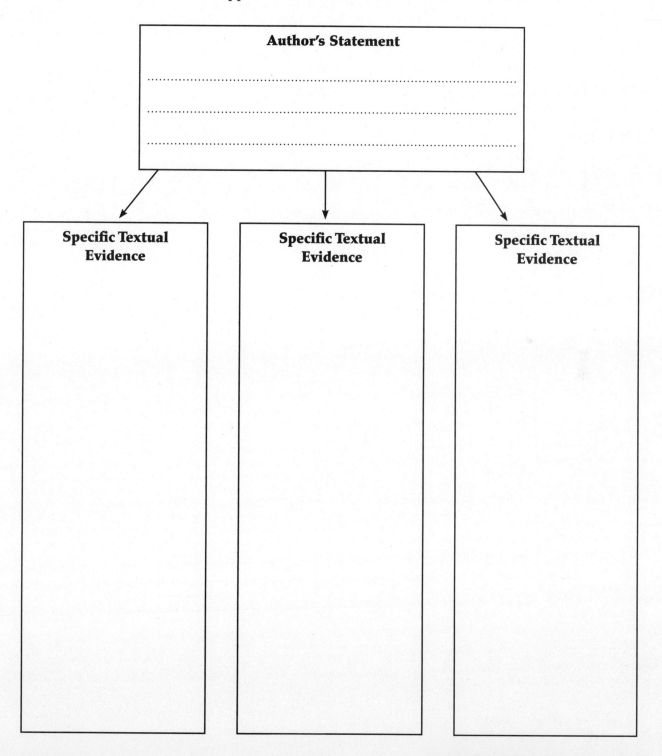

Author's Statement

....

....

....

Specific Textual Evidence

Specific Textual Evidence

Specific Textual Evidence

A

Name _____ Date _____ Assignment _____

Identifying Strong Textual Evidence

Use this organizer to identify textual evidence that supports an important statement made by the author. In the top box, write the author's statement. Then, complete the chart with strong specific textual evidence that serves as support for the statement.

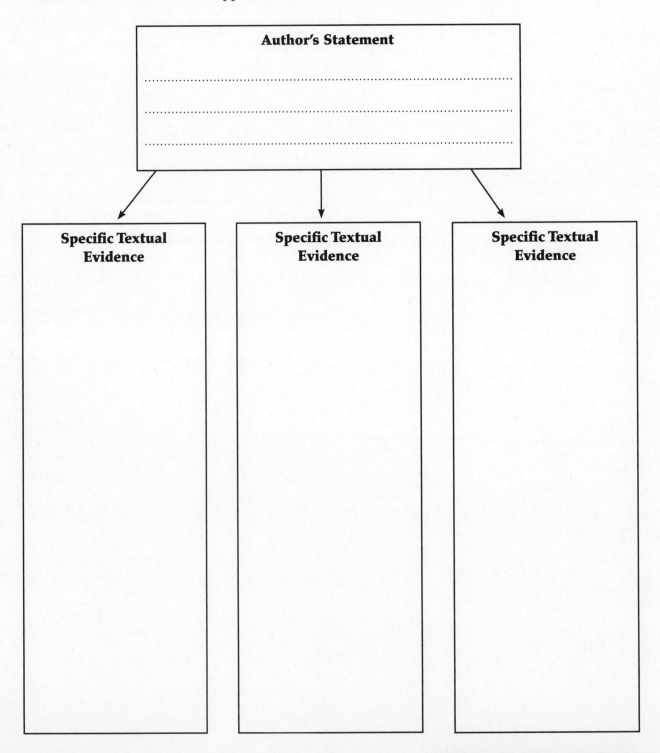

Author's Statement

....

....

....

Specific Textual Evidence

Specific Textual Evidence

Specific Textual Evidence

B

For use with Informational Text 1

Name _____ Date _____ Assignment _____

Identifying Strong Textual Evidence

Use this organizer to identify textual evidence that supports an important statement made by the author. In the top box, write the author's statement. Then, complete the chart with strong specific textual evidence that serves as support for the statement.

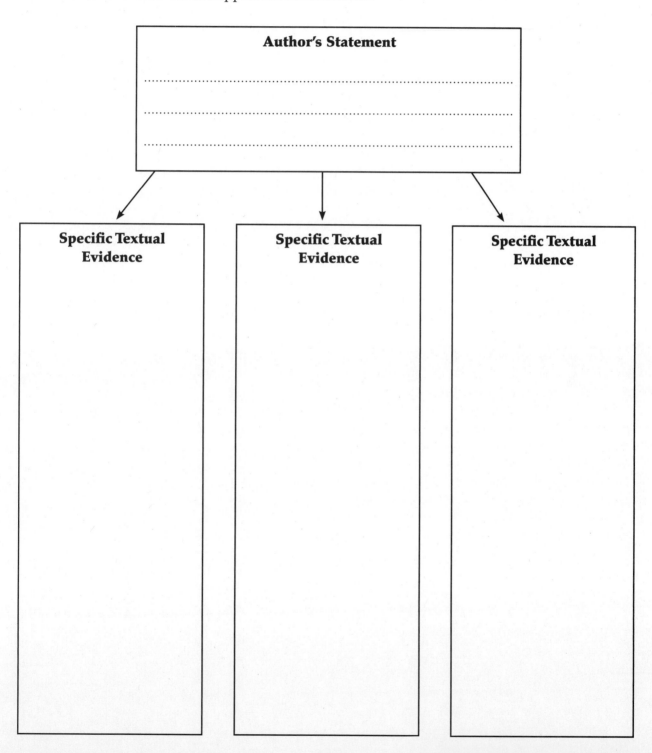

Author's Statement

....

....

....

Specific Textual Evidence

Specific Textual Evidence

Specific Textual Evidence

C

For use with Informational Text 1

Name _____ Date _____ Assignment _____

Identifying Strong Textual Evidence

Use this organizer to identify textual evidence that supports an important statement made by the author. In the top box, write the author's statement. Then, complete the chart with strong specific textual evidence that serves as support for the statement.

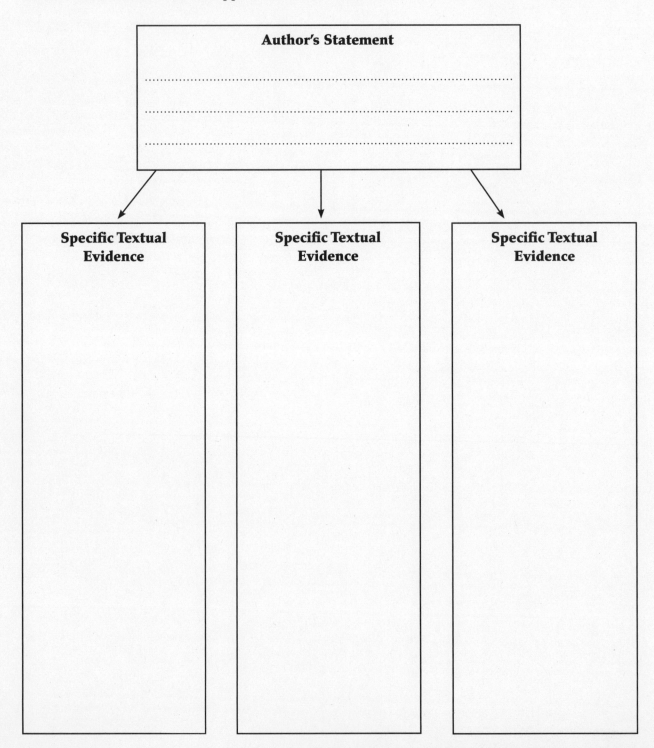

Author's Statement

....

....

....

Specific Textual Evidence	Specific Textual Evidence	Specific Textual Evidence

D

Name _____ Date _____ Assignment _____

Identifying Strong Textual Evidence

Use this organizer to identify textual evidence that supports an important statement made by the author. In the top box, write the author's statement. Then, complete the chart with strong specific textual evidence that serves as support for the statement.

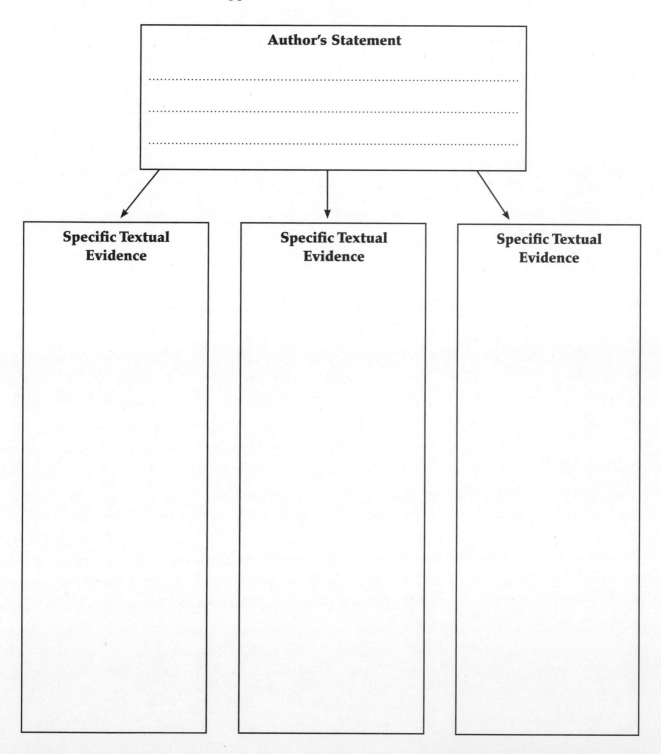

Author's Statement

Specific Textual Evidence

Specific Textual Evidence

Specific Textual Evidence

E

Name _____ Date _____ Assignment _____

Identifying Strong Textual Evidence

Use this organizer to identify textual evidence that supports an important statement made by the author. In the top box, write the author's statement. Then, complete the chart with strong specific textual evidence that serves as support for the statement.

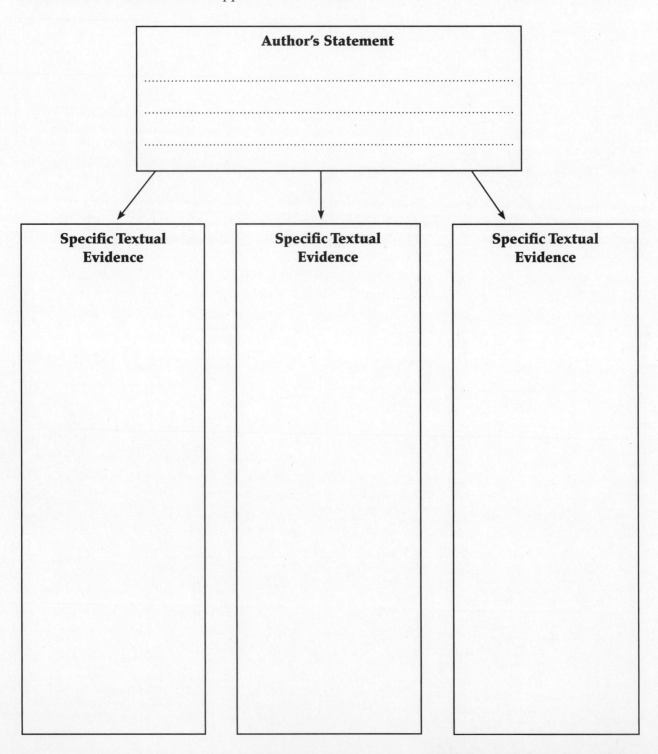

Author's Statement

Specific Textual Evidence

Specific Textual Evidence

Specific Textual Evidence

F

Name _____ Date _____ Assignment _____

Making Inferences

Use this organizer to make an inference and cite textual evidence to support that inference. Write your inference in the center box. Then, write textual evidence that provides strong, thorough support in the outer boxes.

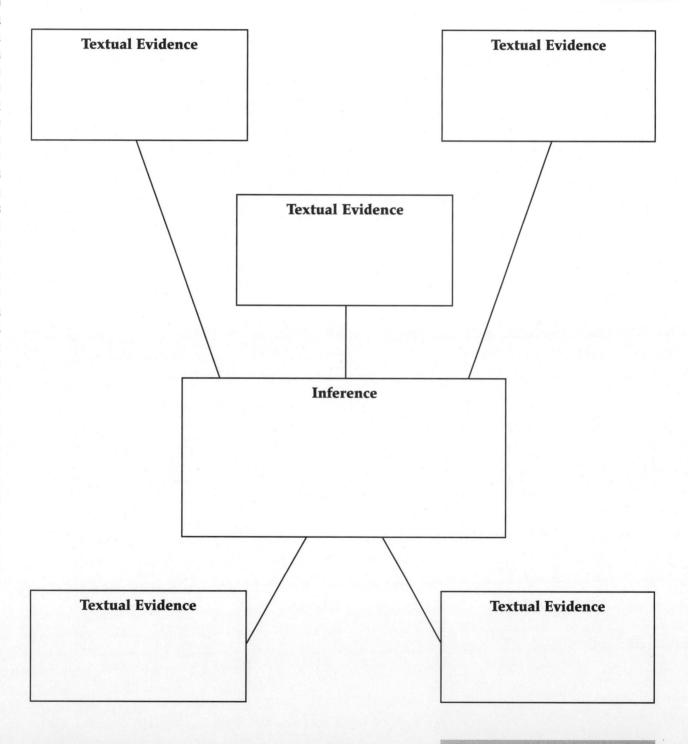

A

Name _____ Date _____ Assignment _____

Making Inferences

Use this organizer to make an inference and cite textual evidence to support that inference. Write your inference in the center box. Then, write textual evidence that provides strong, thorough support in the outer boxes.

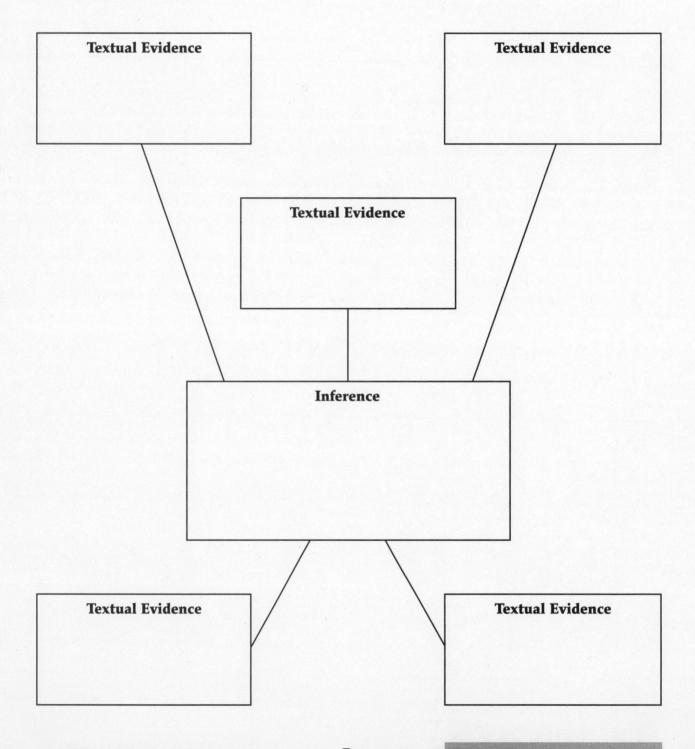

Textual Evidence

Textual Evidence

Textual Evidence

Inference

Textual Evidence

Textual Evidence

B

Name _____ Date _____ Assignment _____

Making Inferences

Use this organizer to make an inference and cite textual evidence to support that inference. Write your inference in the center box. Then, write textual evidence that provides strong, thorough support in the outer boxes.

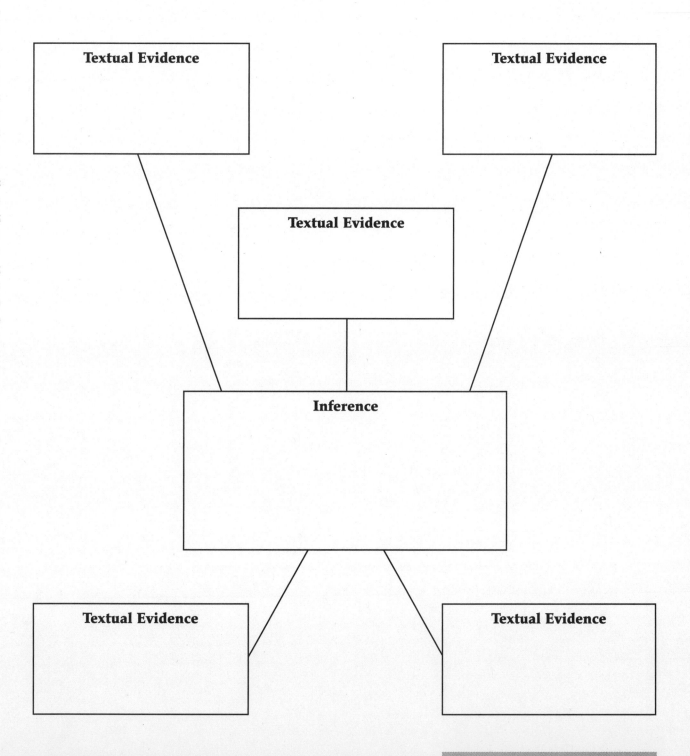

C

For use with Informational Text 1

Name _____ Date _____ Assignment _____

Making Inferences

Use this organizer to make an inference and cite textual evidence to support that inference. Write your inference in the center box. Then, write textual evidence that provides strong, thorough support in the outer boxes.

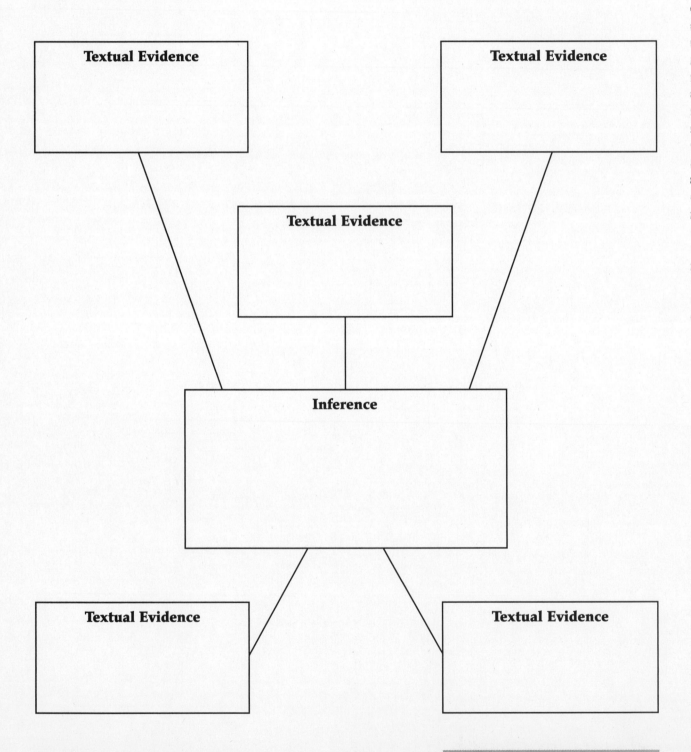

Name _____ Date _____ Assignment _____

Making Inferences

Use this organizer to make an inference and cite textual evidence to support that inference. Write your inference in the center box. Then, write textual evidence that provides strong, thorough support in the outer boxes.

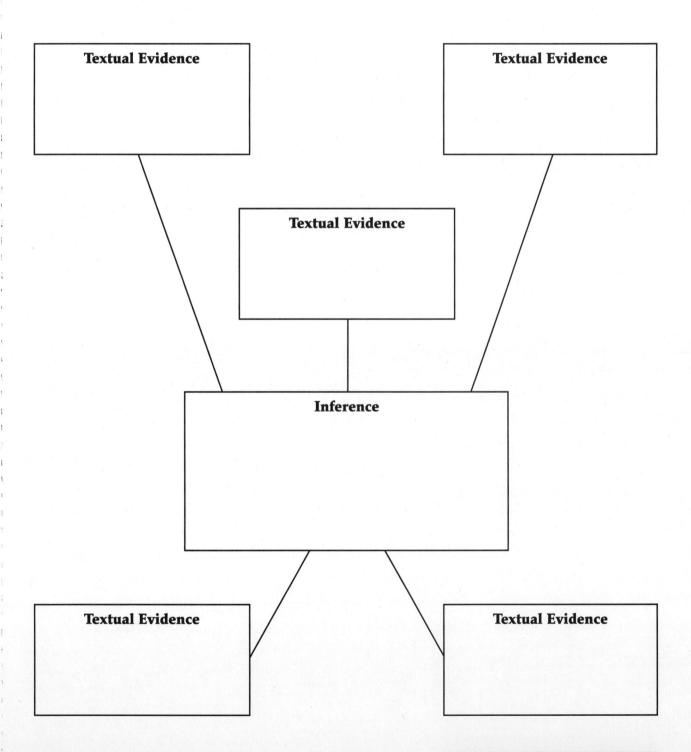

E

Name _____ Date _____ Assignment _____

Making Inferences

Use this organizer to make an inference and cite textual evidence to support that inference. Write your inference in the center box. Then, write textual evidence that provides strong, thorough support in the outer boxes.

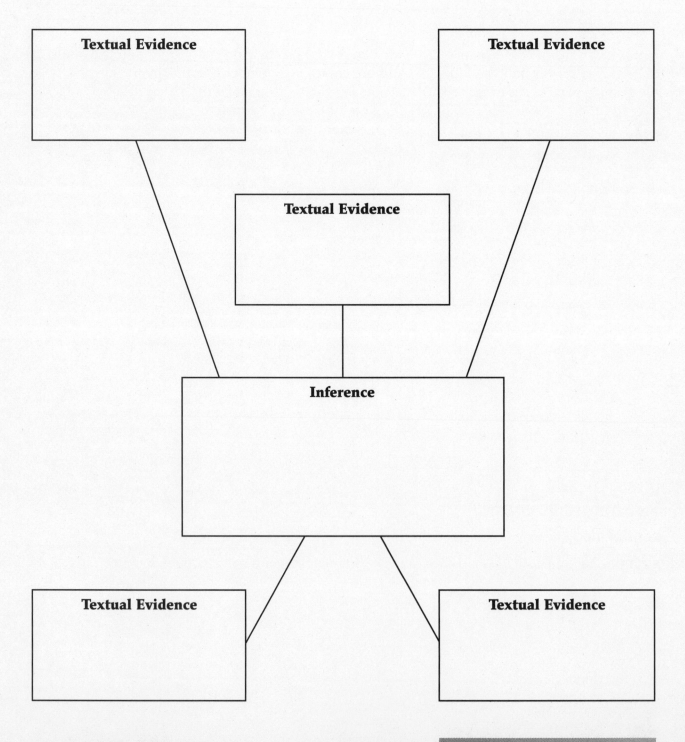

F

Informational Text 2

> 2. **Determine a central idea of a text and analyze its development over the course of the text, including how it emerges and is shaped and refined by specific details; provide an objective summary of the text.**

Explanation

An informational text usually has one **central idea**—a thesis or main point that the author wants to explain or prove about the subject. The author often states or introduces this central idea in the opening paragraphs of the text. Then, in the remaining paragraphs, the author develops and expands upon the central idea with **specific details.** Creating a summary is a good first step when analyzing a text. When you **summarize** a text, you briefly state its main idea and most important details in your own words—without including your opinions.

Examples

- An author often will state the **central idea** of an informational text in the opening paragraphs. For example, in the first paragraph of the essay "Single Room, Earth View," Sally Ride says that traveling in the space shuttle offers astronauts an amazing new perspective on Earth. This is the central idea, or thesis, of her entire essay.

- An author develops a central idea throughout the body paragraphs of his or her work by providing **specific details,** each of which supports the central idea. In "Single Room, Earth View," for example, Sally Ride offers vivid details that serve to shape and refine her thesis. She includes details about how fast the space shuttle travels and how quickly the view outside the window changes. She describes details of the changing landscape she witnessed, states how her observations support scientific theories, and recalls the cities and man-made objects she was able to identify. Additionally, she describes the effects of pollution she was able to observe while in flight, as well as the dramatic changes that occurred from day to night and during thunderstorms. She ends her essay by re-emphasizing how different a space traveler's perspective is from any earthbound experience.

Academic Vocabulary

central idea the main point the author wants to explain or prove; the thesis

summarize to restate the main ideas and important details of a text in your own words

Apply the Standard

Use the worksheets that follow to help you apply the standard as you read. Several copies of each worksheet have been provided for you to use with different informational texts.

- Summarizing the Text

- Analyzing the Central Idea

Name _____ Date _____ Assignment _____

Summarizing the Text

Use the organizer to list only the most important ideas and details in the text. Then, use the main points from your organizer to write a summary. Remember, your summary should be objective and stated in your own words. Tell only what was in the original source.

Topic
Central idea
Most Important Details

Summary

....

....

....

....

....

....

....

....

....

A

Name _____ Date _____ Assignment _____

Summarizing the Text

Use the organizer to list only the most important ideas and details in the text. Then, use the main points from your organizer to write a summary. Remember, your summary should be objective and stated in your own words. Tell only what was in the original source.

Topic
Central idea
Most Important Details

Summary

....

....

....

....

....

....

....

....

....

B

Name _____ Date _____ Assignment _____

Summarizing the Text

Use the organizer to list only the most important ideas and details in the text. Then, use the main points from your organizer to write a summary. Remember, your summary should be objective and stated in your own words. Tell only what was in the original source.

Topic
Central idea
Most Important Details

Summary

....

....

....

....

....

....

....

....

....

C

Name _____ Date _____ Assignment _____

Summarizing the Text

Use the organizer to list only the most important ideas and details in the text. Then, use the main points from your organizer to write a summary. Remember, your summary should be objective and stated in your own words. Tell only what was in the original source.

Topic
Central idea
Most Important Details

Summary

....

....

....

....

....

....

....

....

....

D

Name _____ Date _____ Assignment _____

Summarizing the Text

Use the organizer to list only the most important ideas and details in the text. Then, use the main points from your organizer to write a summary. Remember, your summary should be objective and stated in your own words. Tell only what was in the original source.

Topic
Central idea
Most Important Details

Summary

....

....

....

....

....

....

....

....

....

E

Name _____ Date _____ Assignment _____

Summarizing the Text

Use the organizer to list only the most important ideas and details in the text. Then, use the main points from your organizer to write a summary. Remember, your summary should be objective and stated in your own words. Tell only what was in the original source.

Topic
Central idea
Most Important Details

Summary

....

....

....

....

....

....

....

....

....

F

Name _____ Date _____ Assignment _____

Analyzing the Central Idea

Use this organizer to analyze how an author develops the central idea of an informational text. Write the central idea (the thesis) in the top box. Write specific details from the text that help shape and develop the central idea in the other boxes. Then answer the question at the bottom of the page.

Central Idea:

↓

Detail:

Detail:

Detail:

Detail:

Detail:

How do the details listed help you analyze the central idea?

....

....

....

....

....

....

A | For use with Informational Text 2

Name _____ Date _____ Assignment _____

Analyzing the Central Idea

Use this organizer to analyze how an author develops the central idea of an informational text. Write the central idea (the thesis) in the top box. Write specific details from the text that help shape and develop the central idea in the other boxes. Then answer the question at the bottom of the page.

Central Idea:

↓

Detail:

Detail:

Detail:

Detail:

Detail:

How do the details listed help you analyze the central idea?

....

....

....

....

....

....

B

For use with Informational Text 2

Name _____ Date _____ Assignment _____

Analyzing the Central Idea

Use this organizer to analyze how an author develops the central idea of an informational text. Write the central idea (the thesis) in the top box. Write specific details from the text that help shape and develop the central idea in the other boxes. Then answer the question at the bottom of the page.

Central Idea:

↓

Detail:

Detail:

Detail:

Detail:

Detail:

How do the details listed help you analyze the central idea?

....

....

....

....

....

....

C

For use with Informational Text 2

Name _____ Date _____ Assignment _____

Analyzing the Central Idea

Use this organizer to analyze how an author develops the central idea of an informational text. Write the central idea (the thesis) in the top box. Write specific details from the text that help shape and develop the central idea in the other boxes. Then answer the question at the bottom of the page.

Central Idea:

↓

Detail:

Detail:

Detail:

Detail:

Detail:

How do the details listed help you analyze the central idea?

....

....

....

....

....

....

D

Name _____ Date _____ Assignment _____

Analyzing the Central Idea

Use this organizer to analyze how an author develops the central idea of an informational text. Write the central idea (the thesis) in the top box. Write specific details from the text that help shape and develop the central idea in the other boxes. Then answer the question at the bottom of the page.

Central Idea:

Detail:

Detail:

Detail:

Detail:

Detail:

How do the details listed help you analyze the central idea?

....

....

....

....

....

....

E | For use with Informational Text 2

Name _____ Date _____ Assignment _____

Analyzing the Central Idea

Use this organizer to analyze how an author develops the central idea of an informational text. Write the central idea (the thesis) in the top box. Write specific details from the text that help shape and develop the central idea in the other boxes. Then answer the question at the bottom of the page.

Central Idea:

Detail:

Detail:

Detail:

Detail:

Detail:

How do the details listed help you analyze the central idea?

....

....

....

....

....

....

F

Informational Text 3

> 3. **Analyze how the author unfolds an analysis or series of ideas or events, including the order in which the points are made, how they are introduced and developed, and the connections that are drawn between them.**

Explanation

Authors of informational texts organize ideas and events in a **logical order** that is clear and easy for readers to follow. They use a variety of text structures to introduce and develop ideas and events and to establish or show connections between them. Among the text structures they commonly use are **chronological order, cause-and-effect,** and **comparison-and-contrast.**

As you read, look for words that signal connections between ideas and events. For example, words such as *first, next,* and *then* often signal chronological order. Words such as *because* and *as a result* signal a cause-and-effect connection between ideas, and words such as *by contrast, on the other hand,* and *similarly* signal comparison-and-contrast order.

Examples

- To show connections among ideas or events that happened over a period of time, authors use **chronological order.** For example, suppose that an author's central idea is that the space shuttle is a reliable, convenient way to carry cargo into space. To develop this idea, the author might relate a brief history of space shuttle flights in the order in which they occurred, describing what each mission accomplished.
- Authors use **cause-and-effect order** to illustrate how and why one idea or event influenced another. For example, an author might explain how the failure of an early space shuttle design caused NASA engineers to make changes to improve the shuttle's safety or performance.
- To show how events or ideas are similar and different, authors use a **comparison-and-contrast** text structure. For example, an author might explain how a space shuttle is similar to and different from a rocket or an airplane.

Academic Vocabulary

cause-and-effect a text structure used to explain how and why one event or idea led to or influenced another

chronological order the arrangement of events or ideas in the order in which they actually occurred over a period of time

comparison-and-contrast a text structure used to explain how events or ideas are alike and different

logical order an order or sequence that makes sense and is easy for readers to follow

Apply the Standard

Use the worksheet that follows to help you apply the standard as you read. Several copies of the worksheet have been provided for you to use with different informational texts.

- Analyzing the Development and Connection of Ideas or Events

Name _____ Date _____ Assignment _____

Analyzing the Development and Connection of Ideas or Events

As you read informational texts, use the following organizer to analyze how each author uses a particular text structure to develop and connect important ideas or events.

Ideas or Events Developed	Words Connecting Ideas or Events	Ideas or Events Developed

Type of Connection Between Ideas or Events

Name _____ Date _____ Assignment _____

Analyzing the Development and Connection of Ideas or Events

As you read informational texts, use the following organizer to analyze how each author uses a particular text structure to develop and connect important ideas or events.

Ideas or Events Developed

Words Connecting Ideas or Events

Ideas or Events Developed

Type of Connection Between Ideas or Events

B

For use with Informational Text 3

Name _____ Date _____ Assignment _____

Analyzing the Development and Connection of Ideas or Events

As you read informational texts, use the following organizer to analyze how each author uses a particular text structure to develop and connect important ideas or events.

Ideas or Events Developed	**Words Connecting Ideas or Events**	**Ideas or Events Developed**

Type of Connection Between Ideas or Events

Name _____ Date _____ Assignment _____

Analyzing the Development and Connection of Ideas or Events

As you read informational texts, use the following organizer to analyze how each author uses a particular text structure to develop and connect important ideas or events.

Ideas or Events Developed	Words Connecting Ideas or Events	Ideas or Events Developed

Type of Connection Between Ideas or Events

Name _____ Date _____ Assignment _____

Analyzing the Development and Connection of Ideas or Events

As you read informational texts, use the following organizer to analyze how each author uses a particular text structure to develop and connect important ideas or events.

Ideas or Events Developed	**Words Connecting Ideas or Events**	**Ideas or Events Developed**

Type of Connection Between Ideas or Events

E

Name _____ Date _____ Assignment _____

Analyzing the Development and Connection of Ideas or Events

As you read informational texts, use the following organizer to analyze how each author uses a particular text structure to develop and connect important ideas or events.

Ideas or Events Developed	**Words Connecting Ideas or Events**	**Ideas or Events Developed**

Type of Connection Between Ideas or Events

F

Informational Text 4

> 4. **Determine the meaning of words and phrases as they are used in a text, including figurative, connotative, and technical meanings; analyze the cumulative impact of specific word choices on meaning and tone (e.g., how the language of a court opinion differs from that of a newspaper).**

Explanation

The attitude that a writer expresses about a subject is called **tone**. To determine a text's meaning and tone, analyze the words and phrases the author uses—including their connotative, figurative, and technical meanings. **Connotations** are the ideas and feelings associated with a word. **Figurative language** is language that is not meant to be taken literally. It includes figures of speech, such as similes and metaphors. **Technical terms** are words that have a special meaning in a particular field of study.

Examples

- Authors of different kinds of texts make specific word choices to convey different tones. A magazine article might include colloquial and figurative language to convey a friendly tone. A user's manual might include technical terms to convey a clear meaning and unemotional tone.

- Many words with similar meanings have different connotations. A word's connotation can be positive, negative, or neutral. For example, *frugal* has a more positive connotation than *cheap*.

- Used to state ideas in vivid and imaginative ways, figurative language also affects meaning and tone. For example, describing a person as a *runaway train* expresses disapproval and concern.

- Informational texts often include words with technical meanings. For example, common words, such as *minor* and *key,* have technical meanings in music. In addition, many fields have technical terms that are not common in everyday life. For example, to understand an article about rock climbing, you might need to identify the meanings of the terms *rappelling* and *belaying*.

Academic Vocabulary

connotations the positive, negative, or neutral feelings associated with a word

figurative language writing or speech that is not meant to be taken literally

technical terms words that have a specialized meaning in a particular career or field of study

tone the writer's attitude toward his or her audience and subject

Apply the Standard

Use the worksheets that follow to help you apply the standard as you read. Several copies of each worksheet have been provided for you to use with different informational texts.

- Understanding Connotations, Figurative Language, and Technical Terms

- Analyzing Word Choice

Name _____ Date _____ Assignment _____

Understanding Connotations, Figurative Language, and Technical Terms

Use this organizer to analyze important words and phrases in an informational text, particularly the author's use of technical terms, figurative language, and words with positive or negative connotations.

Word with Connotation	What It Means	Tone It Conveys

+

Figurative Language	What It Means	Tone It Conveys

+

Technical Term	What It Means	Tone It Conveys

A

For use with Informational Text 4

Name _____ Date _____ Assignment _____

Understanding Connotations, Figurative Language, and Technical Terms

Use this organizer to analyze important words and phrases in an informational text, particularly the author's use of technical terms, figurative language, and words with positive or negative connotations.

Word with Connotation	What It Means	Tone It Conveys

+

Figurative Language	What It Means	Tone It Conveys

+

Technical Term	What It Means	Tone It Conveys

B

Name _____ Date _____ Assignment _____

Understanding Connotations, Figurative Language, and Technical Terms

Use this organizer to analyze important words and phrases in an informational text, particularly the author's use of technical terms, figurative language, and words with positive or negative connotations.

Word with Connotation	What It Means	Tone It Conveys

+

Figurative Language	What It Means	Tone It Conveys

+

Technical Term	What It Means	Tone It Conveys

C

For use with Informational Text 4

Name _____ Date _____ Assignment _____

Understanding Connotations, Figurative Language, and Technical Terms

Use this organizer to analyze important words and phrases in an informational text, particularly the author's use of technical terms, figurative language, and words with positive or negative connotations.

Word with Connotation	What It Means	Tone It Conveys

+

Figurative Language	What It Means	Tone It Conveys

+

Technical Term	What It Means	Tone It Conveys

D

For use with Informational Text 4

Name _____ Date _____ Assignment _____

Understanding Connotations, Figurative Language, and Technical Terms

Use this organizer to analyze important words and phrases in an informational text, particularly the author's use of technical terms, figurative language, and words with positive or negative connotations.

Word with Connotation	What It Means	Tone It Conveys

+

Figurative Language	What It Means	Tone It Conveys

+

Technical Term	What It Means	Tone It Conveys

E

Name _____ Date _____ Assignment _____

Understanding Connotations, Figurative Language, and Technical Terms

Use this organizer to analyze important words and phrases in an informational text, particularly the author's use of technical terms, figurative language, and words with positive or negative connotations.

Word with Connotation	What It Means	Tone It Conveys

+

Figurative Language	What It Means	Tone It Conveys

+

Technical Term	What It Means	Tone It Conveys

F

For use with Informational Text 4

Name _____ Date _____ Assignment _____

Analyzing Word Choice

Use this organizer to analyze the overall meaning and tone of an informational text, based on important words and phrases the author uses in the text.

Important Words and Phrases ....
....
....
....
....
....
....
....

Overall Meaning ....
....
....
....
....
....
....
....

Overall Tone ....
....
....
....
....
....
....
....

A

For use with Informational Text 4

Name _____ Date _____ Assignment _____

Analyzing Word Choice

Use this organizer to analyze the overall meaning and tone of an informational text, based on important words and phrases the author uses in the text.

Important Words and Phrases ....

....

....

....

....

....

....

....

Overall Meaning ....

....

....

....

....

....

....

Overall Tone ....

....

....

....

....

....

....

For use with Informational Text 4

Name _____ Date _____ Assignment _____

Analyzing Word Choice

Use this organizer to analyze the overall meaning and tone of an informational text, based on important words and phrases the author uses in the text.

Important Words and Phrases ....

....

....

....

....

....

....

....

Overall Meaning ....

....

....

....

....

....

....

Overall Tone ....

....

....

....

....

....

....

C

For use with Informational Text 4

Name _____ Date _____ Assignment _____

Analyzing Word Choice

Use this organizer to analyze the overall meaning and tone of an informational text, based on important words and phrases the author uses in the text.

Important Words and Phrases ....
....
....
....
....
....
....
....

Overall Meaning ....
....
....
....
....
....
....

Overall Tone ....
....
....
....
....
....
....

Name _____ Date _____ Assignment _____

Analyzing Word Choice

Use this organizer to analyze the overall meaning and tone of an informational text, based on important words and phrases the author uses in the text.

Important Words and Phrases ....
....
....
....
....
....
....

Overall Meaning ....
....
....
....
....
....

Overall Tone ....
....
....
....
....
....

E

For use with Informational Text 4

Name _____ Date _____ Assignment _____

Analyzing Word Choice

Use this organizer to analyze the overall meaning and tone of an informational text, based on important words and phrases the author uses in the text.

Important Words and Phrases ....
....
....
....
....
....
....

Overall Meaning ....
....
....
....
....
....

Overall Tone ....
....
....
....
....
....

F

For use with Informational Text 4

Informational Text 5

> 5. **Analyze in detail how an author's ideas or claims are developed and refined by particular sentences, paragraphs, or larger portions of text (e.g., a section or chapter).**

Explanation

Writers of informational texts develop and refine their ideas by using **text structures,** such as chronological order, cause and effect, and comparison and contrast. They often use these structures to support **claims,** or arguments, that strengthen their overall point. To find sentences and paragraphs that develop an idea or claim, look for key words, such as *before, after, because, since,* and *as a result.* To analyze how larger portions of text develop an idea, pay attention to **text features,** such as titles, headings, and subheadings.

Examples

- To develop a claim, writers frequently will cite several strong reasons and provide several examples. To analyze an author's reasons, look for key words, such as *because, since,* and *why.* Examples often include dates or statistical data with numbers. For instance, an author might give this reason for supporting his opinion that schools should shorten summer vacations: *Long summer vacations disrupt the learning because students forget what they have learned and must be re-taught old information in the fall.* The writer might then support this reason with an example: *For example, 75 percent of English teachers here spend September reviewing information students learned the year before.*

- To identify larger portions of a text that develop and refine key ideas, look for text features. A title usually tells the topic you will learn about in a text or chapter. For example, the title "Team Builds 'Sociable' Robot" prepares readers to learn about a robot that interacts with people. Headings and subheadings within the text tell you which main ideas are developed in different portions of the text. For example, the heading "Inspired by Kids" alerts readers that this portion of the text tells what the robot builders learned by observing children.

Academic Vocabulary

claim a supporting fact or argument in a persuasive text

text features titles, headings, and subheadings that highlight and identify key ideas in a text

text structures ways of organizing textual support in sentences and paragraphs

Apply the Standard

Use the worksheet that follows to help you apply the standard as you read. Several copies have been provided for you to use with different informational texts.

- Analyzing the Development of an Idea or Claim

Name _____ Date _____ Assignment _____

Analyzing the Development of an Idea or Claim

Use this organizer to analyze particular sentences, paragraphs, and sections of a text that develop and refine an author's ideas or claims. Identify the part of the text on the left. Next to it, explain how that part of the text develops the idea or claim.

Portion of the Text	How It Develops an Idea or Claim
Sentence:	
Paragraph:	
Section and Heading:	

Name _____ Date _____ Assignment _____

Analyzing the Development of an Idea or Claim

Use this organizer to analyze particular sentences, paragraphs, and sections of a text that develop and refine an author's ideas or claims. Identify the part of the text on the left. Next to it, explain how that part of the text develops the idea or claim.

Portion of the Text	How It Develops an Idea or Claim
Sentence:	
Paragraph:	
Section and Heading:	

B

Name _____ Date _____ Assignment _____

Analyzing the Development of an Idea or Claim

Use this organizer to analyze particular sentences, paragraphs, and sections of a text that develop and refine an author's ideas or claims. Identify the part of the text on the left. Next to it, explain how that part of the text develops the idea or claim.

Portion of the Text	How It Develops an Idea or Claim
Sentence:	
Paragraph:	
Section and Heading:	

C

For use with Informational Text 5

Analyzing the Development of an Idea or Claim

Use this organizer to analyze particular sentences, paragraphs, and sections of a text that develop and refine an author's ideas or claims. Identify the part of the text on the left. Next to it, explain how that part of the text develops the idea or claim.

Portion of the Text	How It Develops an Idea or Claim
Sentence:	
Paragraph:	
Section and Heading:	

Name _____ Date _____ Assignment _____

Analyzing the Development of an Idea or Claim

Use this organizer to analyze particular sentences, paragraphs, and sections of a text that develop and refine an author's ideas or claims. Identify the part of the text on the left. Next to it, explain how that part of the text develops the idea or claim.

Portion of the Text	How It Develops an Idea or Claim
Sentence:	
Paragraph:	
Section and Heading:	

E

For use with Informational Text 5

Name _____ Date _____ Assignment _____

Analyzing the Development of an Idea or Claim

Use this organizer to analyze particular sentences, paragraphs, and sections of a text that develop and refine an author's ideas or claims. Identify the part of the text on the left. Next to it, explain how that part of the text develops the idea or claim.

Portion of the Text	How It Develops an Idea or Claim
Sentence:	
Paragraph:	
Section and Heading:	

F

Informational Text 6

6. **Determine an author's point of view or purpose in a text and analyze how an author uses rhetoric to advance that point of view or purpose.**

Explanation

The purpose of an informational text may be to inform, explain, describe, persuade, or even entertain. You can determine the **author's purpose,** or reason for writing, by analyzing the details in the text. You can also determine the author's perspective or **point of view,** the beliefs, attitudes, and experiences relating to the subject. Writers advance their point of view by using **rhetoric.** Rhetorical devices commonly used by writers include repetition, parallelism, slogans, and rhetorical questions.

Examples

• **Purpose and Point of View:** Consider what kinds of details the author uses. For example, to describe, the text will focus on sensory details. To inform or explain, the details will be facts. To persuade, the author will offer reasons and examples. Notice the kinds of words and sentences the author uses. For example, if the author uses the words *shouldn't* and *because* in an article about spreading rumors, you know the purpose is to persuade. Examples of the dangers of spreading rumors drawn from the author's life show a negative point of view and reflect firsthand experience. The kinds of details the author uses reflect the purpose.

• **Rhetoric:** To advance the purpose and point of view, authors will often use rhetorical devices. One such rhetorical device is repetition, or the repeating of key words or phrases to emphasize important ideas. Parallelism is another common rhetorical device. It means using similar grammatical structures to express related ideas. For example, *Nasty rumors hurt the target, corrupt the gossipers, and poison the social atmosphere.* Each phrase begins with a present-tense verb. Slogans are another rhetorical device. They are short, catchy phrases that help readers remember the author's point of view. For example, *Don't use words as weapons.* Finally, rhetorical questions have obvious answers and are used for dramatic effect. For example, *Would you like to be the target of a nasty rumor?*

Academic Vocabulary

author's point of view the author's beliefs, attitudes, and experiences relating to a subject

author's purpose the author's main reason for writing a text

rhetoric verbal techniques that advance a point of view by creating emphasis and emotional appeal

Apply the Standard

Use the worksheets that follow to help you apply the standard as you read. Several copies of each worksheet have been provided for you to use with different informational texts.

• Determining Author's Purpose and Point of View

• Analyzing Author's Rhetoric

Name _____ Date _____ Assignment _____

Determining Author's Purpose and Point of View

Use this organizer to determine the author's purpose for writing a text and the point of view the author expresses about the topic.

Kinds of Details

❑ Facts
❑ Reasons
❑ Examples
❑ Sensory details
❑ Other (Explain.) _____

↓

Important Words and Sentences

↓

Author's Purpose and Perspective

Purpose:

❑ to inform or explain
❑ to persuade
❑ to describe
❑ to entertain

Perspective:

A

For use with Informational Text 6

Name _____ Date _____ Assignment _____

Determining Author's Purpose and Point of View

Use this organizer to determine the author's purpose for writing a text and the point of view the author expresses about the topic.

Kinds of Details
- ❏ Facts
- ❏ Reasons
- ❏ Examples
- ❏ Sensory details
- ❏ Other (Explain.) _____

↓

Important Words and Sentences

↓

Author's Purpose and Perspective

Purpose:
- ❏ to inform or explain
- ❏ to persuade
- ❏ to describe
- ❏ to entertain

Perspective:

B

Name _____ Date _____ Assignment _____

Determining Author's Purpose and Point of View

Use this organizer to determine the author's purpose for writing a text and the point of view the author expresses about the topic.

Kinds of Details

❏ Facts
❏ Reasons
❏ Examples
❏ Sensory details
❏ Other (Explain.) _____

↓

Important Words and Sentences

↓

Author's Purpose and Perspective

Purpose:

❏ to inform or explain
❏ to persuade
❏ to describe
❏ to entertain

Perspective:

C

Name _____ Date _____ Assignment _____

Determining Author's Purpose and Point of View

Use this organizer to determine the author's purpose for writing a text and the point of view the author expresses about the topic.

Kinds of Details

❑ Facts
❑ Reasons
❑ Examples
❑ Sensory details
❑ Other (Explain.) _____

↓

Important Words and Sentences

↓

Author's Purpose and Perspective

Purpose:

❑ to inform or explain
❑ to persuade
❑ to describe
❑ to entertain

Perspective:

Name _____ Date _____ Assignment _____

Determining Author's Purpose and Point of View

Use this organizer to determine the author's purpose for writing a text and the point of view the author expresses about the topic.

Kinds of Details

❏ Facts
❏ Reasons
❏ Examples
❏ Sensory details
❏ Other (Explain.) _____

↓

Important Words and Sentences

↓

Author's Purpose and Perspective

Purpose:

❏ to inform or explain
❏ to persuade
❏ to describe
❏ to entertain

Perspective:

E

For use with Informational Text 6

Name _____ Date _____ Assignment _____

Determining Author's Purpose and Point of View

Use this organizer to determine the author's purpose for writing a text and the point of view the author expresses about the topic.

Kinds of Details
- ❑ Facts
- ❑ Reasons
- ❑ Examples
- ❑ Sensory details
- ❑ Other (Explain.) _____

↓

Important Words and Sentences

↓

Author's Purpose and Perspective

Purpose:
- ❑ to inform or explain
- ❑ to persuade
- ❑ to describe
- ❑ to entertain

Perspective:

F

Name _____ Date _____ Assignment _____

Analyzing Author's Rhetoric

Use this organizer to identify the rhetorical devices used in a text and to explain how they advance the author's purpose and point of view.

Rhetorical Device	Example	Effect
repetition		
parallelism		
slogan		
rhetorical question		

For use with Informational Text 6

Name _____ Date _____ Assignment _____

Analyzing Author's Rhetoric

Use this organizer to identify the rhetorical devices used in a text and to explain how they advance the author's purpose and point of view.

Rhetorical Device	Example	Effect
repetition		
parallelism		
slogan		
rhetorical question		

For use with Informational Text 6

Name _____ Date _____ Assignment _____

Analyzing Author's Rhetoric

Use this organizer to identify the rhetorical devices used in a text and to explain how they advance the author's purpose and point of view.

Rhetorical Device	Example	Effect
repetition		
parallelism		
slogan		
rhetorical question		

C

Name _____ Date _____ Assignment _____

Analyzing Author's Rhetoric

Use this organizer to identify the rhetorical devices used in a text and to explain how they advance the author's purpose and point of view.

Rhetorical Device	Example	Effect
repetition		
parallelism		
slogan		
rhetorical question		

D

For use with Informational Text 6

Name _____ Date _____ Assignment _____

Analyzing Author's Rhetoric

Use this organizer to identify the rhetorical devices used in a text and to explain how they advance the author's purpose and point of view.

Rhetorical Device	Example	Effect
repetition		
parallelism		
slogan		
rhetorical question		

E

For use with Informational Text 6

Name _____ Date _____ Assignment _____

Analyzing Author's Rhetoric

Use this organizer to identify the rhetorical devices used in a text and to explain how they advance the author's purpose and point of view.

Rhetorical Device	Example	Effect
repetition		
parallelism		
slogan		
rhetorical question		

F

For use with Informational Text 6

Informational Text 7

> **7. Analyze the various accounts of a subject told in different mediums (e.g., a person's life story in both print and multimedia), determining which details are emphasized in each account.**

Explanation

Nowadays people can find information available in many different **mediums,** or forms of communication, including print, audio CD, DVD, podcast, Internet text, and online video. The format of a specific medium can influence which details about the subject an author might choose to include, leave out, or emphasize. Reading or viewing several accounts of a subject will help you become better informed about a topic, as each account will add details to your overall understanding. Doing so will also help you become a more critical consumer of media. Analyzing which details are emphasized will show the author's purpose and possible biases. You will learn which sources are trustworthy and helpful and which are not.

Examples

- A written text relies on words to convey an impression of a person, topic, or event. Other mediums use sound and images to convey information. As a result, a multimedia account may emphasize details that can be presented dramatically through music, sound effects, video, and graphics. For example, a written biography of Martin Luther King, Jr. might focus on King's education, his training for the ministry, and how he developed his ideas of nonviolent protest and social justice. A multimedia biography, on the other hand, might emphasize dramatic images of King's participation in demonstrations and the sound of his voice in his famous speeches.

- To analyze accounts of a subject presented in different mediums, study each work and note important details, especially which details are stressed (or less emphasized) in each medium. Synthesize information from several accounts to gain a deeper understanding of the subject. Then compare and contrast the ideas and attitudes conveyed by the works, as well as your own response to them. Ask: Does this account include useful information? Does it add to my understanding? Does it leave out important details? Is the author biased?

Academic Vocabulary

medium a particular means or format of communication, such as text, audio, video, or multimedia

Apply the Standard

Use the worksheet that follows to help you apply the standard as you read. Several copies have been provided for you to use with different informational texts and multimedia accounts.

- Analyzing Accounts in Different Mediums

Name _____ Date _____ Assignment _____

Analyzing Accounts in Different Mediums

Use this organizer to analyze and compare accounts of the same subject in two different mediums, detailing what information is shared or exclusive to each. Then answer the questions.

TITLE:

MEDIUM:

TITLE:

MEDIUM:

Emphasis:

Absent:

Message or Attitude:

Emphasis:

Absent:

Message or Attitude:

How did each account add to your understanding?

....

....

....

Were both accounts trustworthy and useful? Explain.

....

....

....

A

Name _____ Date _____ Assignment _____

Analyzing Accounts in Different Mediums

Use this organizer to analyze and compare accounts of the same subject in two different mediums, detailing what information is shared or exclusive to each. Then answer the questions.

TITLE:

MEDIUM:

TITLE:

MEDIUM:

Emphasis:

Absent:

Message or
Attitude:

Emphasis:

Absent:

Message or
Attitude:

How did each account add to your understanding?

....

....

....

Were both accounts trustworthy and useful? Explain.

....

....

....

B

Name _____ Date _____ Assignment _____

Analyzing Accounts in Different Mediums

Use this organizer to analyze and compare accounts of the same subject in two different mediums, detailing what information is shared or exclusive to each. Then answer the questions.

TITLE:

MEDIUM:

TITLE:

MEDIUM:

Emphasis:

Absent:

Message or
Attitude:

Emphasis:

Absent:

Message or
Attitude:

How did each account add to your understanding?

....

....

....

Were both accounts trustworthy and useful? Explain.

....

....

....

C

Analyzing Accounts in Different Mediums

Use this organizer to analyze and compare accounts of the same subject in two different mediums, detailing what information is shared or exclusive to each. Then answer the questions.

TITLE:

MEDIUM:

TITLE:

MEDIUM:

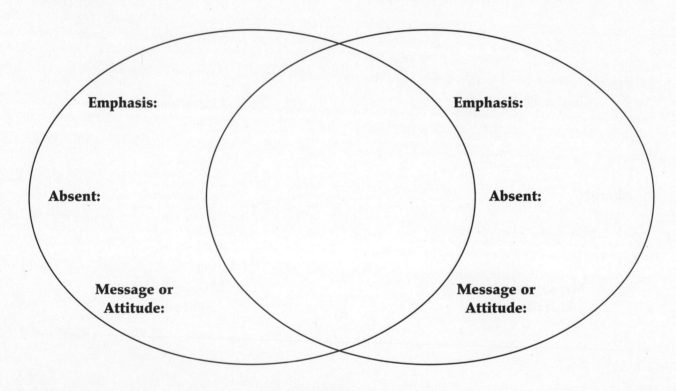

Emphasis:

Absent:

Message or
Attitude:

Emphasis:

Absent:

Message or
Attitude:

How did each account add to your understanding?

....

....

....

Were both accounts trustworthy and useful? Explain.

....

....

....

Name _____ Date _____ Assignment _____

Analyzing Accounts in Different Mediums

Use this organizer to analyze and compare accounts of the same subject in two different mediums, detailing what information is shared or exclusive to each. Then answer the questions.

TITLE:

MEDIUM:

TITLE:

MEDIUM:

Emphasis:

Absent:

Message or Attitude:

Emphasis:

Absent:

Message or Attitude:

How did each account add to your understanding?

....

....

....

Were both accounts trustworthy and useful? Explain.

....

....

....

E

Name _____ Date _____ Assignment _____

Analyzing Accounts in Different Mediums

Use this organizer to analyze and compare accounts of the same subject in two different mediums, detailing what information is shared or exclusive to each. Then answer the questions.

TITLE:

MEDIUM:

TITLE:

MEDIUM:

Emphasis:

Absent:

Message or Attitude:

Emphasis:

Absent:

Message or Attitude:

How did each account add to your understanding?

....

....

....

Were both accounts trustworthy and useful? Explain.

....

....

....

F

Informational Text 8

> 8. **Delineate and evaluate the argument and specific claims in a text, assessing whether the reasoning is valid and the evidence is relevant and sufficient; identify false statements and fallacious reasoning.**

Explanation

In a persuasive text, an author presents an argument or **claim**—the position on an issue that the author wants you to accept. To evaluate the strength and accuracy of an argument, you need to assess the author's supporting evidence and reasoning, the underlying logic that supports the author's claim.

Examples

- Authors should support each claim in an argument with **factual evidence,** statements that can be proven to be true. If you identify any false statements, you can conclude that the argument is not reliable. For example, suppose an author makes this claim: *Watching TV is the best way to learn about history.* The author supports the claim with this faulty evidence: *There are many history programs on TV, and most of them are on subjects you could never learn in a book.* The author's claim about watching TV is unreliable.

- The author should present enough facts to support each claim, and every fact should be relevant to the issue. For example, suppose the author supported the claim about watching TV with this fact: *Ninety percent of teenagers would rather watch TV than read a book.* Whether this statement is true or false, it has no relevance to the claim that watching TV is the best way to learn history.

- Evaluate the author's reasoning to see if the argument makes sense. **Fallacious reasoning,** or false logic, is a sign that an argument is unreliable. Pay close attention to the author's generalizations—broad statements or inferences. For example, in the argument about watching TV, the author might write: *Most people learn better by watching an educational TV show than by reading. I know this is true because everything I know about history I learned from TV shows.* The author tries to support a generalization about "most people" with a fact about his own limited experience. This logic is deeply flawed.

Academic Vocabulary

claim a belief or position on a topic that the author asks readers to accept

factual evidence statements than can be proven to be true

fallacious reasoning false or faulty logic

Apply the Standard

Use the worksheet that follows to help you apply the standard as you read persuasive texts. Several copies of the worksheet have been provided for you.

- Evaluating an Argument

Name _____ Date _____ Selection _____

Evaluating an Argument

Use this organizer to evaluate the argument and claims made by the author of a persuasive text. Consider the evidence the author uses to support his or her argument and why it is or isn't reliable or logical.

Argument or Position	Claim	Factual Evidence	Is the Reasoning Logical?
		true? .... relevant?	Yes, because .... No, because ....
		true? .... relevant?	Yes, because .... No, because ....
		true? .... relevant?	Yes, because .... No, because ....

For use with Informational Texts 8

Name _____ Date _____ Selection _____

Evaluating an Argument

Use this organizer to evaluate the argument and claims made by the author of a persuasive text. Consider the evidence the author uses to support his or her argument and why it is or isn't reliable or logical.

Argument or Position	Claim	Factual Evidence	Is the Reasoning Logical?
		true? .... relevant?	Yes, because .... No, because ....
		true? .... relevant?	Yes, because .... No, because ....
		true? .... relevant?	Yes, because .... No, because ....

Name _____ Date _____ Selection _____

Evaluating an Argument

Use this organizer to evaluate the argument and claims made by the author of a persuasive text. Consider the evidence the author uses to support his or her argument and why it is or isn't reliable or logical.

Argument or Position	Claim	Factual Evidence	Is the Reasoning Logical?
		true? .... relevant?	Yes, because .... No, because ....
		true? .... relevant?	Yes, because .... No, because ....
		true? .... relevant?	Yes, because .... No, because ....

C

Name _____ Date _____ Selection _____

Evaluating an Argument

Use this organizer to evaluate the argument and claims made by the author of a persuasive text. Consider the evidence the author uses to support his or her argument and why it is or isn't reliable or logical.

Argument or Position	Claim	Factual Evidence	Is the Reasoning Logical?
		true? .... relevant?	Yes, because .... No, because ....
		true? .... relevant?	Yes, because .... No, because ....
		true? .... relevant?	Yes, because .... No, because ....

D

Name _____ Date _____ Selection _____

Evaluating an Argument

Use this organizer to evaluate the argument and claims made by the author of a persuasive text. Consider the evidence the author uses to support his or her argument and why it is or isn't reliable or logical.

Argument or Position	Claim	Factual Evidence	Is the Reasoning Logical?
		true? .... relevant?	Yes, because .... No, because ....
		true? .... relevant?	Yes, because .... No, because ....
		true? .... relevant?	Yes, because .... No, because ....

E

Name _____ Date _____ Selection _____

Evaluating an Argument

Use this organizer to evaluate the argument and claims made by the author of a persuasive text. Consider the evidence the author uses to support his or her argument and why it is or isn't reliable or logical.

Argument or Position	Claim	Factual Evidence	Is the Reasoning Logical?
		true? .... relevant?	Yes, because .... No, because ....
		true? .... relevant?	Yes, because .... No, because ....
		true? .... relevant?	Yes, because .... No, because ....

F

Informational Text 9

> **9.** Analyze seminal U.S. documents of historical and literary significance (e.g., Washington's Farewell Address, the Gettysburg Address, Roosevelt's Four Freedoms speech, King's "Letter from Birmingham Jail"), including how they address related themes and concepts.

Explanation

When you analyze and compare historic U.S. documents, you learn about key ideas that have shaped American values. Some of these documents and speeches have played important roles in U.S. history and continue to influence people today. In many instances, these documents present political arguments, positions on important issues, and American ideals. Political arguments usually include both **logical appeals** and **emotional appeals** to persuade their audiences. Many important documents address related themes and concepts.

Examples

- **Logical appeals** use facts and reasons to build an argument and change people's thinking. For example, in his 1933 First Inaugural Address, Franklin Delano Roosevelt presented facts about the effects of the Great Depression before explaining how he proposed to solve the problem. In his 1963 "I Have a Dream" speech, Martin Luther King, Jr., cited facts about segregation, housing discrimination, and voting rights to explain why African Americans had to fight for civil rights.

- **Emotional appeals** use words with strong positive or negative connotations to affect people's feelings about an issue. For example, Roosevelt described banking and business leaders as "unscrupulous money changers" and cited their "callous and selfish wrongdoing" as causes of the Great Depression. King described African Americans as "seared in the flames of withering injustice" and "crippled by the manacles of segregation."

- Although their authors may use different kinds of language, many historical documents address similar **themes** and concepts. These documents often include memorable quotations and images that help people remember the authors' key ideas. For example, most Americans remember Roosevelt's claim that "the only thing we have to fear is fear itself." They also remember this key sentence from King's speech: "I have a dream that my four little children will one day live in nation where they will not be judged by the color of the skin but by the content of their character."

Academic Vocabulary

logical appeal using facts and reasons to persuade an audience

emotional appeal using words with strong positive or negative connotations

theme central idea or message of a text

Apply the Standard

Use the worksheet that follows to help you apply the standard as you read important documents from U.S. history. Several copies of the worksheet have been provided for you.

- Analyzing Historical Documents

Name _____ Date _____ Selection _____

Analyzing Historical Documents

Use this organizer to analyze and compare two historic U.S documents or speeches. Focus on the authors' use of different types of appeals or memorable language to address an important theme or ideas.

	Document 1	**Document 2**
Title		
Author		
Theme		
Logical Appeals		
Emotional Appeals		
Important Concepts		
Memorable Quotations		

A

For use with Informational Texts 9

Analyzing Historical Documents

Use this organizer to analyze and compare two historic U.S documents or speeches. Focus on the authors' use of different types of appeals or memorable language to address an important theme or ideas.

	Document 1	Document 2
Title		
Author		
Theme		
Logical Appeals		
Emotional Appeals		
Important Concepts		
Memorable Quotations		

Name _____ Date _____ Selection _____

Analyzing Historical Documents

Use this organizer to analyze and compare two historic U.S documents or speeches. Focus on the authors' use of different types of appeals or memorable language to address an important theme or ideas.

	Document 1	Document 2
Title		
Author		
Theme		
Logical Appeals		
Emotional Appeals		
Important Concepts		
Memorable Quotations		

C

Name _____ Date _____ Selection _____

Analyzing Historical Documents

Use this organizer to analyze and compare two historic U.S documents or speeches. Focus on the authors' use of different types of appeals or memorable language to address an important theme or ideas.

	Document 1	**Document 2**
Title		
Author		
Theme		
Logical Appeals		
Emotional Appeals		
Important Concepts		
Memorable Quotations		

D

Name _____ Date _____ Selection _____

Analyzing Historical Documents

Use this organizer to analyze and compare two historic U.S documents or speeches. Focus on the authors' use of different types of appeals or memorable language to address an important theme or ideas.

	Document 1	**Document 2**
Title		
Author		
Theme		
Logical Appeals		
Emotional Appeals		
Important Concepts		
Memorable Quotations		

E

Name _____ Date _____ Selection _____

Analyzing Historical Documents

Use this organizer to analyze and compare two historic U.S documents or speeches. Focus on the authors' use of different types of appeals or memorable language to address an important theme or ideas.

	Document 1	**Document 2**
Title		
Author		
Theme		
Logical Appeals		
Emotional Appeals		
Important Concepts		
Memorable Quotations		

F

Informational Texts 10

> **10. By the end of grade 9, read and comprehend literary nonfiction in the grades 9–10 text complexity band proficiently, with scaffolding as needed at the high end of the range.**

Explanation

Nonfiction texts vary in their **complexity,** or how difficult they are to understand and analyze. Some essays and articles have familiar subjects, include an explicitly stated thesis and main ideas, and have a simple style, featuring conversational vocabulary and short sentences. Other essays and articles introduce readers to unfamiliar concepts, have implied main ideas, and include advanced vocabulary and long sentences.

In grade 9, you will read different types of literary nonfiction. You will also be expected to **comprehend,** or understand, the meaning and importance of more complex texts. To comprehend complex nonfiction texts, use reading strategies such as previewing, skimming, asking questions, taking notes, and summarizing.

Examples

- Before you read a nonfiction text, preview it by looking at the title, text features such as headings and bulleted text, and graphic aids such as photos and diagrams. Make predictions about what you will learn. For example, the title "Libraries Face Sad Chapter" tells you the essay will present bad news about libraries. The headings "Built by Carnegie" and "Immigrants' Appreciation" tell you about other ideas the author will present about libraries.

- Then skim the text, quickly reading a paragraph or two, looking for key words to determine the kind of text structure the author uses. Is the author's purpose to inform, to persuade, or simply to reflect on a topic? Skimming the first section of "Libraries Face Sad Chapter," you see that the author describes the effects that libraries had on him as a child. The second section talks about possible cutbacks in library services and what effects they might have. The author's purpose seems to be to convince people not to reduce public library services.

- As you read, take notes on the text's main ideas and details. Ask yourself questions about the parts you don't understand. Then reread the difficult passages, or read ahead to find the answers. Use your notes to summarize the author's perspective and main ideas in your own words.

Academic Vocabulary

complexity the degree to which a text is difficult to understand and analyze

comprehend to understand the meaning and importance of something

Apply the Standard

Use the worksheet that follows to help you apply the standard as you read nonfiction texts. Several copies of the worksheet have been provided for you.

- Comprehending Complex Texts

Name _____ Date _____ Selection _____

Comprehending Complex Texts

Explain what makes the nonfiction text you are reading complex. Then, use the table to explain which reading strategies help you to better comprehend the selection.

Strategy	How I Used It	How It Helped
Previewing		
Skimming		
Asking questions		
Taking notes		
Summarizing		

A

Name _____ Date _____ Selection _____

Comprehending Complex Texts

Explain what makes the nonfiction text you are reading complex. Then, use the table to explain which reading strategies help you to better comprehend the selection.

Strategy	How I Used It	How It Helped
Previewing		
Skimming		
Asking questions		
Taking notes		
Summarizing		

B

Name _____ Date _____ Selection _____

Comprehending Complex Texts

Explain what makes the nonfiction text you are reading complex. Then, use the table to explain which reading strategies help you to better comprehend the selection.

Strategy	How I Used It	How It Helped
Previewing		
Skimming		
Asking questions		
Taking notes		
Summarizing		

C

Name _____ Date _____ Selection _____

Comprehending Complex Texts

Explain what makes the nonfiction text you are reading complex. Then, use the table to explain which reading strategies help you to better comprehend the selection.

Strategy	How I Used It	How It Helped
Previewing		
Skimming		
Asking questions		
Taking notes		
Summarizing		

D

Name _____ Date _____ Selection _____

Comprehending Complex Texts

Explain what makes the nonfiction text you are reading complex. Then, use the table to explain which reading strategies help you to better comprehend the selection.

Strategy	How I Used It	How It Helped
Previewing		
Skimming		
Asking questions		
Taking notes		
Summarizing		

E

Name _____ Date _____ Selection _____

Comprehending Complex Texts

Explain what makes the nonfiction text you are reading complex. Then, use the table to explain which reading strategies help you to better comprehend the selection.

Strategy	How I Used It	How It Helped
Previewing		
Skimming		
Asking questions		
Taking notes		
Summarizing		

F

Writing Standards

Writing 1

> 1. Write arguments to support claims in an analysis of substantive topics or texts, using valid reasoning and relevant and sufficient evidence.*

Writing Workshop: Argument

When you develop an argument in writing, you present a claim and then use details to support your claim. An argument is not just an opinion or just a series of emotional appeals. Sound arguments are reasoned and supported with valid evidence. For example, an essay on school sports might present a claim such as "Participation in school sports should be a requirement for graduation." Details that support that claim form the heart of that argument. If the details are well-reasoned and supported, the argument is sound or effective. If the details are largely based on emotion and are not supported, the argument is not sound.

Assignment

Write an argumentative essay about an issue that confronts your school or community. Include these elements:

✓ a claim, or brief statement of your position on the issue that offers your perspective on the subject

✓ evidence and reasoning to support your position or claim

✓ acknowledgement of opposing positions or claims, pointing out their strengths as well as their limitations

✓ effective and coherent organization

✓ use of rhetorical technique, such as parallel structure

✓ a formal style and objective tone

✓ correct use of language conventions

*Additional Standards

Writing

1. Write arguments to support claims in an analysis of substantive topics or texts, using valid reasoning and relevant and sufficient evidence.

1.a. Introduce precise claim(s), distinguish the claim(s) from alternate or opposing claims, and create an organization that establishes clear relationships among claim(s), counterclaims, reasons, and evidence.

1.b. Develop claim(s) and counterclaims fairly, supplying evidence for each while pointing out the strengths and limitations of both in a manner that anticipates the audience's knowledge level and concerns.

1.c. Use words, phrases, and clauses to link the major sections of the text, create cohesion, and clarify the relationships between claim(s) and reasons, between reasons and evidence, and between claim(s) and counterclaims.

1.d. Establish and maintain a formal style and objective tone while attending to the norms and conventions of the discipline in which they are writing.

1.e. Provide a concluding statement or section that follows from and supports the argument presented.

4. Produce clear and coherent writing in which the development, organization, and style are appropriate to task, purpose, and audience.

6. Use technology, including the Internet, to produce, publish, and update individual or shared writing products, taking advantage of technology's capacity to link to other information and to display information flexibly and dynamically.

Language

1.a. Use parallel structure.

2. Demonstrate command of the conventions of standard English capitalization, punctuation, and spelling when writing.

Name _____ Date _____ Assignment _____

Prewriting/Planning Strategies

Choose a topic. Scan through newspapers or online articles to find a topic that interests you. Notice articles that strike you as unfair, foolish, or harmful. Use one of these topics for your essay.

If you prefer, pair up with a classmate and brainstorm for topics that are important to each of you, noting those topics that cause the most discussion or disagreement. Select an issue that can be argued in more than one way.

Identify your claim. After choosing a topic, decide which aspect of the issue to address in your essay. Write your opinion about the topic in a sentence. That sentence is your claim, a statement of your position that you must now prepare to defend.

Define task, purpose, and audience. At all points of the writing process, consider task, what specifically you are writing; purpose, why you are writing or the effect you want your writing to have; and your audience, the people you want to persuade.

	My Description
Writing task	
Purpose	
Audience	

Name _____ Date _____ Assignment _____

Supporting a Claim

Consider all sides of an issue. Gather evidence from a wide variety of sources to support your claim. In the chart shown below, record evidence on both sides of an issue. Anticipate and address reader's potential expectations, biases, and misunderstandings. Do not ignore information that contradicts or opposes your position. Once you have completed your chart, look again to be sure that your evidence is valid, relevant, and sufficient.

- If any of the points you list are not **valid**, or based on fact or provable, you should strengthen that point or delete it.

- If any of the points you list are not **relevant** or directly related to your claim, delete them.

- If you do not have **sufficient** evidence or reasons to support your claim, add more, or revise your claim.

Evidence or Reasons That Support My Claim	Evidence or Reasons That Support Counterclaims

Name _____ Date _____ Assignment _____

Drafting Strategies

Create a structure for your draft. Plan a strategy for presenting your ideas. Be sure to structure your argument in a logical and effective way.

- Evaluate your evidence. Review all of the points that support your claim and consider their impact on your intended audience. Then, rank them according to persuasiveness.

- Use the graphic organizer below to organize your arguments. Start with your least important point and build to your most persuasive point. In addition, be sure to indicate where you will address counterarguments.

Claim		
Support 1 (least important)	Support 2	Support 3 (most important)
Evidence A	Evidence A	Evidence A
Evidence B	Evidence B	Evidence B

Name _____ Date _____ Assignment _____

Develop your claim.

1. Introduce your claim. Use precise wording to ensure that it accurately states your ideas on the topic.

2. As you draft your claim, be sure to distinguish it from alternate claims, those that would be made by people who hold a different point of view on the topic.

3. Refer to your outline and make clear the relationship between the supporting evidence you provide and the claim you made at the beginning of your essay.

4. Anticipate the audience's knowledge of your topic and likely concerns as you develop your draft. Strive to be fair as you support your claim, pointing out the strengths and limitations of your evidence. Do the same as you address counterclaims.

5. Provide a strong concluding statement that supports and summarizes your argument.

My Claim	Evaluating the Claim
	❏ Is the claim precise?
	❏ Is it distinguishable from other claims?
	❏ Is the claim clearly different from the supporting evidence?
	❏ Does it anticipate the audience's knowledge?
Counterclaims	
	❏ Have I addressed counterarguments?

Style and Tone

Establish a formal style and tone. While an informal style might work for a conversation among fellow students, a formal style is more appropriate for a written piece that will be read by a variety of people. An objective tone invites readers to consider a thought; a subjective tone presents an emotional reaction that may repel readers.

Examples:

Claim: A dress code will ensure appropriate attire in the school while allowing individuals some freedom to choose what they wear.

- **Support, Formal Style:** Schools with uniforms have to design, order, sell, and distribute the uniforms they wish to have for their school.
  Support, Informal Style: Schools with uniforms have to do an awful lot of work to get those uniforms to the kids.

- **Support, Objective Tone:** In addition, school officials spend time and resources making sure they receive payment for uniforms.
  Support, Subjective Tone: I cannot believe how much time school officials waste just nagging students who owe money for uniforms.

As you draft your argumentative essay, choose words and phrases to give your writing a formal style and objective tone.

Use transitional words, phrases, and clauses. Link the ideas in your writing by using transitional words, phrases, and clauses. As you draft, use transitions to indicate relationships among your ideas.

- **Cause and effect:** *consequently, as a result, for this reason, therefore, thus, so then*

- **Comparison and contrast:** *on the one hand, on the other hand, in contrast, on the contrary, similarly, likewise*

- **Illustration:** *for example, for instance, for one thing, as an illustration, as an example*

- **Summarizing:** *after all, in conclusion, in any case, on the whole, in the final analysis, in summary, to sum up*

The clauses in compound and complex sentences can also help clarify the connections among ideas, as follows:

- **A complex sentence can clarify the relationship between claims and reasons:** *The school will lose money because it is not conserving energy.*

- **A compound sentence (with a transitional phrase) can clarify the relationship between reasons and evidence:** *Some schools already have started energy conservation programs; for instance, Edison High School in Brightville has such a program.*

- **A complex sentence can clarify the relationship between claims and counterclaims by putting the counterclaim in a subordinating clause to discount it:** *Although some students object to this plan, they are not fully informed about its benefits.*

Name _____ Date _____ Assignment _____

Conclusion

Provide a strong conclusion. Your argumentative essay should end with a strong conclusion. The best conclusions sum up your argument and reinforce your claim. Review the examples below and decide upon the best way to end your essay.

- **Use a memorable analogy that follows from and supports the argument presented:** *Those who drive while talking on a cell phone may think of themselves as high-powered executives, firmly in charge of their own lives. As I have shown, however, they are more like little kids playing dangerously on the edge of a cliff.*

- **After you have described a problem at length, clearly state the solution and its benefits:** *The problem is clear and so is the solution: Installing a traffic light at this dangerous intersection may cost a few dollars now, but it will save money in the long term by preventing costly accidents. Even more important, it will save lives.*

- **Restate your claim, attacking opponents' credibility in a memorable way:** *Only now, after months of distortion, are students beginning to realize that offering healthy food options in the cafeteria would increase, not reduce, their choices. Only now are they discovering what upgrading the lunch menu means: no elimination of favorite dishes; no school administrators forcing you to "eat your spinach"; and no more credibility for those who always say, "No!"*

My Claim	Evaluating My Conclusion
	❑ Does it sum up my argument? ❑ Does it reinforce my claim? ❑ Is it memorable or does it state a solution?

Name _____ Date _____ Assignment _____

Revising Strategies

Put a checkmark beside each question as you address it in your revision.

	Questions To Ask as You Revise
Writing Task	❑ Have I fulfilled my task? ❑ Does my writing contain the elements of an argumentative essay? ❑ Did I begin with a clearly stated claim? ❑ Does my argument sound persuasive?
Purpose	❑ What details in my writing helped me achieve my purpose? ❑ Are there enough details to support my argument? ❑ Should I add more support to my argument? ❑ What details, if any, are irrelevant and detract from my argument? ❑ Have I provided a strong concluding statement that supports my claim?
Audience	❑ Will my audience be persuaded to agree with my claim? ❑ Do I need to add or adjust details to address readers' knowledge of my topic or their concerns? ❑ Is my style of writing and tone suited to my audience? If not, what words and phrases need revision? ❑ Will my audience be able to follow the ideas presented in my argument? ❑ What transitions should be added to create cohesion and clarify relationships between the ideas?

For use with Writing 1

Revising

Revise for parallel structure. Parallelism is the use of similar grammatical forms or patterns to express similar ideas. Effective use of parallelism adds rhythm and balance to your writing and strengthens connections among ideas. As you revise your essay, look for places to fix nonparallel constructions.

Identifying Nonparallel Constructions

Parallel constructions place equal ideas in words, phrases, or clauses of similar types. Nonparallel constructions present equal ideas in an unnecessary mix of grammatical forms, producing awkward, distracting shifts for readers.

Nonparallel: Dress codes are <u>less restrictive, less costly, and are not a controversial system.</u>

Parallel: Dress codes are <u>less restrictive, less costly, and less controversial.</u>

Fixing Nonparallel Constructions

To revise faulty parallelism, follow these steps:

1. Identify similar or equal ideas within a sentence.

2. Determine whether the ideas are expressed in the same form—for example, all nouns or all prepositional phrases.

3. Rewrite the sentence so that all the elements match the stronger pattern. Choose forms that produce the smoothest rhythm or require the fewest words.

Sample Parallel Forms	
Nouns	sharp eyes, strong hands, nimble fingers
Verbs	to ask, to learn, to share
Phrases	under a gray sky, near an icy river
Adverb clauses	when I am happy, when I am peaceful
Adjective clauses	Those who read with care, those who act with concern

Revision Checklist

❏ Are there equal ideas within a sentence that should be in parallel structure?

❏ Are words in a series (e.g., *to think, to live, to learn*) in parallel structure?

❏ Do the phrases and clauses have a smooth, fluent rhythm?

Editing and Proofreading

Review your draft to correct errors in capitalization, spelling, and punctuation.

Focus on Capitalization: Review your draft carefully to find and correct capitalization errors. If your argumentative essay references organizations or other official groups, be sure that you have capitalized the organization's name.

Incorrect capitalization:	**Correct capitalization:**
School uniforms unlimited	School Uniforms Unlimited

Focus on Spelling: An argumentative essay that includes spelling errors loses its authority to convince. Check the spelling of each word. Look for words that you frequently misspell and make sure they are correct. If you have typed your draft on a computer, use the spell-check feature to double-check for errors. Carefully review each suggested change before accepting the spell-check's suggestions. Also note that spell-check features will not catch all errors. Proofread carefully even after running a spell-check.

Focus on Punctuation: Serial Commas and Semicolons Proofread your writing to find and address punctuation errors. In particular, looks for places in your writing where you list details. Be sure you use serial commas and semicolons correctly.

Rule: Use commas to separate three or more words, phrases, or clauses in a series. *In our school we value courage, dignity, and independent thinking.*

Rule: Use semicolons to avoid confusion when independent clauses or items in a series already contain commas. *Our school colors are red, blue, and white; our motto is "Move forward"; and our spirit is unmatched.*

Revision Checklist

❑ Have you reviewed your paper for words, titles, or names that should be capitalized?

❑ Have you read each sentence and checked that all of the words are spelled correctly?

❑ Do you have words, phrases, or clauses in a series that should be separated by commas?

❑ Do you have places where you might avoid confusion by using a semicolon to join two independent clauses?

Name _____ Date _____ Assignment _____

Publishing and Presenting

Consider one of the following ways to present your writing:

Deliver an oral presentation. Use your argumentative essay as the basis for an oral presentation. Before you read your essay aloud, print out a copy and mark up details you want to emphasize. Rehearse with a peer, and practice your pacing to avoid a monotonous delivery.

Post it online. Produce and publish your essay in electronic form. For example, you could post your essay to an online site your school maintains. Take advantage of technology's capacity to link to other information about your topic or to display links to related sites.

Rubric for Self-Assessment

Find evidence in your writing to address each category. Then, use the rating scale to grade your work. Circle that score that best applies for each category.

Evaluating Your Argument	not very very
Focus: How clearly has your claim been stated?	1 2 3 4 5
Organization: How effectively and coherently have you organized your argument?	1 2 3 4 5
Support/Elaboration: How valid, sufficient, and suited to your audience is your evidence?	1 2 3 4 5
Style: How well have you maintained a formal, objective tone throughout your argument?	1 2 3 4 5
Conventions: How free of errors in grammar, usage, spelling, and punctuation is your argument?	1 2 3 4 5

For use with Writing 1

Writing 2

> **2. Write informative/explanatory texts to examine and convey complex ideas, concepts, and information clearly and accurately through the effective selection, organization, and analysis of content.***

Writing Workshop: Expository Essay

When you write an **expository essay**, your task is to inform or explain something to your reader or audience. In an expository essay, ideas and information can be organized a number of ways, whether by describing a cause-and-effect relationship, comparing or contrasting two situations, or discussing a problem and its solution. No matter what your specific purpose, an expository essay should always provide a clear thesis in the opening paragraph, and then explain and support that thesis in the paragraphs that follow. A successful expository essay depends on using good information—including facts, quotations, and examples.

Assignment

Write an expository essay about a problem and solution in your school or neighborhood. Include these elements:

✓ a clear statement of the problem and the recommended solution(s)

✓ an organization that makes that problem and solution clear and convincing and that includes formatting, graphics, or multimedia as needed or helpful

✓ explanation, sufficient facts, quotations, concrete details, and other development specific to the purpose and audience

✓ appropriate transitional words and phrases

✓ precise language, including words that are specific to your topic, as needed

✓ a formal style and objective tone

✓ a logical and effective conclusion

✓ correct use of language conventions

*Additional Standards

2.a. Introduce a topic; organize complex ideas, concepts, and information to make important connections and distinctions; include formatting (e.g., headings), graphics (e.g., figures, tables), and multimedia when useful to aiding comprehension.

2.b. Develop the topic with well-chosen, relevant, and sufficient facts, extended

definitions, concrete details, quotations, or other information and examples appropriate to the audience's knowledge of the topic.

2.c. Use appropriate and varied transitions to link the major sections of the text, create cohesion, and clarify the relationships among complex ideas and concepts.

2.d. Use precise language and domain-specific vocabulary to manage the complexity of the topic.

2.e. Establish and maintain a formal style and objective tone while attending to the norms and conventions of the discipline in which students are writing.

2.f. Provide a concluding statement or section

that follows from and supports the information or explanation presented (e.g., articulating implications or the significance of the topic).

Language

1. Demonstrate command of the conventions of standard English grammar and usage when writing or speaking.

2.b. Use a colon to introduce a list or a quotation.

Name _____ Date _____ Assignment _____

Prewriting/Planning Strategies

Identify problems. Think about things that bother you, such as dirty locker rooms, too few choices at lunch, a school day that starts too early, or a neighbor's dog that barks all day long. Make a list of problems that you think could be solved. If you can't find an idea, ask your classmates and neighbors what bothers them.

Identify solutions. For each problem you list, identify one or more solutions. As you do so, think about how practical or complex each problem and solution actually is. Make sure that you choose a problem that has a clear and achievable solution.

Identify your audience. If you are writing for your peers, you will not want to choose a topic related to your neighbors' behavior or to your neighbor's dog. Similarly, if you are writing about a change needed in the school cafeteria, you will want to be certain that people who can help bring about change in the cafeteria are among your readers.

Problem	Possible Solutions	Audience
	1. 2. 3.	
	1. 2. 3.	
	1. 2. 3.	

Name _____ Date _____ Assignment _____

Developing a Topic

Explore the problem. Once you have chosen your topic, you should explore it in detail. One way to do this is to complete a who-what-where-when-why organizer. In this organizer, show who is affected by the problem, and where and when the problem occurs.

- As you tell **what** happens, include any facts, concrete details, or examples that come to mind.

- To tell **why,** give details not only about the causes of the problem but also why the problem is significant or has far-reaching implications.

Problem:
Who
What
When
Where
Why

Name _____ Date _____ Assignment _____

Develop the solution. Gather ample support for your solution before you write. For example, if the problem is that the school day starts too early, are there studies that show that getting up two hours later does actually improve teen performance on schoolwork? Can you gather quotations from any faculty members or parents about the wisdom of your solution? What about sleep experts? You might search the Web for useful information, statistics, or even data you can present in a graphic on the topic of teens' needs for late-morning sleep. Before you begin drafting, record evidence for your solution here:

Solution:

Evidence in Support of My Solution
Facts and Statistics
Quotations (from People Who Experience the Problem) in Support of the Solution
Expert Opinions and/or Studies and Reports
Other Concrete Details

Name _____ Date _____ Assignment _____

Organizing Ideas

Organize body paragraphs. Use this chart to organize ideas for your body paragraphs.

Body Paragraph 1: Problem
topic/topic sentence—
key points—

Body Paragraph 2: Solution
topic/topic sentence—
key points—

Drafting

Engage your audience. Create interest by using one of these opening strategies:

- **Personal example.** Provide an example of the problem from your own experience.

- **Anecdote.** Tell a brief story about how the problem affected someone else.

- **Scenario.** Present a realistic but hypothetical picture of future consequences if the problem is not solved.

Support your ideas. You can persuade your audience that your proposal is likely to work by using a variety of well-chosen evidence in your body paragraphs.

- **Facts and statistics.** Always favor facts and data over general statements.

- **Expert opinions.** Include the advice of experts.

- **Quotations.** Quote experts as well as everyday people affected by the problem.

- **Comparable situations.** Describe other real-life difficulties that were resolved by actions similar to the ones you propose.

- **Concrete details.** Remember that general statements, such as "Teens need more sleep" are always less effective than concrete details, such as, "The average teen requires approximately 9 hours of sleep per night."

For use with Writing 2

Address readers' concerns. Anticipate arguments from readers with differing opinions. Include one or two skeptical questions to show that you know both sides of your issue. Then provide well-supported answers that show why your solution is best.

Include formatting, graphics, or multimedia. If and when they are useful, consider using headings, such as "Problem" and "Solution" to break up and help organize your text. Bulleted points can also be helpful for isolating and calling out similar types of information. You may also want to create tables, graphs, or other graphic displays to show data you have gathered or researched. Another option is to embed a hyperlink to the graphic or to a video that illustrates the problem or the solution.

Using Transitions

Use appropriate and varied transitions. Link ideas, sentences, and paragraphs in your writing by using transitional words, phrases, and clauses. Below are some examples:

- To introduce support: *according to, as ___ notes/says/writes, for example, for instance, in one survey, the data show*

- To introduce the solution or to conclude: *as a result, because (of), for the best results, for the common good, for these reasons, in summary, therefore, the best solution*

To link paragraphs, repeat a word or phrase from the last line of the previous paragraph in the first line of the next paragraph.

Paragraph 1 ends: . . . contribute to the lack of <u>choices at lunch</u>.

Paragraph 2 begins: To increase <u>lunch choices</u>, . . .

Making Other Connections

Create coherence. Your goal is to connect all the words, sentences, and paragraphs in your essay so that the reader is never confused or uncertain of your meaning. To help create coherence in a problem-solution essay, you may want to use words such as the following:

- To show when the problem occurs: *after, before, during, prior to, when, whenever*

- To show where the problem occurs: *above, across, behind, beneath, here, next to, on top of, outside, throughout, under*

- To classify issues related to the problem: *one group, one kind, other types, other sorts, the first issue, the last effect*

- To emphasize the significance of the problem or its solution: *as can be plainly seen, even, indeed, in fact, without a doubt*

Name _____ Date _____ Assignment _____

Drafting a Conclusion

Provide a strong conclusion. An expository essay should end with a formal conclusion. This is your last opportunity to stress the importance of the problem and the rightness of your solution. Remind your reader of your purpose in a way that reviews, restates, and emphasizes your main points. Remember that your conclusion must be logically supported by the information in your essay.

Review of main points	
Memorable final thought, quotation, question, or view of the future	

Evaluating Language

Check for precise language. If you call the locker room dirty, you may be accurate, but you will need to be more precise for your reader. For example, you might say that there is mold growing in cracks in two of the shower stalls or that the drains of the showers are often clogged and blocked up. Additionally, you will want to replace all vague words with stronger, more richly connotative language. Replace every inexact word in your paper, such as *really, very, good, great, bad, terrible,* and *awesome* with more specific words.

Check for technical or topic-specific language. Suppose that the problem you are addressing is the need to rebuild a bridge in your town. If so, take time to learn the proper and specific language related to the problem, such as *tower, arch, span,* and *pier,* and use it in your paper. If your audience consists of bridge experts, you will not need to explain these terms. However, if this is not the case, you may need to explain certain terms briefly and concisely the first time you use them. Additionally, you might include an illustration that clearly shows and labels the terms in an easy-to-grasp context.

Evaluating Your Writing Style and Tone

Evaluate your tone. The tone you adopt as you draft depends on your task, your purpose, and your audience. If you have chosen to write about the problem of a school day that begins too early, you will need to address the school board as well as the community at large. Just like your expository task and purpose, this type of audience deserves a serious tone. In most expository situations, you must also sound objective and fair-minded. To do so, you should avoid using the first person (*I, me, my, mine, myself; we, us, ours, ourselves*) and the second person (*you, your, yours, yourself*). Also avoid slang, contractions, and other informal language.

Evaluate your style. The style you choose must also reflect your task, your purpose, and your audience. With an audience of faculty, school board, and community members, you will want your style to be both direct and formal. This means avoiding slang, personal asides, nonstandard spellings or usage, and other choices that might make your writing sound too familiar or too friendly. You must also take care not to show—or even imply—disrespect.

In the following example below, consider why the tone and style choices in bold are inconsistent with the task, purpose, and the audience. Then suggest replacements below.

(1) You might say that the current hours of the school day have been in place now for **(2) 40+ years** and **(3) it's been great** for all that time. **(4) But** for 40 years, Madison High has been the location of the first-period nap. **(5) You may also say** that students have to start early so **(6) there's enuf** time left in the day for afterschool activities and work. **(7) But why couldn't kids** just do afterschool activities or go to work two hours later? **(8) It's totally crazy** to think that **(9) there's some rule** that says that soccer practice must begin at **(10) 3.**

1. ....
2. ....
3. ....
4. ....
5. ....

6. ....
7. ....
8. ....
9. ....
10. ....

For use with Writing 2

Name _____ Date _____ Assignment _____

Revising Strategies

Using the checklist below, put a checkmark beside each question as you address it in your revision.

	Questions To Ask as You Revise
Task	❏ Have I written a problem-solution essay?
	❏ Have I fully explained the problem and the solution?
Purpose	❏ Have I set forth a clear problem and a workable solution?
	❏ Have I fully developed both the problem and the solution with sufficient facts, statistics, quotations, concrete details, and other appropriate forms of development?
	❏ Have I anticipated and addressed a reader's concerns?
	❏ Have I provided a strong conclusion?
Audience	❏ Do I create interest in my opening paragraph?
	❏ Do I need to add, delete, or adjust any details to suit them more effectively to my audience's knowledge and experience?
	❏ Have I sufficiently explained domain-specific language?
	❏ Will my audience think I am objective?
	❏ Have I included graphics, headings, or multimedia if or where they are needed to help my audience understand the problem or solution?
	❏ Have I used transitions, repeated words, and clear pronoun references so that my audience can easily follow my ideas?

Revising

Revise for pronoun-antecedent agreement. Pronouns are words that take the place of nouns, such as *him, her, they,* or *it.* Antecedents are the nouns that the pronouns refer to, such as *Thomas, Ms. Myles, the attendees,* or *the washing machine.*

Identifying Errors in Pronoun-Antecedent Agreement

Pronouns *disagree* with their antecedents when they are mismatched in number, person, or gender. A pronoun should agree with its antecedent in number. For example:

Incorrect: Mrs. Chu and Ms. DiLeva leave <u>her</u> dogs unattended all day long.

Correct: Mrs. Chu and Ms. DiLeva leave <u>their</u> dogs unattended all day long.

Incorrect: Neither Mrs. Chu nor Ms. DiLeva is at home with <u>their</u> dog.

Correct: Neither Mrs. Chu nor Ms. DiLeva is at home with <u>her</u> dog.

A pronoun should agree with its antecedent in person:

Incorrect: When students use the locker room, <u>you</u> don't clean up.

Correct: When students use the locker room, <u>they</u> don't clean up.

A pronoun should agree with its antecedent in gender and be gender-neutral:

Incorrect: The typical swimmer has <u>his</u> own way of using the locker room.

Correct: The typical swimmer has <u>his or her</u> own way of using the locker room.

Gender of Third-Person Singular Pronouns		
Masculine	**Feminine**	**Neuter**
he, him, his, himself	she, her, hers, herself	it, its, itself

Fixing Pronoun-Antecedent Agreement Errors

To correct errors in pronoun-antecedent agreement, first find the antecedent.

1. For compound antecedents joined by *and,* use a plural personal pronoun.

2. For singular antecedents joined by *or* or *nor,* use a singular personal pronoun.

Revision Checklist

❏ Does every pronoun I used clearly refer back to an antecedent?

❏ Does each pronoun agree with its antecedent?

Editing and Proofreading

Review your draft to correct errors in capitalization, spelling, and punctuation.

Focus on Capitalization: Review your draft carefully to find and correct capitalization errors. If your problem-solution essay refers to school subjects or classes, do not capitalize them, except for the names of specific languages (such as *English, Spanish,* or *French*).

> **Incorrect capitalization:** Mr. Thompson admitted that several students have fallen asleep in his first-period <u>Algebra</u> class.

> **Correct capitalization:** Mr. Thompson admitted that several students have fallen asleep in his first-period <u>algebra</u> class.

Focus on Spelling: As you read, circle any words that you are not sure how to spell, frequently misspell, or seldom use. Then, use reference resources such as a dictionary or thesaurus to confirm correct spellings. Follow these steps to find spellings in a dictionary:

- **Check the first letters of a word.** Think of homophones for that sound.

- **Check the other letters.** Once you spell the first sound correctly, try sounding out the rest of the word. Look for likely spellings in the dictionary. If you do not find your word, look for more unusual spellings of the sound.

Focus on Punctuation: Using Colons to Introduce Quotations and Lists Proofread your writing to find and address punctuation errors. In particular, look for places in your writing where you introduce quotations. In some cases, you will want to use colons for this purpose. You might also use a colon to introduce a list.

Rule: Use a colon to introduce a formal quotation that follows an independent clause.
Dog expert Ronni Gomez makes it clear that the problem is not insurmountable: "The average dog can be painlessly trained to stop problem barking in less than two weeks."

Rule: Use a colon to introduce a list of items following an independent clause. *The following changes will make the locker rooms far cleaner and more pleasant: new tiling for the showers, antimicrobial shower curtains, and a few basic changes in student behavior.*

For use with Writing 2

Name _____ Date _____ Assignment _____

Publishing and Presenting

Consider one of the following ways to present your writing:

Send a letter. Send a letter to members of your intended audience. When you receive responses, make sure that you follow established rules for posting your letter and the responses on a class or school website.

Make a video. Practice reading your essay aloud, then make a video of yourself reading the essay. Add heading props or cards, such as "Problem," "Solution," and "Audience Concerns" to break the essay into parts. In addition, include one graphic with facts, statistics, or other key information.

Rubric for Self-Assessment

Find evidence in your writing to address each category listed below. Then, use the rating scale to grade your work. Circle the score that best applies to your essay.

Evaluating Your Expository Essay	not very					very
Focus: Have you clearly described the nature of the problem and what needs to be done to solve it?	1	2	3	4	5	6
Organization: How effectively have you structured your essay? Did you include an interesting introduction, a clear and developed statement of the problem and solution, an acknowledgment of your readers' concerns, and a conclusion?	1	2	3	4	5	6
Support/Elaboration: How good is your evidence? It is well chosen, relevant, and concrete? Does it include quotations or other information and examples that are appropriate to your audience and purpose?	1	2	3	4	5	6
Style: How well have you created a formal style and an objective tone that are appropriate to your task, purpose, and audience? Is your language precise and specific?	1	2	3	4	5	6
Conventions: How free is your essay from errors in grammar, spelling, and punctuation?	1	2	3	4	5	6

For use with Writing 2

Writing 3

> **3.** Write narratives to develop real or imagined experiences or events using effective technique, well-chosen details, and well-structured event sequences.

Writing Workshop: Narrative

When you write a **narrative**, you tell a story in order to entertain your audience. Some narratives are personal; in them, you tell your own story. The most well-known forms of narrative, however, are fictional: these works, which include the short story, spring in part or in full from your imagination. Good short stories create and hold their readers' attention from beginning to end. They contain engaging characters, a problem or conflict, a series of events that rises to a climax, and a satisfying ending.

Assignment

Write a realistic or purely imaginative short story. Include these elements:

- ✓ a clear, consistent single point of view, or clear, effective multiple points of view

- ✓ characters, a setting, and an event that begins the rising action

- ✓ a conflict that focuses the story and helps determine what happens from beginning to end

- ✓ a clear sequence of events that rises to a climax

- ✓ narrative techniques, including natural dialogue, reflection or interior monologue, multiple plot lines, and appropriate pacing

- ✓ precise language and sensory details

- ✓ a satisfying conclusion that arises from the conflict and events

- ✓ correct use of language conventions

*Additional Standards

3.a. Engage and orient the reader by setting out a problem, situation, or observation, establishing one or multiple point(s) of view, and introducing a narrator and/or characters; create a smooth progression of experiences or events.

3.b. Use narrative techniques, such as dialogue, pacing, description, reflection, and multiple plot lines, to develop experiences, events, and/or characters.

3.c. Use a variety of techniques to sequence events so that they build on one another to create a coherent whole.

3.d. Use precise words and phrases, telling details, and sensory language to convey a vivid picture of the experiences, events, setting, and/or characters.

3.e. Provide a conclusion that follows from and reflects on what is experienced, observed, or resolved over the course of the narrative.

Language
1.d. Recognize and correct inappropriate shifts in verb tense.

2. Demonstrate command of the conventions of standard English capitalization, punctuation, and spelling when writing.

Name _____ Date _____ Selection _____

Prewriting/Planning Strategies

Explore plot ideas. The major building blocks of a story's plot include the following:

- **Exposition.** Introduce the characters, setting, and basic situation.

- **Inciting incident.** Introduce the main conflict.

- **Action.** Develop the conflict through rising action that leads slowly to a climax and then falls quickly to the resolution.

- **Resolution.** Provide a general insight or change in the characters.

Jot down ideas for plots in this organizer.

	Idea 1	Idea 2	Idea 3

Exposition
    Characters
 	
    Setting
 	
    Basic Situation			

Action			
Resolution			

Name _____ Date _____ Selection _____

Introducing Characters, Conflict, and Setting

Develop characters. Make a character map for each of your main characters.

Name:
Goals, desires, frustrations, talents, weaknesses:
Appearance:

Create a conflict. You can use a tried-and-true conflict such as a person against nature, a person against another person, or a person against self. Use the organizer to name and describe your conflict.

Character:	**in conflict with:**
What character wants (or problem character must solve):	**How this person or thing stands in the way:**

Name _____ Date _____ Selection _____

Decide on a setting. Establish a time, such as dawn or dismissal time; winter or spring; Egyptian times, colonial times, or the future. Next, choose a place, such as a deserted warehouse, the open plains, a desert, a beach, a crowded subway train, or a concert hall.

Setting	
Time	**Place**

Creating Point of View

Select a point of view. Decide how your story will be told. The narrator may be a character who takes part in the action of the story or someone who simply reports on the action. Your narrator may be biased toward one character or outcome. Whoever you choose, your narrator must use a consistent voice to express the events of the story. Determine the identity of your narrator, whether he or she will be a character, and whether he or she will use the first or third person.

Identity of Narrator:
Inside or Outside Story:
First Person or Third Person:

Another option is to develop more than one point of view. Usually, this means telling events from the viewpoint of two or more characters in the story who take turns relating what is happening or reflecting on events and motives. If you employ this option, take special care with transitions so that your reader follows the shift in point of view.

Name _____ Date _____ Selection _____

Organizing the Narrative

Use different techniques. You can order the events of your narrative in different ways.

- **Straight chronological order.** Start with the earliest event and end with the latest or last event.

- **Foreshadow.** Include hints to what will happen. This is a good way to increase narrative tension and build suspense.

- **Flashback.** Use chronological order, but go back in time to an event, dream, or memory that helped to form the character or contribute to the conflict.

Try arranging your events in chronological order first. Then try adding a flashback or foreshadowing to alter the sequence.

Chronological Order	Alternative Order
1.	1.
2.	2.
3.	3.
4.	4.
5.	5.

Using Narrative Techniques

Write realistic dialogue. Effective dialogue does not sound stiff and unnatural. Instead, it should sound as if real people are talking to each other.

Try writing a dialogue between characters; then read it aloud. Among the things you should hear are everyday language, including contractions and informal language or slang, as well characters focusing on themselves and their needs. Decide whether your dialogue has these qualities.

Besides making dialogue sound natural, you should also do the following:

- **Don't overdo the amount of dialogue.** A few spoken words can often tell a lot about the character. Break up conversations with action.

- **Don't give away the whole story in the dialogue.** Don't rely on dialogue to tell everything that happens. Combine dialogue with other narrative techniques.

- **Use speaker tags with care.** Not every bit of dialogue should be followed with "he said" or "she said." After you identify the first speaker and the respondent, it may be clear who is saying what. Also, when you do repeat speaker tags, strive for variety in the verbs: substitute words such as *mused, offered, pleaded,* and *shouted* for *said.*

Add reflection. A reflection or an interior monologue relates the inner thoughts of a character as she or he reacts to events. In an interior monologue, the character might think to herself that there is a curious smell in the room; she might then panic if she cannot immediately open a window. Similarly, a character might reflect back on the conversation he just had with his best friend and decide that what his friend meant was deeper than what the words alone conveyed.

Consider pacing. To keep your story moving, you must introduce the problem or conflict early in the story. Then, to develop the plot, add details that intensify the problem. The problem or conflict should build up over a sequence of events before the action reaches a climax, or high point of suspense or interest. Think about devoting three-quarters or more of your story to your exposition and this buildup. After the climax, wrap things up quickly to hold your readers' interest.

Create multiple plot lines. Two characters who are in conflict, or even two that are working together, may be doing different things at the same time in the story. An additional plot line can add interest to your story.

For use with Writing 3

Name _____ Date _____ Selection _____

Using Descriptive and Sensory Language

Show, don't tell. Don't just tell what happens. Instead, let your reader experience, for example, the deserted alley through sensory details that appeal to the sense of hearing, such as the crash of glass or other frightening sounds. Use other sensory details to create your setting. Similarly, use a combination of sensory details and other descriptive language, such as precise nouns and action verbs, to show characters. For example, don't say the main character was afraid; instead, note how beads of perspiration formed on her forehead or how her heart began to pound. As you draft, avoid straightforward or dull language in favor of descriptive and sensory language.

Writing and Evaluating a Conclusion

Bring the conflict to a close. The first thing to do is to make sure that your conclusion relates to the inciting incident and conflict. For example, if your character is setting off on a journey to find something at the start of the story, the ending should be the end of that journey, whether something was found or not. Similarly, if you started with a mystery, the conclusion should solve it, or if you started with a rift between dear friends, they should either be united again, or resolved about going their separate ways.

Satisfy your reader. However you end your narrative, remember your purpose of entertaining your reader. You might end with a laugh, a surprise, or a symbolic action of some sort, such as tearing up the letter that was the source of so much woe or returning home from the alien world. At the end of the story, anything can happen, from a world blowing up, a wall falling, a car crashing, people embracing, or a child quietly laying a flower on a grave. If there is a surprise, however, it must arise logically from the details of the story.

Check for closure. To evaluate your conclusion, be sure that it resolves the conflict. It should also tie up any loose ends in the story, so that the reader is not left thinking that it makes no sense that one character would wander off or that the family would have separated. Also make sure that your ending says—through action, dialogue, or other detail—"this is the end." A peer reader can help you determine whether your story has a satisfying sense of closure or not.

For use with Writing 3

Name _____ Date _____ Selection _____

Revising Strategies

Put a checkmark beside each question as you address it in your revision.

	Questions To Ask as You Revise
Task	❏ Have I written a short story? ❏ Have I included the following elements of a short story: characters, setting, and inciting incident; conflict; rising action; climax; and resolution?
Purpose	❏ Have I created an effective and consistent point of view, or have I effectively and clearly used multiple points of view? ❏ Have I included natural sounding dialogue? ❏ Have I paced my story to lead slowly to the climax and more quickly from the climax to the end? ❏ Have I varied narrative techniques, such as by including reflection or interior monologue? ❏ Have I sequenced events effectively?
Audience	❏ Have I kept my reader interested from start to finish? ❏ Have I used sensory and descriptive language to create interest? ❏ Do I need to add, delete, or adjust any details to make the characters or setting more interesting, more convincing, or more appropriate to the conflict and events? ❏ Do I need to add, delete, or adjust any details to make the events clearer, more interesting, or easier to follow in sequence? ❏ Have I provided my readers with a satisfying ending?

For use with Writing 3

Name _____ Date _____ Selection _____

Revising

Revise for inconsistent verb tenses. A tense is a form of a verb that expresses the time of an action. The six tenses are present, present perfect, past, past perfect, future, and future perfect. Inconsistent use of verb tenses causes confusion in a story.

Use of Past and Future Perfect Tenses	
Past action or condition completed before another	Jason had studied the map before they started out.
Future action or condition completed before another	Jason will have memorized the route before they leave.
Continuing past action interrupted by another	Leah had been packing before Jason arrived.
Continuing future action interrupted by another	By the time they reach the site, they will have been traveling for four days.

Identifying Inconsistent Verb Tenses

Inconsistent verb tense occurs when a sentence begins in one verb tense and incorrectly switches to another. Shifts in tense should always reflect a logical sequence.

Incorrect: They <u>will start out</u> today, and they *are* there tomorrow.

Correct: They <u>will start out</u> today, and they *will* be there tomorrow.

Incorrect: By the time they <u>figure out</u> the mystery, Derone *will take* the gold.

Correct: By the time they <u>figure out</u> the mystery, Derone *will have taken* the gold.

Fixing Inconsistent Verb Tense

To correct inconsistent verb tense, scan the verbs in your draft for changes in tense.

1. Determine the reason for each change in tense you find.

2. Determine which actions happened first.
   When two actions occur at different times in the past, use the past perfect tense for the earlier action. When two actions occur at different times in the future, use the perfect tense for the earlier action.

Revision Checklist

❏ Have I used the past perfect tense for the earlier of two actions in the past?

❏ Have I used the future perfect tense for the earlier of two actions in the future?

Name _____ Date _____ Selection _____

Editing and Proofreading

Review your draft to correct errors in capitalization, spelling, and punctuation.

Focus on Capitalization: Review your draft carefully to find and correct capitalization errors. Capitalize the first word in each new bit of dialogue.

> **Incorrect capitalization:** "that map can't be wrong, can it?" Jason asked.

> **Correct capitalization:** "That map can't be wrong, can it?" Jason asked.

Capitalize the first word in dialogue that is a full sentence.

> **Incorrect capitalization:** The sun set slowly in the west. The hikers were tired, but Jason asked, "should we go on?"

> **Correct capitalization:** The sun set slowly in the west. The hikers were tired, but Jason asked, "Should we go on?"

Focus on Spelling: Often suffixes cause no spelling change to a word. Sometimes, though, final *e*'s are dropped or final *y*'s are changed to *i*. The final consonant may change as well, as in *conclude/ conclusion*. Changes in spelling may also occur within the words as they change form, such as in *maintain, maintenance*.

Focus on Punctuation: Punctuating Dialogue Proofread your writing to find and address punctuation errors. In particular, look at the dialogue. Be sure you have used commas, end marks, and quotation marks correctly.

Rule: Use quotation marks to enclose a person's exact speech or thoughts.

Jason said, "Let's head toward those trees."

Rule: Always place a comma inside the final quotation mark.

"I'm not sure that's right," Leah said.

Rule: Place a question mark or an exclamation mark inside the final quotation mark if the end mark is part of the quotation.

"Just do it!" Jason shouted.

For use with Writing 3

Name _____ Date _____ Selection _____

Publishing and Presenting

Consider one of the following ways to present your writing:

Deliver a dramatic reading. Prepare and record sound effects or background music to integrate with a dramatic reading of your story. Practice delivering the reading as you synch the proper effects. Then give the reading to the class.

Create an anthology. Work with your classmates to illustrate and collect your stories into a single print or online anthology. Choose a method of organization, such as by theme, type of fiction (realistic fiction, science fiction, mystery, and so on), type of conflict, or settings.

Rubric for Self-Assessment

Find evidence in your writing to address each category. Then, use the rating scale to grade your work. Circle the score that best applies for each category.

Evaluating Your Narrative	not very			very		
Focus: How clear are the characters, the setting, and the conflict?	1	2	3	4	5	6
Organization: How effectively have you presented the sequence of events? Have you used appropriate pacing, dialogue, and other narrative techniques?	1	2	3	4	5	6
Support/Elaboration: How well have you used descriptive details to establish the setting, create the characters, and show the action?	1	2	3	4	5	6
Style: How well have you engaged the reader with an interesting conflict, a consistent or effective point of view, and precise words that create a vivid picture of the characters?	1	2	3	4	5	6
Conventions: How free is your essay from errors in grammar, spelling, and punctuation?	1	2	3	4	5	6

Writing 4

---

4. Produce clear and coherent writing in which the development, organization, and style are appropriate to task, purpose, and audience.

Explanation

When you write, one important goal is to produce writing that is both clear and coherent. Equally important is ensuring that the writing you produce is appropriate for your task, purpose, and audience.

- Your **task** is the specific reason you are writing, such as an essay assignment.

- Your **purpose** is the goal you want your writing to achieve. Presenting a strong argument, explaining a given topic, and telling an entertaining story are common purposes for writing.

- Your **audience** is the person or people who will read your writing.

Your task, purpose, and audience should affect nearly every decision you make as you write. Knowing why and for whom you are writing helps you develop and organize your ideas, as well as select an appropriate writing style.

Development Develop your writing by including information, evidence, and details that are suited to your task, purpose, and audience. For example, a letter to the editor of your school newspaper in favor of a longer school day could include evidence that more time in school leads to better opportunities after graduation. With an adventure story, fast pacing and vivid descriptions will keep readers excited.

Organization Sequence ideas and information—or the events in your narrative—appropriately for your task and purpose. For example, if you are writing an essay about a recycling program, explain how the program works before describing its effects. Include such transitions as "because" and "as a result" to help your audience recognize how the facts and ideas in your essay are related.

Style Selecting language and a tone that are appropriate for your task, purpose, and audience is especially important. An essay on recycling requires a formal style and objective tone. A letter to the editor could be less formal but should still remain objective so it does not offend readers who disagree. An adventure story requires precise words and descriptive details to engage the audience.

Academic Vocabulary

development the use of information, evidence, and details in writing to present and build an argument, a topic, or a narrative

organization the way ideas, information, and other elements are arranged and connected in writing

style the language and tone used by a writer to communicate clearly and engage readers

Apply the Standard

Use the worksheet that follows to help you apply the standard as you write. Several copies of the worksheet have been provided for you to use with different assignments.

- Writing to a Specific Task, Purpose, and Audience

Name _____ Date _____ Assignment _____

Writing to a Specific Task, Purpose, and Audience

Identify your writing task, purpose for writing, and audience. Then use the organizer to describe an appropriate development, organization, and style for your writing.

Task:

....

....

Purpose:

....

....

Audience:

....

....

Development	Organization	Style

A

Name _____ Date _____ Assignment _____

Writing to a Specific Task, Purpose, and Audience

Identify your writing task, purpose for writing, and audience. Then use the organizer to describe an appropriate development, organization, and style for your writing.

Task:

....

....

Purpose:

....

....

Audience:

....

....

Development	Organization	Style

B

For use with Writing 4

Name _____ Date _____ Assignment _____

Writing to a Specific Task, Purpose, and Audience

Identify your writing task, purpose for writing, and audience. Then use the organizer to describe an appropriate development, organization, and style for your writing.

Task:
....
....
Purpose:
....
....
Audience:
....
....

Development	Organization	Style

C

Name _____ Date _____ Assignment _____

Writing to a Specific Task, Purpose, and Audience

Identify your writing task, purpose for writing, and audience. Then use the organizer to describe an appropriate development, organization, and style for your writing.

Task:

....

....

Purpose:

....

....

Audience:

....

....

Development	Organization	Style

D

For use with Writing 4

Name _____ Date _____ Assignment _____

Writing to a Specific Task, Purpose, and Audience

Identify your writing task, purpose for writing, and audience. Then use the organizer to describe an appropriate development, organization, and style for your writing.

Task:

....

....

Purpose:

....

....

Audience:

....

....

Development	Organization	Style

E

For use with Writing 4

Name _____ Date _____ Assignment _____

Writing to a Specific Task, Purpose, and Audience

Identify your writing task, purpose for writing, and audience. Then use the organizer to describe an appropriate development, organization, and style for your writing.

| **Task:** |
| .... |
| .... |
| **Purpose:** |
| .... |
| .... |
| **Audience:** |
| .... |
| .... |

Development	**Organization**	**Style**

Writing 5

> 5. Develop and strengthen writing as needed by planning, revising, editing, rewriting, or trying a new approach, focusing on addressing what is most significant for a specific purpose and audience.

Explanation

Finished pieces of writing are not produced without effort. Writers first **develop** their writing by generating ideas and gathering information about issues, topics, or subjects. Writers also **strengthen** their writing by reviewing what they have written and making changes to improve it. In developing and strengthening their writing, writers ensure it achieves its purpose, or the goal they want it to achieve. They also ensure that their writing meets the needs of the audience.

Develop and strengthen your writing by **planning** before you begin and by **revising** and **editing** after you finish. As you plan, revise, and edit, focus on what is most important for your **purpose** and **audience.**

- **Planning:** Find ideas and information that will help you achieve your purpose for writing. If you are planning an expository essay on pollution, for example, your purpose might be to explain how air pollution affects people's health. Information about illnesses caused by air pollution will help you address your purpose. Include all the information your audience will need to understand your topic.

- **Revising:** Carefully review what you have written, keeping your purpose and audience in mind. For example, if you are writing an argument in favor of a dress code at your school, ask yourself: Are my reasons persuasive? Have I included enough evidence to convince readers? Is my tone objective and fair to my audience? Be prepared to add or delete details, sentences, or even whole paragraphs in order to address your purpose and audience.

- **Editing:** After revising, check what you have written for errors in grammar, spelling, and punctuation. Correcting errors will help your audience read and understand what you have written. For example, if you are writing a short story, make sure you have used verb tenses consistently to help readers keep track of what happens to your characters.

If your writing does not address what is most important for your purpose and audience, be prepared to rewrite what you have written and try a new approach.

Academic Vocabulary

develop building an argument, topic, or narrative with information, evidence, and details

editing checking a piece of writing and correcting errors in grammar, spelling, and punctuation

revising reviewing and making changes to writing to better address the purpose and audience

Apply the Standard

Use the worksheet that follows to help you apply the standard as you write. Several copies of the worksheet have been provided for you to use with different assignments.

- Developing and Strengthening Your Writing

Name _____ Date _____ Assignment _____

Developing and Strengthening Your Writing

Use the organizer to describe how you plan, revise, and edit your writing. Then answer the questions at the bottom of the page.

Your Purpose for Writing: ....

Your Audience: ....

PLANNING
Ideas:
Information:

REVISING	EDITING
Add:	Grammar:
Delete:	Spelling:
Change:	Punctuation:

How well does your writing achieve your purpose?

....

....

How well does your writing meet the needs of your audience?

....

....

A

For use with Writing 5

Name _____ Date _____ Assignment _____

Developing and Strengthening Your Writing

Use the organizer to describe how you plan, revise, and edit your writing. Then answer the questions at the bottom of the page.

Your Purpose for Writing: ....

Your Audience: ....

PLANNING

Ideas:

Information:

REVISING

Add:

Delete:

Change:

EDITING

Grammar:

Spelling:

Punctuation:

How well does your writing achieve your purpose?

....
....

How well does your writing meet the needs of your audience?

....
....

Name _____ Date _____ Assignment _____

Developing and Strengthening Your Writing

Use the organizer to describe how you plan, revise, and edit your writing. Then answer the questions at the bottom of the page.

Your Purpose for Writing: ....

Your Audience: ....

PLANNING

Ideas:

Information:

REVISING

Add:

Delete:

Change:

EDITING

Grammar:

Spelling:

Punctuation:

How well does your writing achieve your purpose?

....

....

How well does your writing meet the needs of your audience?

....

....

C

For use with Writing 5

Name _____ Date _____ Assignment _____

Developing and Strengthening Your Writing

Use the organizer to describe how you plan, revise, and edit your writing. Then answer the questions at the bottom of the page.

Your Purpose for Writing: ....

Your Audience: ....

PLANNING

Ideas:

Information:

REVISING

Add:

Delete:

Change:

EDITING

Grammar:

Spelling:

Punctuation:

How well does your writing achieve your purpose?

....

....

How well does your writing meet the needs of your audience?

....

....

D

Name _____ Date _____ Assignment _____

Developing and Strengthening Your Writing

Use the organizer to describe how you plan, revise, and edit your writing. Then answer the questions at the bottom of the page.

Your Purpose for Writing: ....

Your Audience: ....

<table>
<tr><td colspan="2" align="center">PLANNING</td></tr>
<tr><td>Ideas:</td><td></td></tr>
<tr><td>Information:</td><td></td></tr>
</table>

<table>
<tr><td align="center">REVISING</td><td align="center">EDITING</td></tr>
<tr><td>Add:</td><td>Grammar:</td></tr>
<tr><td>Delete:</td><td>Spelling:</td></tr>
<tr><td>Change:</td><td>Punctuation:</td></tr>
</table>

How well does your writing achieve your purpose?

....

....

How well does your writing meet the needs of your audience?

....

....

Name _____ Date _____ Assignment _____

Developing and Strengthening Your Writing

Use the organizer to describe how you plan, revise, and edit your writing. Then answer the questions at the bottom of the page.

Your Purpose for Writing: ....

Your Audience: ....

PLANNING

Ideas:

Information:

REVISING

Add:

Delete:

Change:

EDITING

Grammar:

Spelling:

Punctuation:

How well does your writing achieve your purpose?

....

....

How well does your writing meet the needs of your audience?

....

....

F

Writing 6

> 6. Use technology, including the Internet, to produce, publish, and update individual or shared writing products, taking advantage of technology's capacity to link to other information and to display information flexibly and dynamically.

Explanation

Technology provides today's writers with many powerful tools. The Internet gives writers quick access to the information they need to develop ideas. Word processing software makes writing, revising, and editing easier. Using the appropriate applications, writers can present information in a range of formats, incorporating **links** that readers can click on to call up related Web pages. Through Internet formats such as **blogs** and **wikis,** writers can collaborate on shared writing products, publish their writing online, and update what they have posted in the past.

- **Produce, publish, and update writing:** Select the appropriate format for producing and presenting your writing, whether as a printed laid out page or as a blog on a classroom Web site. Explore the technology you will need to produce writing in this format, and use it to publish your work. If you are publishing online, consider whether you should offer periodic updates to the information or invite and respond to comments posted by others.

- **Link to other information:** Use links to connect your word processing document or Web page to a related Web page. For example, if you are posting an argument to a class Web site in support of a new recycling program, you might create a link to an Internet journal article about the benefits of recycling.

- **Display information in flexible, dynamic formats suited to your topic:** Most word processing programs include tools for creating charts, graphs, or tables. Use these tools for presenting statistics, rates, and other quantitative information. You may also include multimedia information, such as photographs, audio clips, or video clips, in your writing products. For multimedia you find on the Web, always check the site to ensure that you have permission to use the multimedia. Correctly cite your sources.

Academic Vocabulary

blog (short for "Web log") an online journal in which the writer or writers post entries over time

link a word, phrase, button, or other feature in a Web page or other document that readers click on to open up a designated Web page or document on the Internet

wiki (short for *wikkiwikki,* "quick" in Hawaiian) a collaborative Web site on which visitors create, add, remove, and edit material

Apply the Standard

Use the worksheet that follows to help you apply the standard as you write. Several copies have been provided for you to use with different assignments.

- Using Technology

Name _____ Date _____ Assignment _____

Using Technology

Identify your topic and audience. Then, use the organizer to plan how you will employ technology to produce, publish, and update your work, as well as to link to and display information.

Topic on Which You Are Writing: ....

Audience for Your Work: ....

USE TECHNOLOGY AND THE INTERNET TO . . .			
Produce, Publish, and Update Work	**Link to Other Information**	**Display Information: Charts, Graphs, Tables**	**Display Information: Multimedia**
Format (word processor document, Web page, and so on):	Sources to link to:	Information to be displayed:	Multimedia pieces to be included:
Software needed:	Sections of source to link to:	Format (chart, graph, table):	Source:
Collaboration with/ comments from others:	Where link will appear in your writing product:	Where graphic will appear in your writing product:	Where multimedia will appear in your writing product:
Updates (give reasons to include or omit):	Why link is appropriate to your topic and useful to your reader:	Why graphic is appropriate to your topic and useful to your reader:	Why multimedia is appropriate to your topic and useful to your reader:

For use with Writing 6

Name _____ Date _____ Assignment _____

Using Technology

Identify your topic and audience. Then, use the organizer to plan how you will employ technology to produce, publish, and update your work, as well as to link to and display information.

Topic on Which You Are Writing: ....

Audience for Your Work: ....

USE TECHNOLOGY AND THE INTERNET TO . . .			
Produce, Publish, and Update Work	**Link to Other Information**	**Display Information: Charts, Graphs, Tables**	**Display Information: Multimedia**
Format (word processor document, Web page, and so on):	Sources to link to:	Information to be displayed:	Multimedia pieces to be included:
Software needed:	Sections of source to link to:	Format (chart, graph, table):	Source:
Collaboration with/ comments from others:	Where link will appear in your writing product:	Where graphic will appear in your writing product:	Where multimedia will appear in your writing product:
Updates (give reasons to include or omit):	Why link is appropriate to your topic and useful to your reader:	Why graphic is appropriate to your topic and useful to your reader:	Why multimedia is appropriate to your topic and useful to your reader:

For use with Writing 6

Name _____ Date _____ Assignment _____

Using Technology

Identify your topic and audience. Then, use the organizer to plan how you will employ technology to produce, publish, and update your work, as well as to link to and display information.

Topic on Which You Are Writing: ....

Audience for Your Work: ....

USE TECHNOLOGY AND THE INTERNET TO . . .			
Produce, Publish, and Update Work	**Link to Other Information**	**Display Information: Charts, Graphs, Tables**	**Display Information: Multimedia**
Format (word processor document, Web page, and so on):	Sources to link to:	Information to be displayed:	Multimedia pieces to be included:
Software needed:	Sections of source to link to:	Format (chart, graph, table):	Source:
Collaboration with/ comments from others:	Where link will appear in your writing product:	Where graphic will appear in your writing product:	Where multimedia will appear in your writing product:
Updates (give reasons to include or omit):	Why link is appropriate to your topic and useful to your reader:	Why graphic is appropriate to your topic and useful to your reader:	Why multimedia is appropriate to your topic and useful to your reader:

C

For use with Writing 6

Name _____ Date _____ Assignment _____

Using Technology

Identify your topic and audience. Then, use the organizer to plan how you will employ technology to produce, publish, and update your work, as well as to link to and display information.

Topic on Which You Are Writing: ....

Audience for Your Work: ....

USE TECHNOLOGY AND THE INTERNET TO . . .			
Produce, Publish, and Update Work	**Link to Other Information**	**Display Information: Charts, Graphs, Tables**	**Display Information: Multimedia**
Format (word processor document, Web page, and so on):	Sources to link to:	Information to be displayed:	Multimedia pieces to be included:
Software needed:	Sections of source to link to:	Format (chart, graph, table):	Source:
Collaboration with/ comments from others:	Where link will appear in your writing product:	Where graphic will appear in your writing product:	Where multimedia will appear in your writing product:
Updates (give reasons to include or omit):	Why link is appropriate to your topic and useful to your reader:	Why graphic is appropriate to your topic and useful to your reader:	Why multimedia is appropriate to your topic and useful to your reader:

D

For use with Writing 6

Name _____ Date _____ Assignment _____

Using Technology

Identify your topic and audience. Then, use the organizer to plan how you will employ technology to produce, publish, and update your work, as well as to link to and display information.

Topic on Which You Are Writing: ....

Audience for Your Work: ....

USE TECHNOLOGY AND THE INTERNET TO . . .			
Produce, Publish, and Update Work	**Link to Other Information**	**Display Information: Charts, Graphs, Tables**	**Display Information: Multimedia**
Format (word processor document, Web page, and so on):	Sources to link to:	Information to be displayed:	Multimedia pieces to be included:
Software needed:	Sections of source to link to:	Format (chart, graph, table):	Source:
Collaboration with/ comments from others:	Where link will appear in your writing product:	Where graphic will appear in your writing product:	Where multimedia will appear in your writing product:
Updates (give reasons to include or omit):	Why link is appropriate to your topic and useful to your reader:	Why graphic is appropriate to your topic and useful to your reader:	Why multimedia is appropriate to your topic and useful to your reader:

E

For use with Writing 6

Name _____ Date _____ Assignment _____

Using Technology

Identify your topic and audience. Then, use the organizer to plan how you will employ technology to produce, publish, and update your work, as well as to link to and display information.

Topic on Which You Are Writing: ....

Audience for Your Work: ....

USE TECHNOLOGY AND THE INTERNET TO . . .			
Produce, Publish, and Update Work	**Link to Other Information**	**Display Information: Charts, Graphs, Tables**	**Display Information: Multimedia**
Format (word processor document, Web page, and so on):	Sources to link to:	Information to be displayed:	Multimedia pieces to be included:
Software needed:	Sections of source to link to:	Format (chart, graph, table):	Source:
Collaboration with/ comments from others:	Where link will appear in your writing product:	Where graphic will appear in your writing product:	Where multimedia will appear in your writing product:
Updates (give reasons to include or omit):	Why link is appropriate to your topic and useful to your reader:	Why graphic is appropriate to your topic and useful to your reader:	Why multimedia is appropriate to your topic and useful to your reader:

F

Writing 7

7. Conduct short as well as more sustained research projects to answer a question (including a self-generated question) or solve a problem; narrow or broaden the inquiry when appropriate; synthesize multiple sources on the subject, demonstrating understanding of the subject under investigation.

Explanation

Research projects vary in their scope and can have different goals. Some research projects are short and focused on very narrow topics. Complex subjects, however, require more **sustained research**, or in-depth investigation involving multiple sources. As you conduct research, you may need to narrow or broaden your **inquiry**. A narrow inquiry is appropriate for a short research project, while a broader inquiry may be appropriate for a more sustained project.

- **Narrowing an inquiry:** For a short research project, you may need to narrow a question or problem. For example, "strategies for conserving energy" is probably too broad a topic for a short research project. You might narrow it, choosing to focus on conserving electricity. If the problem is still too broad for the scope of your project, narrow it again. For example, you might focus on reducing electricity use in your home.

- **Broadening an inquiry:** For a more sustained research project, you may need to broaden a question or problem. For example, the question "How was William Shakespeare's *Romeo and Juliet* first performed?" might be too limited for a long-term project. You might broaden it to "How have performances of *Romeo and Juliet* changed over time?"

To develop an understanding of your subject, gather ideas and information from several different sources. When you present the results of your research, demonstrate your understanding by supporting your answer or solution with information from each of these multiple sources. Do not just repeat points from each source. Instead, **synthesize,** or creatively combine, information. First, show the connections and conflicts between information and theories in different sources. Then, build your own conclusions about the research question or problem based on the ideas and information that you have gathered.

Academic Vocabulary

inquiry the process of looking for information to answer questions about a topic or to solve a problem

sustained research in-depth investigation or inquiry involving multiple sources

synthesize combine information from different sources to present a new answer or solution

Apply the Standard

Use the worksheets that follow to help you apply the standard as you write. Several copies of each worksheet have been provided for you to use with different assignments.

- Researching to Answer Questions or Solve Problems
- Synthesizing Information from Different Sources

Name _____ Date _____ Assignment _____

Researching to Answer Questions or Solve Problems

To use the organizer, begin by identifying your topic, the scope of the project, and your initial problem or question. Narrow or broaden your inquiry as appropriate. Then, use the organizer to gather ideas and information from multiple sources.

Subject: ....

Scope of Research Project: ❏ Short project ❏ Sustained project

Initial Question or Problem: ....

....

❏ Narrow Inquiry ❏ Broaden Inquiry

Narrowed/Broadened Question or Problem: ....

....

Source 1	Source 2	Source 3	Source 4
Title, Author, Publisher, Date of Publication, Medium:	Title, Author, Publisher, Date of Publication, Medium:	Title, Author, Publisher, Date of Publication, Medium:	Title, Author, Publisher, Date of Publication, Medium:
Ideas and Information:	Ideas and Information:	Ideas and Information:	Ideas and Information:

For use with Writing 7

Name _____ Date _____ Assignment _____

Researching to Answer Questions or Solve Problems

To use the organizer, begin by identifying your topic, the scope of the project, and your initial problem or question. Narrow or broaden your inquiry as appropriate. Then, use the organizer to gather ideas and information from multiple sources.

Subject: ....

Scope of Research Project: ❑ Short project   ❑ Sustained project

Initial Question or Problem: ....

....

❑ Narrow Inquiry   ❑ Broaden Inquiry

Narrowed/Broadened Question or Problem: ....

....

Source 1	Source 2	Source 3	Source 4
Title, Author, Publisher, Date of Publication, Medium:	Title, Author, Publisher, Date of Publication, Medium:	Title, Author, Publisher, Date of Publication, Medium:	Title, Author, Publisher, Date of Publication, Medium:
Ideas and Information:	Ideas and Information:	Ideas and Information:	Ideas and Information:

For use with Writing 7

Name _____ Date _____ Assignment _____

Researching to Answer Questions or Solve Problems

To use the organizer, begin by identifying your topic, the scope of the project, and your initial problem or question. Narrow or broaden your inquiry as appropriate. Then, use the organizer to gather ideas and information from multiple sources.

Subject: ....

Scope of Research Project: ❏ Short project ❏ Sustained project

Initial Question or Problem: ....

....

❏ Narrow Inquiry ❏ Broaden Inquiry

Narrowed/Broadened Question or Problem: ....

....

Source 1	Source 2	Source 3	Source 4
Title, Author, Publisher, Date of Publication, Medium:	Title, Author, Publisher, Date of Publication, Medium:	Title, Author, Publisher, Date of Publication, Medium:	Title, Author, Publisher, Date of Publication, Medium:
Ideas and Information:	Ideas and Information:	Ideas and Information:	Ideas and Information:

C

For use with Writing 7

Name _____ Date _____ Assignment _____

Synthesizing Information from Different Sources

Use the organizer below to record information about a question or problem from multiple sources. Then, synthesize the information to produce your own answer or solution, calling out the ideas and information that most clearly support your conclusion.

Subject: ....

Question or Problem: ....

....

Information from Source 1:
Information from Source 2:
Information from Source 3:
Information from Source 4:

⇩

SYNTHESIS
Your Answer/Solution: ....
....
Most Relevant Support:

A

For use with Writing 7

Name _____ Date _____ Assignment _____

Synthesizing Information from Different Sources

Use the organizer below to record information about a question or problem from multiple sources. Then, synthesize the information to produce your own answer or solution, calling out the ideas and information that most clearly support your conclusion.

Subject: ....

Question or Problem: ....

....

Information from Source 1:
Information from Source 2:
Information from Source 3:
Information from Source 4:

⇩

SYNTHESIS
Your Answer/Solution: ....
....
Most Relevant Support:

Name _____ Date _____ Assignment _____

Synthesizing Information from Different Sources

Use the organizer below to record information about a question or problem from multiple sources. Then, synthesize the information to produce your own answer or solution, calling out the ideas and information that most clearly support your conclusion.

Subject: ....

Question or Problem: ....

....

Information from Source 1:
Information from Source 2:
Information from Source 3:
Information from Source 4:

⇩

SYNTHESIS
Your Answer/Solution: ....
....
Most Relevant Support:

Writing 8

> **8. Gather information from multiple print and digital sources, using advanced searches effectively; assess the usefulness of each source in answering the research question; integrate information into the text selectively to maintain the flow of ideas, avoiding plagiarism and following a standard format for citation.**

Writing Workshop: Research Report

When you write a **research report,** your task is to inform. To do so, you must decide on a topic, read about it in a number of sources, narrow it down to an appropriate scope and focus, arrive at a thesis, and then gather information to support that thesis. Gathering information requires time and care as you evaluate what you find, take notes from your sources, and use what you have learned to refine your thesis. As you draft, you must integrate that information smoothly into your paper.

At the same time, research writing requires you to keep in mind all the qualities of good writing, including clarity; smooth transitions; an appropriate structure with an interesting opener, an appropriate ending, and well-documented body paragraphs; as well as a clear sense of your audience and purpose from start to finish.

Assignment

Write a research report about an event or development in history. Include these elements:

✓ a topic that is narrow enough to be covered in the length of your paper

✓ a clear, specific thesis that functions as the controlling idea

✓ body paragraphs that clearly relate to and develop that thesis

✓ relevant and substantial support for the thesis

✓ appropriately quoted or paraphrased information from credible sources

✓ accurate, correctly formatted citations within the paper

✓ an accurate, correctly formatted Works Cited list or bibliography

✓ correct use of language conventions and manuscript conventions throughout

*Additional Standards

Language
1.b. Use various types of phrases (nouns, verb, adjectival, adverbial, participial, prepositional, absolute) and clauses (independent, dependent; noun, relative, adverbial) to convey

specific meanings and add variety and interest to writing or presentations.

2.a. Use a semicolon (and perhaps a conjunctive adverb) to link two or more closely related independent clauses.

3.a. Write and edit work so that it conforms to the guidelines in a style manual (e.g., *MLA Handbook,* Turabian's *Manual for Writers*) appropriate for the discipline and writing type.

Name _____ Date _____ Selection _____

Prewriting/Planning Strategies

Brainstorm categories. Identify an area of general interest and list categories. For example, if you are interested in technology, you might list personal computers, computer games, smartphones, or technology using unlicensed portions of the radio spectrum. Repeating that process, you might narrow your topic from computer games to a specific computer game or to the first computer game with a widespread or lasting audience.

Notebook review. Flip through the notebooks you keep for each class in school to find subjects or ideas that spark your interest or that lead you to new ideas. Choose an idea from your review. This idea, too, will probably need narrowing by focusing in on specific aspects of the topic:

Subject from class notebook:				
Who?	**What Happened?**	**When?**	**Why?**	**What Else?**

Ask an open-ended research question. Before you begin researching, compose a question about your topic. The answer to this question may be your thesis, or, more likely, the beginning of it. The question will also help focus your research into a flexible search plan, as well as prevent you from gathering details that are too broad for your purpose.

Questions:

1. _____

2. _____

3. _____

Write a working thesis. Because you have not yet started to read, the thesis you start with won't be the one you end with. Yet, it's a good idea to commit an idea to paper now; it will help you focus your research.

Identify your audience. If your audience has not already been specified, decide who would be most interested by your topic or most likely to benefit by learning about it. Keep this audience in mind throughout all the stages of your writing process. Even if you are writing for your peers, however, think of a research report as a formal task for which you should create an objective tone and formal style.

Working Thesis:
Audience:

Researching from Print and Digital Sources

Begin reading. The purpose of a research report is to inform your audience about a topic; therefore, plan to do some serious reading. The best place to start is with a general overview of your topic. For this, consult encyclopedias or general reference works.

The reading doesn't end there. You must consult sources at least twice. At the start of the research process, you must read to develop a general sense of your topic and to narrow it to a specific focus and thesis. Later, you will read again to find additional information in support of your specific thesis. The success of your paper will depend, in part, on choosing a variety of reliable and appropriate sources.

Use reference works. Reference works you might turn to at the beginning of your research process, as well as later on, include specialized encyclopedias, such as encyclopedias of science, animal life, inventions, the Civil War, the Cold War, and so on. When you are seeking to narrow your topic, take a look at the specific subheadings in these reference works. They can help you understand at a glance the smaller "chunks" or aspects of a large topic. Look for reference works online as well as in your public library system.

Use a variety of other sources. Web sites offer worlds of information, but they are not the only source of information, and they are not always the best source. For most topics, you will want to use both primary and secondary sources. Primary sources offer firsthand or original accounts. They may include, for example, the letters written by soldiers or people who were actually at a battle or living nearby. Histories, textbook accounts, and biographies from a later date are all examples of secondary sources.

Sources you should consult include the following:

- **Books.** Find these on the shelves of your library, online in your library catalog, in the Gutenberg online library (Project Gutenberg), or through Google.

- **Magazines and newspapers.** Access these through the *Reader's Guide to Periodicals* or through other library databases.

- **Databases.** There are specialized databases for every topic from literary criticism and health and wellness to biographies and general science resources. Databases can also lead you to magazines, newspapers, general and specialized encyclopedias, and scholarly journals. You can access databases from terminals in your local library. To access them from home, you usually need a library card number.

- **Government documents.** These documents are on subjects ranging from law and government issues to agricultural planning.

- **Consumer, workplace, and other public documents.** Consumer documents include everything from the descriptions of goods and services to warranties and guarantees for them. Workplace documents include business correspondence, as well as items such as task force reports. Public documents also span a broad range. Anything your town, city, or state government keeps on who lives where, what taxes they pay, and how your laws came about is a public document.

Do advanced searching. Take time to learn about advanced searches in your favorite search engine as well as in your library system. Often, there is a link called "Advanced Search" that you can select on the home page. In a search engine, you can limit your search to documents with some words but not others; you might be able to limit your search strictly to .gov items or another domain. In a library catalog, you might be able to limit the results to the material type (book, CD, periodical, software, and so on); to the collection type (adult or children's); and to the publication date.

Stop to evaluate your topic. After you have gathered a variety of sources and begun to read with a specific thesis in mind, stop. Make sure the topic you haven chosen is the right match for your task, your purpose, and your audience. Ask yourself these questions:

- ❏ Is this the right topic for me? Am I interested enough in it to interest my audience?

- ❏ Is this the right topic for meeting the requirements of the assignment?

- ❏ Is this topic narrow enough?

- ❏ Am I going to be able to find the information I need?

- ❏ How well does my thesis reflect my focus at this point?

Name _____ Date _____ Selection _____

Evaluating Credibility and Usefulness of Your Sources

Evaluate Web sites. Anyone can create a Web site. No one has to check it over, edit it, or make sure the facts are correct: that is, a Web site does not have to be credible to be on the Web. As a potential user of a Web site, the job of establishing credibility is up to you.

You must also decide how potentially useful the site is for your purpose, so check the sitemap for a fuller picture of what the site has to offer. Use this form to record information about Web sites and make decisions about their credibility and usefulness to you.

Web site URL:
Author or Sponsoring Institution (such as the Smithsonian):
Is the author/institution a respected authority on this subject? Explain:
Are there footnotes, a bibliography, or other list of sources on which the information is based? Does the information come from respectable sources?
What is the site's purpose? Is it selling anything? Is there a bias, such as a political agenda?
Is the information current? Is there a copyright date?
How useful is this source to me? Why?

Evaluate Other Sources. Carefully judge other online or print sources. Weed out lower quality and popular items.

- **Magazines and Newspapers.** Popular magazines are generally not good sources. If you are writing about the history of aerobics, prefer a researched book to, for example, a magazine called *Men Get Fit Fast.* The quality of newspapers varies widely. You may find excellent articles in your local paper, or you may find great inaccuracies. Large city newspapers such as *The New York Times* and the *Washington Post* are generally considered reliable.

- **Books.** Again, popular books are usually not credible. Use some of the same criteria to evaluate books that you use to evaluate Web sites: information about the author and whether he or she is an authority on the topic; publication date; the presence or absence of footnotes, endnotes, and/or bibliography; and the copyright date.

Taking Notes

Make source cards. Create a card, a listing, or a separate electronic file for every source you use. Assign a number or letter to each source, beginning with 1 or A.

- **Books.** If your source is a book, your source card should list the title, the author, the publisher, the city, and the copyright date.

- **Web sites.** If your source is a Web site, your source card should list the name and Web address of the site, the author and sponsoring institution if available, and the date you accessed the site.

Make notecards. Create a separate notecard, a listing, or an electronic file listing every bit of information you take from your sources. Number or letter each source card or listing in the upper right hand corner. Use the number or letter you assigned to the source when you made its source card. Then write the information you find interesting or useful.

Revisit your thesis. As you research and take notes, you should be getting nearer and nearer to a specific thesis. Keep refining the idea for your thesis as you go along.

Name _____ Date _____ Selection _____

Avoiding Plagiarism

Use sources honestly. The correct and honest use of sources begins at the moment when you view your first source. Careful, honest recordkeeping will also save you time and trouble, as you will not have to scramble at the end to locate the source of a great quotation or paraphrased information that you have to credit or cite. As you take notes, follow these guidelines.

- **Paraphrase.** Paraphrase as much as possible. To do this in the best possible way, read the entire source or source part, such as a chapter or Web page, and then, without referring to the source, write down your understanding of what you read in your own words. If it is too hard to do that, try the same method with smaller chunks of the text, such as information covered under just one subheading or in just one paragraph.

  You can also paraphrase sentence by sentence, but you have to use extreme care with this method. It's fine to copy words such as *the* and *and.* You can also copy core nouns that are essential to your topic. For example, if you are writing about a battle, words such as *battle, soldier, casualties, command,* and so on can also go straight onto your notecards without change. Otherwise, however, the words should be your own. If you do happen to use just one keyword or phrase in your paraphrase, or copy exactly any unique way of saying anything, be sure to enclose it in quotation marks.

- **Summarize.** Sometimes, you will want just the main idea of what a source says. In that case, it may be possible to boil down a paragraph, a Web page, or other large chunk of text into a single sentence or two. Even though you are doing a lot of work by summarizing, the words you come up with still have to be documented. To be sure you don't forget to do that, put your summary on a notecard, and don't forget to assign the letter or number of the source to it.

- **Quote.** Occasionally, the exact words of your source will be too good to pass up. In that case, you will want to record your source word for word. If you do so, remember to enclose those words in quotation marks on your notecard. Keep in mind that your finished paper should not be a patchwork of quotations. Furthermore, you will want to keep long quotations to a minimum. Therefore, quote only when the words are perfect for your purpose and audience. When you quote, you may decide to leave a word, phrase, sentence, or entire section out. To show this omission, use an ellipsis (. . .).

Name _____ Date _____ Selection _____

Developing a Structure

Write a specific thesis. Make your thesis as specific as possible before you begin to draft. Your thesis should take a position and be supported by most of your research. Your thesis statement will serve as the controlling idea of your report.

Relate the content of your body paragraphs to your thesis. Record your specific thesis. Then develop main idea sentences or topic sentences that reflect your research and relate specifically back to your controlling idea:

Thesis:	
	Topic Sentence:
	Topic Sentence:
	Topic Sentence:

Choose a text structure. Use your thesis statement, your possible topic sentences, and knowledge of your audience to choose an organizational structure. Consider these options, as well as any logical order that fits your purpose and your information:

- **Chronological order.** Present events in the order in which they occur. This structure is ideal for reporting a subject's history or a series of events.

- **Order of importance.** Present details in order of increasing or decreasing significance. This structure is ideal for building an argument.

- **Comparison.** Present similarities and differences. This method is ideal for addressing two or more related subjects.

Plan for visuals. You may include visual aids, such as charts, tables, and graphs, to organize and display information in your report. Whenever you include additional information—whether it is visuals or quotations—be sure to make a clear link from your thesis to the data you include. Also be sure to include a source line, which documents the source of the information or the graphic, by following the rules of the style manual you are using.

Name _____ Date _____ Selection _____

Organizing and Drafting Your Report

Organize support. Begin organizing your notes into blocks and chunks that are related to your topic sentences or to a specific aspect of your thesis. Use this chart to list specific, ample support from your notes that you will include in your body paragraphs.

Topic sentence: Support—
Topic sentence: Support—
Topic sentence: Support—

Drafting

Lead into and out of your information. Your quoted, paraphrased, or summarized information will not introduce itself or create its own links to other ideas. Think about introducing all significant quoted and paraphrased material with a transitional word or phrase, such as "[Author's name] notes," "According to…," or "In [title of work]." Other transitional words and phrases, such as *furthermore, therefore, as a result, on the other hand* should also be used to link ideas within sentences, to link sentences, and to link paragraphs.

Your information will also not explain itself. You have to do that. Make clear connections for your audience between what you cite and your thesis.

Citing Sources

Give credit within the paper. You must give proper credit to the people whose ideas and words you have borrowed. Failing to do this raises legal and ethical issues. Libel, slander, copyright infringement, and plagiarism are serious accusations. Responsible writers are thorough and accurate in citing all of their sources.

When citing sources, follow a specific format such as MLA (Modern Language Association) style or APA (American Psychological Association) style. MLA style calls for citations in parentheses directly following the material being cited.

- **Print works.** Provide the author's or editor's name followed by a page number. If the work does not have an author, use a key word or short phrase from the title.

- **Web sources.** Give the author's name, title of the article, if any, or title of the site.

Make a list of all your sources. At the end of your paper, give information for each source you cite. MLA style calls for a works cited list. It should be arranged alphabetically by author's or editor's last name. If the author's or editor's last name is not given, then alphabetize by the first word of the title.

- **Books.** Give the author's name (last name first), the title of the work, the city of publication, the name of the publisher, and the year of publication.

- **Periodicals.** Give the author's last name, first name, title of the article, the name of the magazine, the date of the issue, the volume and issue number, and the pages of the article. For any month with more than four letters, abbreviate the month by using the first three letters followed by a period.

- **Web sites.** Give any of the information that is available in this order: the author's name, the title of the page, the title of the site, the date of last update, and the name of the sponsoring organization. Give the date you accessed the Web site and its full URL, or Web address.

Use a style reference. There are many different kinds of sources and variations within them, such as multiple authors, multivolume works, translations, pamphlets, and so on. Additionally, you may use sound recordings, interviews, or other less common sources. Do not guess how to cite these works. Instead, refer to the specific style manual that your teacher requires.

Name _____ Date _____ Selection _____

Revising Strategies

Put a checkmark beside each question as you address it in your revision.

	Questions To Ask as You Revise
Task	❑ Does my research report inform? ❑ Is my topic appropriate to the assignment requirements? ❑ Have I correctly and honestly cited all my sources? ❑ Have I relied on one style or style manual for all citations? ❑ Have I formatted my paper according to the conventions for a research report?
Purpose	❑ Do I need to make my thesis more specific? ❑ Do I need to revise my thesis to make it more adequately reflect the content of my paper? ❑ Have I fully developed my thesis by introducing and explaining ample, relevant information? ❑ What details, if any, do not relate to my purpose and should be deleted? ❑ Where do I need to add more details or explanation to achieve my purpose?
Audience	❑ Will my audience be interested in my topic? ❑ Will my audience be able to identify my thesis? ❑ Have I provided enough support for my thesis? ❑ Have I led smoothly into and out of my support and clearly linked it to my thesis? ❑ Do I sound objective? Have I limited myself to formal and standard word choices? ❑ Are the sources of all my ideas clear?

For use with Writing 8

Revise to combine sentences using adverb clauses. Adverb clauses can be used to combine information from two sentences into one sentence. Often, the revised sentence will make the intended meaning more obvious.

Two sentences: Few people know about this battle. It is a minor battle.
Combined: Few people know about this battle because it is a minor battle.

Identifying Adverb Clauses

A clause is any group of words with a subject and a verb. An independent clause can stand by itself as a complete sentence; a subordinate clause is not complete because it does not express a complete thought. An adverb clause is a subordinate clause that modifies a verb, an adjective, or another adverb in the sentence. It begins with a subordinating conjunction that tells where, when, in what way, to what extent, under what condition, or why.

When: *After* Forrest's men surrounded him, Bloodgood surrendered.
Under what condition: *If* the 2nd Brigade had not cut the telegraph, Bloodgood might not have surrendered.
In what way: To the Union commander, the enemy troops appeared *as if* they were a larger force.
Why: The Union wanted to hold Brentwood *so that it* could control the railroad line.

Combining Sentences with Adverb Clauses

When combining two short sentences using adverb clauses, follow these steps:

1. Look for a relationship between the ideas of the two sentences.

2. Select the appropriate subordinating conjunction to show that relationship. Place the adverb clause at the beginning or end of the combined sentence—wherever it conveys your intent more clearly.

3. Use a comma after the subordinate clause only when the subordinate clause begins the sentence.

Revision Checklist

❏ Are there short sentences that I could effectively combine with adverb clauses?

❏ Do the sentences I have combined accurately convey my intended meaning?

Editing and Proofreading

Review your draft to correct errors in format, capitalization, spelling, and punctuation.

Focus on Format: Follow manuscript requirements by including an appropriate title page, pagination, spacing and margins, and citations. Make sure you have used the preferred manual or set of guidelines for crediting sources in your paper and for bibliographical sources at the end. Double-check all punctuation and capitalization. If you are using MLA style, follow these rules for your Works Cited page:

- Begin a new page with the centered title "Works Cited."

- Double space all the entries; do not add extra lines of space between them.

- Create a hanging indent for entries that are more than one line long.

- Use the same one-inch margins on all sides that you used in the rest of the paper.

Focus on Spelling: Some words are difficult to spell because they contain unusual combinations of consonants or silent consonants. Certain consonant groupings in a single syllable, such as the *mb* in *comb*, do not appear in many words. Other consonant groupings that are hard to hear or contain a silent letter include the *c* sound in *muscle* and *indict;* the *th* in clothes; the *n* in *condemn;* and the *g* in *diaphragm, reign, campaign,* and *gnome.*

Focus on Punctuation: Semicolons to Join Independent Clauses Proofread your writing to find places where you have joined two independent clauses with only a comma. Some of these sentences may include a conjunctive adverb. Use a semicolon to join them correctly.

Rule: Use a semicolon to join independent clauses that are not already joined by a conjunction. *The inventor of Tetris did not patent the game; there were no individual property rights in Russia at the time to cover his invention.*

Rule: Use a semicolon to join independent clauses separated either by a conjunctive adverb or by a transitional expression. *The game is considered addictive; in fact, early fans reported not being able to leave the computer. The game seems deceptively simple at first; however, the speed and challenge pick up over time.*

Name _____ Date _____ Selection _____

Publishing and Presenting

Consider one of the following ways to present your writing:

Give a power presentation. Prepare a talk that presents all or some of the major points of your paper, including your thesis. Make slides with all key points. Practice integrating these slides with your talk, and then present your report to the class.

Organize a panel discussion. If several of your classmates have written on a similar topic, plan a discussion to compare and contrast your findings. Speakers can summarize their research before opening the panel to questions from the class.

Rubric for Self-Assessment

Find evidence in your writing to address each category. Then, use the rating scale to grade your work. Circle the score that best applies for each category.

Evaluating Your Research Report	not very very
Focus: How clearly have you presented a thesis on a topic that is appropriate to the length of your paper? How well have you stuck to that thesis throughout your report?	1 2 3 4 5 6
Organization: How well have you chosen a logical method of organization? How clearly have you linked all your ideas to your thesis and to each other?	1 2 3 4 5 6
Support/Elaboration: How well have you supplied ample support for your thesis?	1 2 3 4 5 6
Style: How effectively have you created a formal style and objective tone that are appropriate to your task, your purpose, and your audience? Have you consistently followed one manual of style for all citations?	1 2 3 4 5 6
Conventions: How free is your research report from errors in grammar, spelling, and punctuation?	1 2 3 4 5 6

Writing 9a

> **9a. Draw evidence from literary or informational texts to support analysis, reflection, and research.**
> - **Apply *grades 9–10 Reading standards* to literature (e.g., "Analyze how an author draws on and transforms source material in a specific work [e.g., how Shakespeare treats a theme or topic from Ovid or the Bible or how a later author draws on a play by Shakespeare]").**

Explanation

When you write about a literary text, you need to support your analysis with evidence from the text. The evidence you supply must be accurate and relevant to the point you are supporting. Always provide appropriate citations to the work from which your evidence comes, following a standard style. Textual evidence may take these forms:

- **Quotations** Use quotations, or excerpts taken word-for-word from a source, when analyzing the meaning of a passage, making a point about the author's style, and so on.
- **Paraphrases** For clarity or brevity, you may wish to restate a writer's descriptions or ideas in your own words.
- **Summaries** Summarize, or repeat key ideas in your own words, when you wish to supply your readers with necessary background or context.

In one type of literary analysis, you might be asked to show how an author drew from a source to develop his or her own work. To support your analysis, you would need to give textual evidence both from the writer's work and from his or her source. For example, to analyze how Shakespeare used Arthur Brooke's *The Tragicall Historye of Romeus and Juliet* to write *Romeo and Juliet*, you might take these steps:

1. Read the **primary sources.** Read Shakespeare's play and then Brooke's work. Note characters, plot elements, or language in Brooke's work that is similar to the characters, plot elements, or language in *Romeo and Juliet*.
2. Consult **secondary sources** in which scholars analyze how Shakespeare used Brooke.
3. Present a conclusion about Shakespeare's use of Brooke, supporting your analysis with evidence from your sources. Quote from the plays to illustrate specific points about language and character; summarize to make larger comparisons of the plots.

Academic Vocabulary

primary source a document from a given period, such as an original literary work

secondary source a document that analyzes a historical event, period, or literary work

Apply the Standard

Use the worksheet that follows to help you apply the standard as you write. Several copies have been provided for you to use with different assignments.

- Analyzing Literature

Name _____ Date _____ Assignment _____

Analyzing Literature

Use the organizer below to record supporting evidence for your analysis of a literary text.

My Topic: .... **My Thesis (Main Idea):** ....

Primary Source 1

Bibliographic Information:

Evidence (with page numbers):

Primary Source 2

Bibliographic Information:

Evidence (with page numbers):

Secondary Source 1

Bibliographic Information:

Evidence (with page numbers):

Secondary Source 2

Bibliographic Information:

Evidence (with page numbers):

For use with Writing 9a

Name _____ Date _____ Assignment _____

Analyzing Literature

Use the organizer below to record supporting evidence for your analysis of a literary text.

My Topic: .... **My Thesis (Main Idea):** ....

Primary Source 1
Bibliographic Information:
Evidence (with page numbers):

Primary Source 2
Bibliographic Information:
Evidence (with page numbers):

Secondary Source 1
Bibliographic Information:
Evidence (with page numbers):

Secondary Source 2
Bibliographic Information:
Evidence (with page numbers):

B

For use with Writing 1

Name _____ Date _____ Assignment _____

Analyzing Literature

Use the organizer below to record supporting evidence for your analysis of a literary text.

My Topic: .... **My Thesis (Main Idea):** ....

Primary Source 1

Bibliographic Information:

Evidence (with page numbers):

Primary Source 2

Bibliographic Information:

Evidence (with page numbers):

Secondary Source 1

Bibliographic Information:

Evidence (with page numbers):

Secondary Source 2

Bibliographic Information:

Evidence (with page numbers):

C

For use with Writing 9a

Writing 9b

> **9. Draw evidence from literary or informational texts to support analysis, reflection, and research.**
>
> - Apply *grades 9–10 Reading standards* to literary nonfiction (e.g., "Delineate and evaluate the argument and specific claims in a text, assessing whether the reasoning is valid and the evidence is relevant and sufficient; identify false statements and fallacious reasoning").

Explanation

In an argument, a writer states a position on an issue. This position is called the **claim.** When you write an evaluation of an argument, you examine the evidence the writer uses to support the claim. You evaluate whether the writer's reasoning is valid or not. Based on the evidence in the text, you determine if the writer's argument is sound.

Choose a text that contains an argument to evaluate, such as an editorial or a speech. Then take notes for your essay. Here are some points to keep in mind as you take notes:

- A sound argument usually begins with a clearly stated opinion.

- A valid claim is supported by several reasons and evidence, such as facts, examples, statistics, and expert testimony.

- Reasons are logical and presented in an order that makes sense.

- The writer acknowledges and gives evidence against opposing points of view.

- The writer does not use claims that rely solely on readers' emotions.

In your evaluation, be sure to identify any false statements or **fallacious** reasoning that the writer uses to support his or her argument. These are some common fallacies:

bandwagon—a call to do something because everyone else is doing it

celebrity endorsement—a celebrity thinks this should be done; therefore, do it

overgeneralization—an inference based on too little evidence

either/or argument—a false assumption that only two choices are possible

Academic Vocabulary

claim a brief statement of position on an issue that offers the writer's perspective

fallacious containing or involving a mistaken belief or idea; untrue; faulty

Apply the Standard

Use the worksheet that follows to help you apply the standard as you complete your writing assignments. Several copies of the worksheet have been provided for you.

- Evaluating an Argument

Name _____ Date _____ Selection _____

Evaluating an Argument

Use the organizer to take notes for an essay in which you evaluate a writer's argument. Use specific details from the text to explain your responses.

Title:	Form (e.g., essay, speech):	
Writer's claim:		
What does the writer want readers to believe or do?		
Evaluation Questions	**Response**	**Evidence from Text**
Is an opinion clearly stated?	❏ Yes ❏ No	
Is the claim supported by reasons and evidence?	❏ Yes ❏ No	
Do the reasons make sense? Is the evidence factual?	❏ Yes ❏ No	
Are reasons and evidence presented in an order that makes sense?	❏ Yes ❏ No	
Does the writer acknowledge and give evidence against an opposing point of view?	❏ Yes ❏ No	

Has the writer included any logical fallacies or false statements? Give examples.

❏ **Bandwagon:** _____

❏ **Celebrity endorsement:** _____

❏ **Overgeneralization:** _____

❏ **Either/or argument:** _____

❏ **Other:** _____

Name _____ Date _____ Selection _____

Evaluating an Argument

Use the organizer to take notes for an essay in which you evaluate a writer's argument. Use specific details from the text to explain your responses.

Title:	Form (e.g., essay, speech):	
Writer's claim:		
What does the writer want readers to believe or do?		
Evaluation Questions	**Response**	**Evidence from Text**
Is an opinion clearly stated?	❏ Yes ❏ No	
Is the claim supported by reasons and evidence?	❏ Yes ❏ No	
Do the reasons make sense? Is the evidence factual?	❏ Yes ❏ No	
Are reasons and evidence presented in an order that makes sense?	❏ Yes ❏ No	
Does the writer acknowledge and give evidence against an opposing point of view?	❏ Yes ❏ No	

Has the writer included any logical fallacies or false statements? Give examples.

❏ **Bandwagon:** _____

❏ **Celebrity endorsement:** _____

❏ **Overgeneralization:** _____

❏ **Either/or argument:** _____

❏ **Other:** _____

For use with Writing 9b

Name _____ Date _____ Selection _____

Evaluating an Argument

Use the organizer to take notes for an essay in which you evaluate a writer's argument. Use specific details from the text to explain your responses.

Title:	Form (e.g., essay, speech):	
Writer's claim:		
What does the writer want readers to believe or do?		
Evaluation Questions	**Response**	**Evidence from Text**
Is an opinion clearly stated?	❏ Yes ❏ No	
Is the claim supported by reasons and evidence?	❏ Yes ❏ No	
Do the reasons make sense? Is the evidence factual?	❏ Yes ❏ No	
Are reasons and evidence presented in an order that makes sense?	❏ Yes ❏ No	
Does the writer acknowledge and give evidence against an opposing point of view?	❏ Yes ❏ No	

Has the writer included any logical fallacies or false statements? Give examples.

❏ **Bandwagon:** _____

❏ **Celebrity endorsement:** _____

❏ **Overgeneralization:** _____

❏ **Either/or argument:** _____

❏ **Other:** _____

C

For use with Writing 9b

Writing 10

> 10. Write routinely over extended time frames (time for research, reflection, and revision) and shorter time frames (a single sitting or a day or two) for a range of tasks, purposes, and audiences.

Explanation

Some writing tasks, such as essays or research reports, may need a week or more to complete. Other writing activities can be finished in one class period or over a day or two. A business letter is a type of writing that can be completed in a shorter time frame. You might write a business letter for a variety of purposes. For example, you might request information or ask to schedule an interview. You might lodge a complaint, share praise, or offer a proposal. Effective business letters are clear, direct, courteous, and well formatted. They are also brief and to the point. Follow these steps to plan, write, and revise your letter.

Prewriting:

- Determine your purpose and audience.
- Gather information that helps explain why you are writing or what you want.
- Brainstorm key points that will make your purpose clear to your reader.

Drafting:

- Create your format: two choices are **block format** or **modified block format.**
- Be sure to include the six main parts of a business letter: the heading, inside address, greeting, body, closing, and signature.
- Make your purpose clear right away, starting in the first sentence of the body.
- Include only necessary information—and nothing more.
- Use a courteous tone and formal language.

Revising and Editing:

- Check your format: Have you consistently and correctly formatted your letter?
- Check your tone and word choice: Is it appropriate to your audience?

Academic Vocabulary

block format each part of the letter begins at the left margin, and a double space is used between paragraphs

modified block format some parts of the letter are indented to the center of the page

Apply the Standard

Use the worksheet that follows to help you apply the standard as you complete your writing assignments.

- Writing a Business Letter

Name _____ Date _____ Selection _____

Writing a Business Letter

Use the organizer to plan your business letter and the checklist to check your formatting.

Purpose:	
Audience:	

Important Background Information:	**Key Points:**

Checklist

❏ I have used the block or modified block format.

❏ The inside address tells where the letter will be sent.

❏ The greeting is punctuated with a colon.

❏ The body paragraphs are not indented and I've used a double space between them.

❏ I have included a closing (e.g., *Sincerely, Respectfully yours, Yours truly*), my signature, and my typed name.

Writing 10

10. Write routinely over extended time frames (time for research, reflection, and revision) and shorter time frames (a single sitting or a day or two) for a range of tasks, purposes, and audiences.

Explanation

An editorial is an example of writing that may be completed over an extended time frame. An editorial is a brief persuasive essay that presents and defends an opinion. You might write an editorial to present your position on an issue facing your school or your community. Effective editorials focus on presenting an argument and developing it with strong evidence. They are written in a formal style and maintain an objective tone.

Prewriting:

- Write a thesis statement that clearly states your perspective on an issue.

- Gather evidence from sources to support your argument.

- Consider **counterarguments**, or opposing viewpoints and perspectives your audience might have, and gather evidence that will help you **refute** them.

Drafting:

- Present the major points in support of your thesis in order, from least important to most important. Then acknowledge and respond to at least one counterargument.

- Use evidence such as facts, statistics, expert opinions, personal observations, and testimonials to support each point you make.

- Conclude by restating your thesis. End with a final, memorable thought.

Revising and Editing:

- Replace vague or predictable words with powerful words.

- As needed, add information, explanation, and evidence that show you understand your audience's counterarguments.

Academic Vocabulary

counterargument a response to an argument that opposes the original argument

refute prove to be inaccurate or incorrect

Apply the Standard

Use the worksheet that follows to help you apply the standard as you complete your writing assignments. Several copies of the worksheet have been provided for you.

- Writing an Editorial

Name _____ Date _____ Selection _____

Writing an Editorial

Use the organizer to plan an editorial.

Thesis:

Main Point 1:
 	
  Evidence/Explanation A:
 	
  Evidence/Explanation B:

Main Point 2:
 	
  Evidence/Explanation A:
 	
  Evidence/Explanation B:

Main Point 3:
 	
  Evidence/Explanation A:
 	
  Evidence/Explanation B:

Counterargument:
 	
  Acknowledge and explain counterargument:
 	
  Evidence/Explanation to refute counterargument:

A

For use with Writing 10b

Name _____ Date _____ Selection _____

Writing an Editorial

Use the organizer to plan an editorial.

Thesis:

Main Point 1:
 	
    Evidence/Explanation A:
 	
    Evidence/Explanation B:

Main Point 2:
 	
    Evidence/Explanation A:
 	
    Evidence/Explanation B:

Main Point 3:
 	
    Evidence/Explanation A:
 	
    Evidence/Explanation B:

Counterargument:
 	
    Acknowledge and explain counterargument:
 	
    Evidence/Explanation to refute counterargument:

For use with Writing 10b

Name _____ Date _____ Selection _____

Writing an Editorial

Use the organizer to plan an editorial.

Thesis:

Main Point 1:
 	
    Evidence/Explanation A:
 	
    Evidence/Explanation B:

Main Point 2:
 	
    Evidence/Explanation A:
 	
    Evidence/Explanation B:

Main Point 3:
 	
    Evidence/Explanation A:
 	
    Evidence/Explanation B:

Counterargument:
 	
    Acknowledge and explain counterargument:
 	
    Evidence/Explanation to refute counterargument:

For use with Writing 10b

Writing 10

> 10. Write routinely over extended time frames (time for research, reflection, and revision) and shorter time frames (a single sitting or a day or two) for a range of tasks, purposes, and audiences.

Explanation

A reflective essay is an example of writing that can be completed in one or two class periods or over a day or two. A reflective essay describes a personal experience, memory, object, or idea and explains why it is significant. For example, you might write a reflective essay about your favorite place. Effective reflective essays are written in the first person and use clear, concrete language, vivid imagery, and a personal style.

Prewriting:

- Choose a topic that you can describe vividly. Your idea for writing must have a personal meaning or significance that you can share with an audience.

- Brainstorm a list of sensory images you associate with your topic.

Drafting:

- Use a pattern of organization that makes sense, such as chronological order for narrating a series of events or order of importance for reflecting on an object.

- Use the first person and enliven your writing with **figurative language**.

- End by emphasizing the significance of the event, memory, object, or idea.

Revising and Editing:

- Check for **unity:** Does every word or phrase in the essay contribute to describing the experience, memory, object, or idea?

- Check for word choice: Do the words help to keep your audience's interest?

Academic Vocabulary

figurative language words and phrases that describe a thing in terms of something else

unity a quality that exists when everything in a piece of writing works together to support a single idea or to create one dominant impression

Apply the Standard

Use the worksheet that follows to help you apply the standard as you complete your writing assignments.

- Writing a Reflective Essay

Name _____ Date _____ Selection _____

Writing a Reflective Essay

Use the organizer to plan a reflective essay.

Experience, Memory, Idea, or Object:
Time and Place:
Sensory Details:
Events in Time Order or Ideas in Order of Importance: **1.**   **2.**   **3.**
Significance:

A

Writing 10

10. **Write routinely over extended time frames (time for research, reflection, and revision) and shorter time frames (a single sitting or a day or two) for a range of tasks, purposes, and audiences.**

Explanation

A how-to essay is an example of writing that can be completed in one class period or over a day or two. A how-to essay provides step-by-step instructions for completing a specific task. For example, you might write a how-to essay to give your audience instructions for conducting research, or for cooking your favorite meal. Effective how-to essays are well organized and written in a very clear, direct style.

Prewriting:

- List any materials needed to complete the activity and any other requirements.

- Jot down each step in the process of completing the activity.

- Note important rules for safety, or any other details that may be easy to forget but are important for successfully completing the activity.

Drafting:

- Begin by stating your purpose and listing materials that your audience will need.

- List the activity's steps in **sequential order.** Include examples to demonstrate the steps and solutions to common problems that may occur.

- Consider using bullets or numbering to make the sequence clear, or add drawings or other graphics to illustrate the steps.

Revising and Editing:

- Check for clarity: Can your reader perform each step based on your instructions?

- Check your transitions: Do numbers, bullets, and words and phrases such as *first*, *next*, and *then* help readers follow the sequence?

Academic Vocabulary

sequential order the organization of steps or events in order, from first to last

Apply the Standard

Use the worksheet that follows to help you apply the standard as you complete your writing assignments.

- Writing a How-to Essay

Name _____ Date _____ Selection _____

Writing a How-to Essay

Use the organizer to plan a how-to essay.

Purpose:
Materials:
Safety and Other Requirements:
Steps in Order: 1. 2. 3. 4. 5.

A

For use with Writing 10d

Speaking and Listening Standards

Speaking and Listening 1

> **1. Initiate and participate effectively in a range of collaborative discussions (one-on-one, in groups, and teacher-led) with diverse partners on grades 9–10 topics, texts, and issues, building on others' ideas and expressing their own clearly and persuasively.***

Workshop: Deliver a Technical Presentation

A **technical presentation** is an expository, or explanatory, speech that provides specialized information on a particular subject. There are technical aspects to most activities, including hobbies such as bike riding, cooking, drawing, playing computer games, and skateboarding. When you give a technical presentation, you explain specific and complex information.

Assignment

Deliver a technical presentation to your class on a topic that interests you. In your presentation, include these elements:

- ✓ technical language that is clear and useful for your purpose and occasion
- ✓ effective visual aids, such as diagrams, charts, and sample objects to illustrate technical ideas
- ✓ a main idea that is supported by detailed evidence
- ✓ a coherent, logical organization of your ideas
- ✓ appropriate eye contact, adequate volume, and clear pronunciation
- ✓ language that is formal and precise and that follows the rules of standard English

*Additional Standards

Speaking and Listening

1. Initiate and participate effectively in a range of collaborative discussions with diverse partners on grades 9–10 topics, texts, and issues, building on others' ideas and expressing their own clearly and persuasively.

1.a. Come to discussions prepared, having read and researched material under study; explicitly draw on that preparation by referring to evidence from texts and other research on the topic or issue to stimulate a thoughtful, well-reasoned exchange of ideas.

1.b. Work with peers to set rules for collegial discussions and decision-making, clear goals and deadlines, and individual roles as needed.

1.c. Propel conversations by posing and responding to questions that relate the current discussion to broader themes or larger ideas; actively incorporate others into the discussion; and clarify, verify, or challenge ideas and conclusions.

1.d. Respond thoughtfully to diverse perspectives, summarize points of agreement and disagreement, and, when warranted, qualify or justify their own views and understanding and make new connections in light of the evidence and reasoning presented.

2. Integrate multiple sources of information presented in diverse media or formats evaluating the credibility and accuracy of each source.

4. Present information, findings, and supporting evidence clearly, concisely, and logically such that listeners can follow the line of reasoning and the organization, development, substance, and style are appropriate to purpose, audience, and task.

5. Make strategic use of digital media (e.g., textual, graphical, audio, visual, and interactive elements) in presentations to enhance understanding of findings, reasoning, and evidence and

to add interest.

6. Adapt speech to a variety of contexts and tasks, demonstrating command of formal English when indicated or appropriate.

Language

6. Acquire and use accurately general academic and domain-specific words and phrases, sufficient for reading, writing, speaking, and listening at the college and career readiness level; demonstrate independence in gathering vocabulary knowledge when considering a word or phrase important to comprehension or expression.

COMMON CORE COMPANION • COMMON CORE COMPANION • COMMON CORE COMPANION

Plan and Research Your Presentation

Choose a technical topic of interest to you and determine the main idea on which you will focus. Then, work with a small group to help you refine your main idea. Once you have made your final decision, you will need to gather information and do research.

Identify your main idea. Decide on the main idea you will discuss in your report. For example, you may want to present information about computer functions. Specifically, you may want to talk about how to build an effective Web page. Next, think about how much the audience may already know about the topic. Doing so will help you determine what ideas you will need to explain.

Then, hold a collaborative discussion with a small group of your classmates. Discuss the ideas you are considering and ask students for feedback about your ideas, including whether the topic is too narrow or too broad. Listen for good suggestions about your ideas, and respond to and ask questions of the group to help clarify your main idea.

Research your topic. Formulate a plan to conduct research.

- To learn about a topic, gather a variety of print and media sources.

- First, read through each source and take notes. Gather background information, examples, quotations, facts, and statistics.

- Then, look for similarities and differences among your sources. Conduct further research to settle any discrepancies you find among your sources.

- Be sure to consider the reliability of sources as you plan. Evaluate each one. Ask yourself: Is it useful? Is it free of bias? Is it authoritative?

Use the graphic organizer to help you research and take notes.

Source	Useful Information	Reliability
(Name, type, author, date)		Is this source ❏ useful? ❏ current? ❏ accurate? ❏ free from bias?
(Name, type, author, date)		Is this source ❏ useful? ❏ current? ❏ accurate? ❏ free from bias?
(Name, type, author, date)		Is this source ❏ useful? ❏ current? ❏ accurate? ❏ free from bias?

Choose and Clarify Technical Terms

The words you use in a technical presentation must be carefully chosen, so that listeners can follow along with you and understand any new or unfamiliar concepts. Take time before you begin writing your presentation to think through the language you will use in your talk.

Use technical language effectively. Technical terms are the words and phrases that have special meaning in a particular field—for example, *software, hard drive,* and *USB port* are technical terms used in computer science. Include technical language that will be useful for your purpose and occasion, but avoid language that seems unnecessarily complex. Ask yourself: Which technical words and concepts will my audience know? Which will I need to explain?

Make a list of technical terms and prepare simple definitions your audience can remember. You should use the same terms throughout the presentation, so the audience can follow along. Work with a small group to brainstorm a number of technical terms related to your topic. Decide together which terms most listeners will know and which will need explaining.

Then make note cards to define each technical term. Look up each word in a dictionary. On the card, write the word's common meaning, the profession or field that word comes from, and the technical meaning. Then come up with an analogy that might help a listener better understand the term. For example:

Word: monitor

Common Definition: a person who observes or warns

Technical Definition: a video screen for displaying data, graphic images, and so on

Analogy: A monitor is to a computer as a screen is to a television.

Name _____ Date _____ Assignment _____

Organize Your Technical Presentation

Use the graphic organizer to arrange your presentation so that your main idea and the most important points are easy to follow. Answer the questions and jot notes as you plan what you will say.

Technical Topic: ....

What is the purpose of your presentation?
What is the occasion of your presentation?
Who is your audience? What are the needs of your audience?
Introduction (introduce the main idea):   ....
Point 1:   ....
Support (facts, examples, statistics, reasons, quotations, etc):   ....
Point 2:   ....
Support (facts, examples, statistics, reasons, quotations, etc):   ....
Point 3:   ....
Support (facts, examples, statistics, reasons, quotations, etc):   ....
Conclusion (restate the main idea):   ....

Name _____ Date _____ Assignment _____

Rehearse Your Presentation

The way you deliver your technical presentation is as important as how well you have written it. Practice your presentation in front of a mirror so that you can decide which gestures and facial expressions are most effective. Remember to point to your visual aids.

Use presentation techniques. Use these tips to help you practice your delivery:

- **Eye contact:** Use eye contact to connect with your audience. Speak *to* your listeners rather than *at* them.

- **Speaking rate:** Speak slowly when explaining new concepts. Pause for effect or to emphasize important ideas.

- **Volume:** Project your voice so everyone in your audience can hear you. You can also increase or decrease your volume for dramatic effect, but do not overuse this device.

- **Enunciation:** Pronounce words clearly, especially technical words that are unfamiliar to your audience. If you know you have trouble pronouncing a word, practice saying it beforehand.

- **Gestures:** Use gestures to illustrate ideas and emphasize important points. While you present, be aware of movements that may be distracting.

- **Language conventions:** Use academic and domain-specific words and phrases correctly.

Preview the presentation checklist to anticipate how your audience will evaluate your presentation.

Presentation Technique	Listening Rubric
Eye contact	❑ Did the speaker maintain eye contact? ❑ Did you feel the speaker was speaking directly to you?
Speaking rate	❑ Was the speaker's delivery slow enough to help you understand new concepts? ❑ Did you feel the speaker used pauses effectively?
Volume	❑ Was the speaker loud enough for everyone to hear? ❑ Did the speaker vary his or her tone for dramatic effect?
Enunciation	❑ Was the speaker's delivery easy to understand? ❑ Did the speaker exhibit control over the language in his or her report?
Gestures	❑ Did the speaker use effective gestures to emphasize important points in the presentation?
Language conventions	❑ Did the speaker use standard English? ❑ Was the language clear and precise?

For use with Speaking and Listening 1

Name _____ Date _____ Assignment _____

Visuals and Multimedia

In order to enhance your presentation, make strategic use of visual displays, including charts, diagrams, and multimedia elements.

Use visual displays and multimedia components. Visual displays present complex information quickly and easily. Multimedia elements, such as audio and video clips, can also highlight portions of a presentation. Work with a small group to brainstorm ideas for visuals and multimedia to use in your presentation. Discuss the main idea and important technical language needed for your presentation so the group can generate strong ideas. It is important to select the appropriate medium for each part of your presentation.

Use the chart to plan how you will integrate visuals and multimedia into your presentation. In order to effectively integrate these elements, you must edit and weave them together to create a coherent presentation. Remember to choose a few strong elements that have a clear meaning and a clear relevance to the presentation. Try to use them throughout the presentation, instead of clustering their use at one point.

Visual Element or Multimedia Component	Main Idea or Evidence It Supports	Where to Include It

Name _____ Date _____ Assignment _____

Discuss and Evaluate

After you complete your presentation, take time to participate in a group discussion of the content and delivery of your speech.

Discuss and evaluate the technical presentation. If possible, reach a consensus on the strengths and weaknesses of your presentation. If it is not possible to agree, then summarize the points of agreement and disagreement among group members. Refer to the Guidelines below to ensure that your discussion is productive.

Guidelines for Discussion

In order to prepare for the discussion, review the rubric for evaluating a critique, below.

- Help the group set goals for the discussion and assign roles, such as leader and note-taker, as applicable.

- Ask questions and answer others' questions and clarify, verify, or challenge ideas and conclusions.

- Be open to new ideas suggested by others and change your own thinking to take such ideas into account when appropriate.

- Make sure all group members have a chance to participate and express his or her views.

Guidelines for Group Discussion

Discussion Rubric	Notes
❏ Did each group member participate in the discussion? ❏ Was each group member able to freely express his or her opinion?	
❏ Was a leader guiding the discussion? ❏ Did someone take notes for everyone to share at the end of the discussion?	
❏ Did people in the group ask questions and answer those posed by others? ❏ Did group members' questions and answers stay focused on the topic?	
❏ Did participants accept comments from others? ❏ Were participants open to new ideas or perspectives suggested by others?	

For use with Speaking and Listening 1

Name _____ Date _____ Assignment _____

Self-Assessment

After you've completed your presentation, you should reflect on your speech. Ask yourself how well you thought it went. Was your speech organized and logical? Was your delivery effective? Did you clearly define any unfamiliar terms and phrases for your audience? Did you integrate visual and multimedia elements effectively? Consider how your classmates reacted to your presentation and whether or not the group discussions helped you to realize anything about your speech.

Use a rubric for self-assessment. Combine your self-evaluation with what you learned from your classmates' response to your speech. Then, apply those insights as you fill in the rubric below. Use the rating scale to grade your work, and circle the score that best applies to each category.

Self-Assessment Rubric

Criteria	Rating Scale					
	not very					very
Focus: How effectively did my presentation use technical language that met the needs of my audience, purpose, and occasion?	1	2	3	4	5	6
Organization: How logical and well-organized was my presentation so that listeners could easily follow it?	1	2	3	4	5	6
Support/Elaboration: How well did I support the main idea with examples and detailed evidence, using visual displays and multimedia components where appropriate?	1	2	3	4	5	6
Delivery: How well did I create a relaxed but formal tone, making eye contact with listeners, maintaining an adequate volume, and speaking clearly?	1	2	3	4	5	6
Conventions: How free was my presentation from errors in grammar, spelling, and punctuation?	1	2	3	4	5	6

For use with Speaking and Listening 1

Speaking and Listening 2

> **2. Integrate multiple sources of information presented in diverse media or formats (e.g., visually, quantitatively, orally) evaluating the credibility and accuracy of each source.**

Explanation

When you give a multimedia presentation, you must **integrate**, or bring together, both print media sources (such as printed books, newspapers, journals, and so on) and nonprint media sources (such as television programs, videos, Internet sites, and music CDs). Your presentation may also include visual and quantitative data, such as charts, graphs, maps, and diagrams.

Before you decide to use a source, you must determine if it is **credible** (whether it can be believed and trusted) and if it is **accurate** (whether the information presented is factual, truthful, and error-free). To help determine if a source is credible and accurate, ask yourself if the information is being presented in a fair and evenhanded manner, reflecting both sides of an issue.

Examples

- To learn about a topic, gather information from different media sources. Your first step should be to read, view, or listen to each source and take notes if the information being presented relates to the subject of your report. For example, if you are presenting a report on the benefits of recycling, you should seek out relevant facts and statistics that support your argument, such as experts in the fields of recycling or environmental science.

- Evaluate each source. Ask yourself these questions: Is it useful? Is it free of bias? Is it authoritative? Is it the best source for the topic? Is the source up-to-date?

- Evaluating sources is especially important on the Internet. Many Web pages are written by people who are not experts. They may include information that is unreliable, invalid, or inaccurate. Drawing complex conclusions about the quality of the information you find online is a key part of performing research on the Web.

- Choose photos and video clips carefully. They should provide information not available from your text sources or be used to provoke a specific response from your audience.

Academic Vocabulary

integrate to combine information from a variety of print and nonprint sources

accurate something that is correct; factual

credibility the power to inspire belief; trustworthiness

Apply the Standard

Use the worksheet that follows to help you apply the standard. Several copies of the worksheet have been provided for you to use with different assignments.

- Integrating Multiple Sources of Information

Name _____ Date _____ Selection _____

Integrating Multiple Sources of Information

Use the first column in this chart to evaluate the credibility and accuracy of multiple sources of information on the same topic. Then, complete the chart by deciding how to integrate each source into your presentation.

Source	Where to Include It
Name and Type of Source: .... Information Provided in Source: .... Audience and Purpose of Source: .... Is this source ❏ useful? ❏ accurate? ❏ current? ❏ free from bias?	
Name and Type of Source: .... Information Provided in Source: .... Audience and Purpose of Source: .... Is this source ❏ useful? ❏ accurate? ❏ current? ❏ free from bias?	
Name and Type of Source: .... Information Provided in Source: .... Audience and Purpose of Source: .... Is this source ❏ useful? ❏ accurate? ❏ current? ❏ free from bias?	

A

For use with Speaking and Listening 2

Name _____ Date _____ Selection _____

Integrating Multiple Sources of Information

Use the first column in this chart to evaluate the credibility and accuracy of multiple sources of information on the same topic. Then, complete the chart by deciding how to integrate each source into your presentation.

Source	Where to Include It
Name and Type of Source: .... Information Provided in Source: .... Audience and Purpose of Source: .... Is this source ❏ useful? ❏ accurate? ❏ current? ❏ free from bias?	
Name and Type of Source: .... Information Provided in Source: .... Audience and Purpose of Source: .... Is this source ❏ useful? ❏ accurate? ❏ current? ❏ free from bias?	
Name and Type of Source: .... Information Provided in Source: .... Audience and Purpose of Source: .... Is this source ❏ useful? ❏ accurate? ❏ current? ❏ free from bias?	

Name _____ Date _____ Selection _____

Integrating Multiple Sources of Information

Use the first column in this chart to evaluate the credibility and accuracy of multiple sources of information on the same topic. Then, complete the chart by deciding how to integrate each source into your presentation.

Source	Where to Include It
Name and Type of Source: .... Information Provided in Source: .... Audience and Purpose of Source: .... Is this source ❏ useful? ❏ accurate? ❏ current? ❏ free from bias?	
Name and Type of Source: .... Information Provided in Source: .... Audience and Purpose of Source: .... Is this source ❏ useful? ❏ accurate? ❏ current? ❏ free from bias?	
Name and Type of Source: .... Information Provided in Source: .... Audience and Purpose of Source: .... Is this source ❏ useful? ❏ accurate? ❏ current? ❏ free from bias?	

C

For use with Speaking and Listening 2

Speaking and Listening 3

> **3. Evaluate a speaker's point of view, reasoning, and use of evidence and rhetoric, identifying any fallacious reasoning or exaggerated or distorted evidence.**

Explanation

Evaluating a presentation involves judging how well the speaker communicates his or her point of view. Speakers must use **reasoning** and relevant **evidence** to support and defend their ideas. Relevant evidence includes statistics, expert opinions, and testimonials. Reasoning can include appeals to logic or emotion. Speakers also use **rhetorical devices.** They include:

- parallelism—using similar grammatical structures to express similar ideas
- restatement—stressing key points by expressing the same idea in different words
- analogy—illustrating an unfamiliar idea by comparing it to something familiar

When evaluating a speech, it is also important to identify distorted evidence and fallacious, or flawed, reasoning. Some common logical fallacies are:

- *ad hominem* attack—assaulting a person's character, rather than his or her arguments
- overgeneralization—using scant evidence to reach a broad conclusion

Examples

- Reasoning includes logical and emotional appeals. For example, if your point of view is that the school day is too short, you might appeal to logic by citing the fact that students with longer school days perform better on standardized tests.
- Rhetorical devices add emphasis and help persuade. For example, suppose your coach is trying to inspire your team. She says, "We will keep working. We will keep practicing, and we will keep winning." She is using parallelism (*we will keep*) to emphasize her point.
- Fallacious reasoning is unsupported and weak. For example, in a political debate, one candidate might respond to the other by saying, "You have a history of overreacting." The speaker has attacked the opponent personally, rather than responding to ideas or facts.

Academic Vocabulary

evidence something that provides proof

reasoning using reason to make judgments or form conclusions

rhetorical device a technique used to add emphasis and persuade

Apply the Standard

Use the worksheet that follows to help you apply the standard. Several copies of each worksheet have been provided for you to use with different assignments.

- Evaluating Point of View and Reasoning
- Evaluating Evidence

Name _____ Date _____ Assignment _____

Evaluating Point of View and Reasoning

Use this chart to evaluate a speaker's point of view and reasoning. Then identify any rhetorical devices and their effects.

Topic:
What is the speaker's point of view? How clearly is it stated? How convincing is it?
What type of reasoning does the speaker use? How sound is the speaker's reasoning?
What rhetorical devices does the speaker use? ❏ Parallelism Example: .... Effect: .... ❏ Restatement Example: .... Effect: .... ❏ Analogy Example: .... Effect: ....

For use with Speaking and Listening 3

Name _____ Date _____ Assignment _____

Evaluating Point of View and Reasoning

Use this chart to evaluate a speaker's point of view and reasoning. Then identify any rhetorical devices and their effects.

Topic:
What is the speaker's point of view? How clearly is it stated? How convincing is it?
What type of reasoning does the speaker use? How sound is the speaker's reasoning?

What rhetorical devices does the speaker use?

❏ Parallelism

Example: ....

Effect: ....

❏ Restatement

Example: ....

Effect: ....

❏ Analogy

Example: ....

Effect: ....

Name _____ Date _____ Assignment _____

Evaluating Point of View and Reasoning

Use this chart to evaluate a speaker's point of view and reasoning. Then identify any rhetorical devices and their effects.

Topic:
What is the speaker's point of view? How clearly is it stated? How convincing is it?
What type of reasoning does the speaker use? How sound is the speaker's reasoning?
What rhetorical devices does the speaker use? ❏ Parallelism Example: .... Effect: .... ❏ Restatement Example: .... Effect: .... ❏ Analogy Example: .... Effect: ....

C

For use with Speaking and Listening 3

Name _____ Date _____ Assignment _____

Evaluating Evidence

Use this chart to analyze the relevance, quality, and credibility of a speaker's evidence.

Topic: ....
Speaker's Point of View: ....
What evidence supports the speaker's point of view?
Is the evidence   ❏ relevant, or connected to the topic?   ❏ of good quality, or based on facts and research?   ❏ credible, or reliable and believable?   ❏ exaggerated or distorted?
How well does the evidence support the speaker's point of view?

Name _____ Date _____ Assignment _____

Evaluating Evidence

Use this chart to analyze the relevance, quality, and credibility of a speaker's evidence.

Topic: .... **Speaker's Point of View:** ....
What evidence supports the speaker's point of view?
Is the evidence ❏ relevant, or connected to the topic? ❏ of good quality, or based on facts and research? ❏ credible, or reliable and believable? ❏ exaggerated or distorted?
How well does the evidence support the speaker's point of view?

For use with Speaking and Listening 3

Name _____ Date _____ Assignment _____

Evaluating Evidence

Use this chart to analyze the relevance, quality, and credibility of a speaker's evidence.

Topic: ....
Speaker's Point of View: ....
What evidence supports the speaker's point of view?
Is the evidence   ❑ relevant, or connected to the topic?   ❑ of good quality, or based on facts and research?   ❑ credible, or reliable and believable?   ❑ exaggerated or distorted?
How well does the evidence support the speaker's point of view?

Speaking and Listening 4

> **4. Present information, findings, and supporting evidence clearly, concisely, and logically such that listeners can follow the line of reasoning, and the organization, development, substance, and style are appropriate to purpose, audience, and task.**

Explanation

To present a speech effectively, keep your audience, purpose, and occasion in mind as you prepare. Determine what your audience already knows about the subject. Then gather **evidence,** or factual information, that supports the main points of your presentation. Organize the speech **logically**—in a way that is clear and easy for the audience to follow and understand. The organizational structure you choose depends on the information you are presenting. Below are a few possible approaches:

- *Order of importance:* Present the most important facts first and the least important facts last.

- *Problem/Solution:* First, describe a problem. Then, explain how it can be solved.

- *Chronological order:* Offer information in the sequence in which it happened.

Examples

- Suppose you wanted to motivate people to clean up a park in your community. You could do so with a problem/solution organizational structure. The main cause of the problem is a lack of funds for improving or replacing equipment in the park. Possible solutions to the problem might include hosting a community fund-raiser or lobbying local businesses for sponsorships.

- If you want to give a presentation about the events that helped women achieve the right to vote, the main point will be to show how the movement began and then grew. Thus, it makes sense to provide a sequence of events, or to use chronological organization.

- Suppose your point of view could be summed up as the following: "To stop global warming, we need to address each of its numerous causes." Chronological order does not work because many causes of global warming occur simultaneously. Instead, you might address each cause separately, in the order of their importance.

Academic Vocabulary

evidence factual proof

logically based on logic or evidence

Apply the Standard

Use the worksheets that follow to help you apply the standard. Several copies of each worksheet have been provided for you to use with different assignments.

- Presenting a Speech Effectively

- Organizing Information

Name _____ Date _____ Assignment _____

Presenting a Speech Effectively

After choosing a topic and position for your speech, fill out the chart below. Use your notes to help you effectively deliver your presentation.

Topic of presentation: _____

Who is your audience?	
What is your purpose?	
What is the occasion or task?	

How will you focus your point of view?	What evidence or reasoning can you provide to support your point of view?

Name _____ Date _____ Assignment _____

Presenting a Speech Effectively

After choosing a topic and position for your speech, fill out the chart below. Use your notes to help you effectively deliver your presentation.

Topic of presentation: _____

Who is your audience?

What is your purpose?

What is the occasion or task?

How will you focus your point of view?	What evidence or reasoning can you provide to support your point of view?

B

Name _____ Date _____ Assignment _____

Presenting a Speech Effectively

After choosing a topic and position for your speech, fill out the chart below. Use your notes to help you effectively deliver your presentation.

Topic of presentation: _____

Who is your audience?	
What is your purpose?	
What is the occasion or task?	
How will you focus your point of view?	What evidence or reasoning can you provide to support your point of view?

Name _____ Date _____ Assignment _____

Organizing Information

Use the graphic organizer below to help you decide which pattern of organization works best for your speech. Try filling out each section. Then explain which structure works best for your topic.

Chronological Order

First ....

Second ....

Third ....

Problem/Solution

Thesis/Problem: ....

Who is affected? ....

What causes the problem?

1) ....

2) ....

3) ....

What are the possible solutions?

1) ....

2) ....

3) ....

Order of Importance
Most to Least or Least to Most

1) ....

2) ....

3) ....

Which organizational structure works best and why?

Name _____ Date _____ Assignment _____

Organizing Information

Use the graphic organizer below to help you decide which pattern of organization works best for your speech. Try filling out each section. Then explain which structure works best for your topic.

Chronological Order
First ....
Second ....
Third ....
Problem/Solution
Thesis/Problem: ....
Who is affected? ....
What causes the problem?
1) ....
2) ....
3) ....
What are the possible solutions?
1) ....
2) ....
3) ....
Order of Importance   Most to Least or Least to Most
1) ....
2) ....
3) ....
Which organizational structure works best and why?

B

Name _____ Date _____ Assignment _____

Organizing Information

Use the graphic organizer below to help you decide which pattern of organization works best for your speech. Try filling out each section. Then explain which structure works best for your topic.

Chronological Order
First ....
Second ....
Third ....

Problem/Solution
Thesis/Problem: ....
Who is affected? ....
What causes the problem?
1) ....
2) ....
3) ....
What are the possible solutions?
1) ....
2) ....
3) ....

Order of Importance
Most to Least or Least to Most
1) ....
2) ....
3) ....

Which organizational structure works best and why?

C

For use with Speaking and Listening 4

Speaking and Listening 5

> **5. Make strategic use of digital media (e.g., textual, graphical, audio, visual, and interactive elements) in presentations to enhance understanding of findings, reasoning, and evidence and to add interest.**

Explanation

A good multimedia presentation makes **strategic,** or well-planned, use of digital media. Digital media include a variety of formats:

- **textual elements,** such as titles and captions

- **graphical elements,** such as charts, maps, and diagrams

- **audio elements,** such as music and sound effects

- **visual elements,** such as still pictures and video

- **interactive elements,** such as a message board or game

Use media to emphasize key points in your presentation, and try to use it throughout, instead of clustering these elements at the beginning or end. Visuals should be large enough to be seen at a distance. Also, try not to let the audio drown out your voice in the presentation. Strategic use of multimedia means you have considered the effect of each element on your audience, as well as how the elements work together to convey your message.

Examples

- Choose a few strong visual elements that have clear meaning and relevance. For example, a few dramatic pictures of a single damaging hurricane may be more effective than many slides showing hurricanes in several places.

- Visual and textual elements communicate information differently. For example, a photograph of trees bending in a hurricane prompts an emotional response. A caption about the force of hurricane winds can expand on the effect of the photograph.

- Audio elements can be used to appeal to or change an audience's emotional response. For example, audio of a hurricane's roar might emphasize the power of the storm by recreating the feeling of it with your audience.

Academic Vocabulary

strategic done as part of a carefully made plan

Apply the Standard

Use the worksheet that follows to help you apply the standard.

- Using Digital Media

Name _____ Date _____ Assignment _____

Using Digital Media

Use this chart to help you plan where to use digital media elements in your presentation.

Topic: ....

Digital Media Element	How does this element enhance understanding?	Where should I include this element?
❑ textual ❑ graphical ❑ audio ❑ visual ❑ interactive Describe:		
❑ textual ❑ graphical ❑ audio ❑ visual ❑ interactive Describe:		
❑ textual ❑ graphical ❑ audio ❑ visual ❑ interactive Describe:		

A

Speaking and Listening 6

> **6. Adapt speech to a variety of contexts and tasks, demonstrating command of formal English when indicated or appropriate.**

Explanation

To present a speech effectively, first identify the **context,** or situation, and the audience. For example, is it a formal presentation or an impromptu speech? Then identify the task, or purpose. Is your purpose to persuade, to explain, to describe, or to entertain?

Keep your audience and purpose in mind as you **adapt,** or adjust, the delivery of your presentation. Remember to use eye contact, gesture purposefully, enunciate words, and speak using an appropriate volume and rate.

The language you use must be easily understood. Communicate your ideas by using correct grammar and word usage, so your audience will understand what you mean. Use standard American English, the version of English taught in school, and avoid use of informal language unless the situation calls for it.

Examples

- Identify ways to adapt your speech to the given context and task. For example, use formal language for a classroom presentation, informal language for a group discussion, and casual but polite language when working with a partner. Speak expressively and use pauses, gestures, and facial expressions when seeking to entertain. Vary volume for emphasis when attempting to persuade. Speak with authority and conviction when your purpose is to inform.

- Monitor your command of formal English in presentations that require you to use it. Pay attention to common usage problems, including incorrect pronouns and verb tenses. For example, "Him and John were on the debate team" is incorrect. It should be "He and John were on the debate team."

- Look out for the use of slang, including frequent use of temporizing words and phrases. These include *like, you know,* and *I mean.*

Academic Vocabulary

adapt to change for a specific situation

context a situation or environment

Apply the Standard

Use the worksheets that follow to help you apply the standard. Several copies of each worksheet have been provided for you.

- Adapting a Speech

- Using Appropriate Language

Name _____ Date _____ Selection _____

Adapting a Speech

Use this chart to help you adapt a speech to the appropriate context, audience, and task.

Topic: ....

What is the context, or situation?

Who is your audience?

What is your task, or purpose?

Adaptations I Will Make	Reason for Change
1.	
2.	
3.	

Name _____ Date _____ Selection _____

Adapting a Speech

Use this chart to help you adapt a speech to the appropriate context, audience, and task.

Topic: ....

What is the context, or situation?

Who is your audience?

What is your task, or purpose?

Adaptations I Will Make	**Reason for Change**
1.	
2.	
3.	

For use with Speaking and Listening 6

Name _____ Date _____ Selection _____

Adapting a Speech

Use this chart to help you adapt a speech to the appropriate context, audience, and task.

Topic: ....

What is the context, or situation?

Who is your audience?

What is your task, or purpose?

Adaptations I Will Make	**Reason for Change**
1.	
2.	
3.	

C

For use with Speaking and Listening 6

Name _____ Date _____ Selection _____

Using Appropriate Language

Before you give a speech, use the checklist to evaluate your use of language.

Audience: ....

Context: ....

Speaking Task: ....

	Speech Checklist
Language	❑ Is my language appropriate for the context and speaking task? ❑ Have I avoided slang and filler words? ❑ Is my language and word choice precise and engaging enough to keep the listeners interested?
Sentences	❑ Are my sentences varied enough? ❑ Can I change sentence length to vary my pace and tempo? ❑ Do I use short sentences for dramatic effect or to emphasize important points?
Pronouns	❑ Are there too many pronouns in my speech? ❑ Can I substitute proper names and specific nouns to avoid confusion? ❑ Is who or what my pronouns refer to absolutely clear?

Name _____ Date _____ Selection _____

Using Appropriate Language

Before you give a speech, use the checklist to evaluate your use of language.

Audience: ....

Context: ....

Speaking Task: ....

	Speech Checklist
Language	❑ Is my language appropriate for the context and speaking task? ❑ Have I avoided slang and filler words? ❑ Is my language and word choice precise and engaging enough to keep the listeners interested?
Sentences	❑ Are my sentences varied enough? ❑ Can I change sentences lengths to vary my pace and tempo? ❑ Do I use short sentences for dramatic effect or to emphasize important points?
Pronouns	❑ Are there too many pronouns in my speech? ❑ Can I substitute proper names and specific nouns to avoid confusion? ❑ Is who or what my pronouns refer to absolutely clear?

Name _____ Date _____ Selection _____

Using Appropriate Language

Before you give a speech, use the checklist to evaluate your use of language.

Audience: ....

Context: ....

Speaking Task: ....

	Speech Checklist
Language	❏ Is my language appropriate for the context and speaking task? ❏ Have I avoided slang and filler words? ❏ Is my language and word choice precise and engaging enough to keep the listeners interested?
Sentences	❏ Are my sentences varied enough? ❏ Can I change sentences lengths to vary my pace and tempo? ❏ Do I use short sentences for dramatic effect or to emphasize important points?
Pronouns	❏ Are there too many pronouns in my speech? ❏ Can I substitute proper names and specific nouns to avoid confusion? ❏ Is who or what my pronouns refer to absolutely clear?

Language Standards

Language 1a

1a. Demonstrate command of the conventions of standard English grammar and usage when writing or speaking.

- **Use parallel structure.**

Explanation

Parallelism means the use of similar grammatical forms or patterns to express similar ideas. Use of parallelism adds rhythm and balance to writing and strengthens the connections among ideas.

Examples

Sentences with parallel structure contain **repeated grammatical patterns** or **repeated types of phrases or clauses.**

- **Repeated grammatical patterns**
  - **Nonparallel:** *Last summer, we **swam, played** baseball, and **trips** to the beach.*
    (The two verbs *swam* and *played* are followed by the noun *trips*.)
  - **Parallel:** *Last summer, we **swam, played** baseball, and **went** to the beach.*
    (Here the three verbs *swam*, *played*, and *went* create a parallel structure.)

- **Repeated types of phrases**
  - **Nonparallel:** *Marcus enjoys hiking **in the mountains** and **to hike around the lake.***
    (A prepositional phrase is followed by an infinitive phrase.)
  - **Parallel:** *Marcus enjoys hiking **in the mountains** and **around the lake.***
    (The two prepositional phrases create a parallel structure.)
  - **Nonparallel:** *Julia works **after school** and **Saturdays.***
    (A prepositional phrase is followed by a noun.)
  - **Parallel:** *Julia works **after school** and **on Saturdays.***
    (The two prepositional phrases create a parallel structure.)

- **Repeated types of clauses**
  - **Nonparallel:** *My favorite stories are those **that are exciting** or **lots of action.***
    (A noun clause is followed by a noun and a prepositional phrase.)
  - **Parallel:** *My favorite stories are those **that are exciting** or **that have lots of action.***
    (The two noun clauses create a parallel structure.)
  - **Nonparallel:** *I feel really happy **when I am exercising** and **during a run.***
    (An adverbial clause is followed by a prepositional phrase.)
  - **Parallel:** *I feel really happy **when I am exercising** and **when I am running.***
    (The two adverbial clauses create a parallel structure.)

Name _____ Date _____ Assignment _____

Apply the Standard

Rewrite each sentence so that it contains parallel structures.

1. Ana likes playing the guitar and to sing folk songs.

....

2. Last Saturday, she sang and was playing the guitar in the talent show.

....

3. She is both a musician and someone who entertains.

....

4. Ana's grandfather gave her singing lessons and how to play the guitar.

....

5. As a young man, he was a famous singer, and he was famous as a guitar player.

....

6. Many times he appeared on television and playing in concerts.

....

7. Ana loves to watch DVDs and listening to recordings of his performances.

....

8. Her grandfather is very proud, very talented, and he is a very smart man.

....

9. He taught Ana to listen, to practice, and playing music.

....

10. Ana has a younger brother who is ten and a six-year-old sister.

....

11. She will teach them to play music and sing when they are older.

....

12. Then she will play and sing with her grandfather, her brother, and sister.

....

For use with Language 1a

Language 1b

1b. **Demonstrate command of the conventions of standard English grammar and usage when writing or speaking.**

• **Use various types of phrases (noun, verb, adjectival, adverbial, participial, prepositional, absolute) and clauses (independent, dependent, noun, relative, adverbial) to convey specific meanings and add variety and interest to writing or presentations.**

Explanation

A **phrase** is a group of words that does not contain a subject and a verb. Types of phrases include prepositional phrases, appositive phrases, infinitive phrases, participial phrases, and gerund phrases. A **clause** is a group of words that *does* contain a subject and a verb. There are two types of clauses: main clauses and subordinate clauses.

Examples

A **prepositional phrase** includes a preposition (*at, in, for*) and a noun or pronoun that is the object of the preposition. Types of prepositional phrases include an adjective phrase and an adverb phrase.

> **An adjective phrase modifies a noun or pronoun.**
>
> *The girl **in the blue coat** is my sister.* (Answers the question, Which girl?)

> **An adverb phrase modifies a verb, an adjective, or an adverb.**
>
> *We'll practice **in the morning.*** (Answers the question, When?)

An **appositive phrase** is a noun or pronoun with modifiers, placed next to a noun or pronoun to add information and details. Appositive phrases are usually set off by commas.

> *My uncle, **a published author,** will speak to our science class today.*

An **infinitive phrase** contains an infinitive (*to walk, to do*) and its modifiers or complements. In a sentence, an infinitive phrase might act as a noun, an adjective, or an adverb.

> *Someday, I hope **to be an astronaut.***

A **participial phrase** contains a present or past participle (*walking, walked*) and its modifiers or complements. In a sentence, a participial phrase acts as an adjective.

> ***Grabbing his coat,** Jack ran to catch the bus.*

A **gerund phrase** contains a gerund (*acting, smiling*) and its modifiers or complements. In a sentence, a gerund phrase acts as a noun.

> ***Writing a thank-you note** is always a good idea.*

A **main clause** expresses a complete thought. Therefore, it can stand alone as a complete sentence. A **subordinate clause** does *not* express a complete thought. Therefore, it cannot stand alone as a complete sentence. A subordinate **adjective clause** modifies a noun, and a subordinate **adverb clause** modifies a verb. You can use adjectival or adverbial clauses to combine simple sentences.

Name _____ Date _____ Assignment _____

Apply the Standard

A. Underline the answer that correctly identifies each phrase or clause. Then use each phrase or clause in a sentence.

1. on Tuesday (prepositional phrase, infinitive phrase)

....

2. to win a race (participial phrase, infinitive phrase)

....

3. playing basketball (infinitive phrase, gerund phrase)

....

4. she is the captain (main clause, adjective clause)

....

5. because we won (adverb clause, adjective clause)

....

B. Combine each pair of simple sentences to form a new sentence. Follow the directions.

Example: Nancy lives in Cleveland. She is my cousin. (Use an adjective clause to modify *Nancy.*)

 Nancy, who lives in Cleveland, is my cousin.

1. Nancy's brother is a fine student. He goes to college. (Use an appositive phrase to modify *brother.*)

....

2. He goes to Bett College. It has a great art program. (Use an adverb clause to modify *Bett College.*)

....

3. He has a goal. He will be a famous artist. (Use an infinitive phrase to modify *goal.*)

....

4. He works in an art gallery. He works there while on school vacations. (Use an adverb clause to tell *when* he works there.)

....

Language 2a

2a. **Demonstrate command of the conventions of standard English capitalization, punctuation, and spelling when writing.**

- **Use a semicolon (and perhaps a conjunctive adverb) to link two or more closely related independent clauses.**

Explanation

Use a comma and a conjunction (*and, but, or*) to join two or more independent clauses in order to form a compound sentence. Use a **semicolon** to join independent clauses that are *not* joined by a conjunction. You can also use a semicolon and a **conjunctive adverb** (*however, for example, nevertheless*) to join two independent clauses.

Examples

1. Use a comma and a conjunction

My family came from Puerto Rico, **and** *Mary's family came from Canada.*

My report is due tomorrow, **but** *I have not finished writing it.*

2. Use a semicolon when the clauses are *not* joined by a conjunction

Our team is ready; **let** *the games begin.*

Please clean your room; **guests** *are coming.*

3. Use a semicolon and a conjunctive adverb, followed by a comma

We were late; **therefore,** *we missed the bus.*

I usually enjoy rice; **however,** *this rice is too salty.*

I'll wash the dishes; **meanwhile,** *please put away the leftover food.*

As a babysitter, Jan is very patient; **furthermore,** *she loves to read to children.*

My sister collects many things; **for example,** *she collects stamps and coins.*

Note that a comma should appear after the conjunctive adverb.

Here is a list of **commonly used conjunctive adverbs.** Note their different meanings and uses.

consequently, therefore	something happens as a result of something else
however, nevertheless	something happens despite something else
meanwhile, in the mean time	something happens at the same time as something else
furthermore, moreover	something happens in addition to something else
for example, for instance	something is an example of something else

Name _____ Date _____ Assignment _____

Apply the Standard

A. Each sentence is missing a semicolon. Add the semicolon in its proper place.

Example: The floor is dirty get the mop.

The floor is dirty; get the mop.

1. My little brother wanted a dog therefore, we went to a shelter to find one.

2. We walked in the door all the dogs began to bark.

3. My brother thought he wanted a shaggy, brown dog however, he changed his mind.

4. A little white dog jumped up and licked my brother's hand our search was over.

5. That little dog won my brother's heart consequently, she's our new companion animal!

B. Rewrite each pair of simple sentences as a single sentence. Follow the directions. Remember to place a comma after a conjunctive adverb.

1. My mother goes to a cooking school. She brings home samples. (Use a semicolon and *consequently.*)

....

2. One day she brought home some muffins. We were eager to try them. (Use a semicolon.)

....

3. They were moist. They were *very* sweet. (Use a semicolon and *moreover.*)

....

4. I didn't care for them. Jenny loved them. (Use a semicolon and *however.*)

....

5. Jenny finished the muffins. I served myself a slice of apple pie. (Use a semicolon and *meanwhile.*)

....

C. Write an original sentence using the elements that are shown. Remember to place a comma after the conjunctive adverb.

1. semicolon ....

2. semicolon and *however* ....

3. semicolon and *for example* ....

4. semicolon and *therefore* ....

For use with Language 2a

Language 2b

> **2b. Demonstrate command of the conventions of standard English capitalization, punctuation, and spelling when writing.**
> • **Use a colon to introduce a list or quotation.**

Explanation

The **colon** is a punctuation mark that has three main functions.

- **To introduce a list**

  Use a colon to introduce a list of items that follows an independent clause.

- **To introduce a direct quotation**

  When you include a direct quotation from another text in your writing, you may choose to introduce it with an independent clause followed by a colon.

- **To end the salutation of a business letter**

  When you write an informal personal letter, you end the salutation with a comma. However, when you write a formal business letter, you end the salutation with a colon.

Examples

- **To introduce a list that follows an independent clause**

  At the costume store, she was able to buy everything: the powdered wig, the spectacles, and a large hat.

  Do *not* use a colon if the list is the direct object of the verb.

  At the costume store, she was able to buy the powdered wig, the spectacles, and a large hat.

- **To introduce a direct quotation from another work of literature**

  Abraham Lincoln's Gettysburg Address has a strong beginning: "Four score and seven years ago, our fathers brought forth on this continent a new nation, conceived in liberty, and dedicated to the proposition that all men are created equal."

- **To end the salutation of a business letter**

  Dear Dr. Rodriguez:

  Dear Ms. Wallace:

Name _____ Date _____ Assignment _____

Apply the Standard

A. Add colons where they are needed. If a sentence or phrase is correctly punctuated and does not require the addition of a colon, write *No colon* on the line.

    Example: Martin Luther King, Jr.'s faith and optimism are clear: "I have a dream."

1. Some of my favorite writers include Ernest Hemingway, Mark Twain, and Judith Ortiz.

    ....

2. Can you answer these questions Which one of you took my pencil?, What were you thinking?, How

    many people were involved? ....

3. John Donne spoke of our connection to one another "No man is an island."

    ....

4. A story that is filled with suspense is Edgar Allan Poe's "The Tell-Tale Heart." ....

5. The club now has four new members John, Ramon, Shelly, and Mason. ....

6. Dear Senator Byron ....

7. The Beatles had four members John, Paul, George, and Ringo. ....

8. Dear Grandma, ...

9. Indiana Jones delivered this line in a funny way "Snakes! Why did they have to be snakes?"

    ....

10. The camping gear that I need to borrow includes a flashlight, a compass, and a sleeping bag.

    ....

B. Follow each direction.

1. Write an original sentence in which a colon introduces a list.

    ....

2. Write a correctly punctuated salutation for a business letter.

    ....

3. Write a correctly punctuated salutation for an informal personal letter.

    ....

Language 2c

2c. Demonstrate command of the conventions of standard English capitalization, punctuation, and spelling when writing.

• **Spell correctly.**

Explanation

An essay in which you present a carefully crafted and convincing argument could become weak and confusing to a reader if it contains spelling errors. These guidelines will help you to prevent —or correct—spelling errors.

Examples

Words with suffixes can present spelling problems. Follow these guidelines.

- Keep the silent *e* when adding a suffix that begins with a consonant *(move + ment = movement)*.

- Drop the silent *e* when adding a suffix that begins with a vowel *(move + ing = moving)*.

- If a word ends in a consonant and *y*, change the *y* to *i* before adding a suffix *(hurry + ed = hurried)*.

- If the last syllable of a multisyllabic word is accented and ends in a consonant, double the final consonant before adding a suffix that starts with a vowel *(occur + ing = occurring)*.

- Remember that some base words change their form when suffixes are added *(suspend, suspension; maintain, maintenance)*. Keep a file on these words to remind you of the changes.

Tricky letter combinations and silent letters can also cause spelling problems. Keep a file on these words, too. The following are examples.

<u>g</u>nat   <u>kn</u>owledge   sil<u>h</u>ouette   r<u>h</u>ythm   ex<u>h</u>ibit   w<u>h</u>ile   av<u>e</u>rage   rest<u>au</u>rant

Some words are easily confused. A spell checker will not help you catch such errors because you have not really spelled the word incorrectly. Instead you have used the wrong word. This chart lists some examples. Learn their differences and use them correctly.

capital—"a city that is the seat of government" *Augusta is the capital of Maine.*	**capitol**—"a building in the capital city" *The flag is raised on the roof of the capitol.*
loose—"free, not close or tight" *Wear loose clothing while exercising.*	**lose**—"to suffer loss" *I hope we don't lose the game.*
already—"previously" *I have already heard that story.*	**all ready**—"prepared" *The players are all ready for the game to begin.*
affect—(verb) "to influence or change" *Will the rain affect our plans?*	**effect**—(noun) "result or consequence" *The music had a soothing effect on the children.*

Name _____ Date _____ Assignment _____

Apply the Standard

A. Correct all the misspelled or misused words in the following sentences. Circle each error. Then, write the correct spelling on the line provided. If the sentence is correct, write *Correct* on the line.

1. I had packed up my clothes and was already for moveing day.

....

2. We were worryed that the movers might be late because traffic was heavy around the capital building.

....

3. It was therefore surpriseing when the movers nocked on our door two hours earlyer than we had expected.

....

4. My mother said, "Let's get out of their way wile they are working. We'll sit altogether out on the patio."

....

5. The movers worked for sevral hours before they took a break.

....

6. The affect of all of that heavy work was that one man seemed altogether exausted.

....

7. "You've been hurring too much," Mom said, "and it is effecting your health. Come sit with us for a while."

....

8. He prefered to keep carrying our furniture because he was an exellent worker.

....

B. Use each pair of words in a sentence.

1. *loose, lose* ....

2. *affect, effect* ....

3. *capital, capitol* ....

Language 3a

> **3a. Apply knowledge of language to understand how language functions in different contexts, to make effective choices for meaning or style, and to comprehend more fully when reading or listening.**
>
> • Write and edit work so that it conforms to the guidelines in a style manual (e.g., *MLA Handbook,* Turabian's *Manual for Writers*) appropriate for the discipline and writing type.

Explanation

The **Modern Language Association (MLA)** has created a style guide that instructs writers on the correct rules to follow regarding grammar, punctuation, and capitalization, as well as the appropriate formats to use when citing reference sources in the bibliography (or Works Cited page) at the end of a report or essay. Following the guidelines of an established style manual will help you to revise and present your written work effectively.

Examples

• **Underlines or Italics in Titles:** Underline or italicize the titles of books, encyclopedias, periodicals, plays, movies, CDs, and DVDs. Underline or italicize *the* only if it is part of the title. **Do not underline or italicize** *the* before the name of a magazine or newspaper.

> *The Way We Were*, a movie
>
> the *New York Times*, a newspaper

• **Quotation Marks in Titles:** Use quotation marks to punctuate the titles of stories, articles, poems, Internet Web pages, radio or television transcripts, and editorials.

> "The Tell-Tale Heart," a story by Edgar Allan Poe
>
> "No Second Troy," a poem by William Butler Yeats

• **Capitalization in Titles:** Capitalize **the first word and all important words** in the titles of books, periodicals, plays, poems, stories, and articles. However, **do not capitalize articles** (*a, an, the*) unless they are the first word. **Do not capitalize coordinating conjunctions** (*and, or, but*) or **prepositions of fewer than five letters** (*with, in, on* but *Under, Within*).

> *A Farewell to Arms*, a novel by Ernest Hemingway
>
> *Desire Under the Elms*, a play by Eugene O'Neil
>
> "Stopping by Woods on a Snowy Evening," a poem by Robert Frost

• **Formats for Bibliographies or Works Cited Lists:** Follow this order for each entry. List the entries in alphabetical order (by author's last name).

1. Name of author, editor, translator, or group responsible (last name first)
2. Title of the work (article first, then volume)
3. Place of publication, publisher, and date of publication

> Fischer, William T. "Minor League Baseball." *Century of Sports.* New York: Dial, 2010.
>
> Scott, Henry P. *Baseball Greats.* New York: Prentice Hall, 2009.

Name _____ Date _____ Assignment _____

Apply the Standard

A. Each of these titles needs punctuation and capitalization. On the line, rewrite each one correctly.

1. a novel: somewhere over the rainbow ....

2. a poem: my heart belongs to nature ....

3. a newspaper: the houston chronicle ....

4. an article: the amphibians of australia ....

5. a nonfiction book: the adventures of marco polo ....

B. On the lines provided, write an entry for a Works Cited page for each of these items. Be sure to use underlining, quotation marks, capitalization, and the appropriate format for each one.

1. a novel: when we were a colony, published by Penguin in 2008 in London, and authored by Bev Bright

....

2. an article: heroes of ancient Greece, authored by Cyrus Reese. It appears in a book titled myths and legends, which was published in 1999 in New York by Crawford.

....

....

3. a poem: a glimpse beneath the bed, which appears in a book titled the best poems of 1995. The poem is by Katherine Salle, and the book was published by Horn in 1996 in Chicago.

....

....

4. a play: a curious adventure within his past, by Walter A. Gibbons. It was published by Crocker in Boston in 2007.

....

....

Language 4a

> **4a.** Determine or clarify the meaning of unknown and multiple-meaning words and phrases based on *grades 9–10 reading and content,* choosing flexibly from a range of strategies.
>
> - Use context (e.g., the overall meaning of a sentence, paragraph, or text; a word's position or function in a sentence) as a clue to the meaning of a word or phrase.

Explanation

When you come to an unfamiliar word in your reading, the **words and phrases surrounding that word** may provide **context clues** regarding the word's meaning. Additionally, you might find **context clues** in the **unknown word's position or function in the sentence.** Finally, the overall meaning of the sentence or even the main idea of the paragraph might also provide clues.

Examples

Clues in Nearby Words and Phrases Examples of this type of context clue include:

- **Restatement or definition:** The meaning of the word may be restated in other ways.
  *They performed a **farandole,** a lively and traditional dance from southern France.*
  (The clue suggests that *farandole* is a type of dance.)

- **Opposite or contrast:** An antonym or a contrasting phrase may provide clues.
  *We worried that the loud party would disturb him, but he remained **insouciant.***
  (The clues suggest that *insouciant* means "calm and untroubled.")

- **Illustration:** The context may provide an illustration or example that contains clues.
  *The old, shabby neighborhood had been completely **gentrified.** The old buildings had new paint, the windows had been replaced, and trees had been planted along the sidewalk.*
  (The clues suggest that *gentrified* means "renewed" or "renovated.")

Clues in the Word's Function in the Sentence Study the unfamiliar word's position and function in the sentence. If, for example, it comes before a noun, it is an adjective. If it follows an article or an adjective, it is a noun. If it expresses action, it is a verb. If it modifies a verb, it is an adverb. Use that information to determine the unfamiliar word's meaning.

> *In the fifteenth century, Spanish traders sailed to faraway ports in three-masted **galleons.***

(*Galleons* follows an adjective. Therefore, it is probably a noun. That information helps to determine that a *galleon* was a large sailing ship.)

Clues in the Overall Meaning of the Sentence or Passage Think about the meaning of the sentence or main idea of the paragraph. Often the overall meaning will provide context clues.

> *At the aquarium, we saw schools of tiny, colorful **rasbora** swimming in large freshwater tanks.*
> (The overall meaning of the sentence suggests that *rasbora* are a type of small freshwater fish.)

If you are still unsure of the meaning after studying context clues, consult a dictionary.

Name _____ Date _____ Assignment _____

Apply the Standard

Study context clues in nearby words, the overall meaning of the sentence, and the underlined word's function and position in the sentence. Then write its definition on the line provided.

1. The restaurant served a large platter of <u>havarti</u> and other cheeses. ....

2. After two hours at the <u>raucous</u> party, Shirley relaxed in her quiet living room. ....

3. Is the basement <u>accessible</u> from the inside of the house? ....

4. I didn't think the artist's humorous <u>caricature</u> resembled me at all. ....

5. In the <u>ornithology</u> seminar, we studied several different kinds of birds. ....

6. The sculptor molded a <u>kea</u>, a strange green parrot. ....

7. He pretends to be rich and important, with a fancy car and <u>ostentatious</u> gifts. ....

8. It is hard to get comfortable in this <u>oppressive</u> heat. ....

9. The candidate stepped to the <u>rostrum</u>, adjusted the mike, and began to speak. ....

10. I find most vegetables delicious, but I <u>detest</u> brussels sprouts. ....

11. An aura of dignity seemed to surround the highly respected judge. ....

12. Because he could not attend, the senator sent me as an <u>emissary</u>. ....

13. Bring the children inside at once! A swiftly moving storm is <u>imminent</u>. ....

14. <u>Marsupials</u>, such as kangaroos and opossums, carry their young in pouches. ....

15. That little boy is such a <u>rapscallion</u>. He is always doing pranks and tricks. ....

16. The giant sequoia tree had such a broad <u>girth</u> we could hide behind it. ....

17. I don't think I want to study <u>ophiology</u> because I do not like snakes. ....

18. Because Al's directions were <u>inscrutable</u>, we had trouble finding our way. ....

19. She collects fine china. I collect a <u>hodgepodge</u> of "treasures" from garage sales. ....

20. Please give me a straight "yes" or "no," not an <u>equivocal</u> "maybe." ....

Language 4b

4b. Determine or clarify the meaning of unknown and multiple-meaning words and phrases based on *grades 9–10 reading and content,* choosing flexibly from a range of strategies.

- Identify and correctly use patterns of word changes that indicate different meanings or parts of speech (e.g., *analyze, analysis, analytical; advocate, advocacy*).

Explanation

When you come to an unfamiliar word in your reading, try breaking the word down into its parts. Look for **affixes**, word parts that are added to a root or base word in order to change its meaning. There are two kinds of affixes—**prefixes**, which are attached *before* the root or base word, and **suffixes**, which are attached *after* the root or base word.

Knowing the meanings of suffixes is important because **suffixes determine both the meaning and the part of speech of the root or base word**.

Examples

This chart shows the meanings and specific functions of some common suffixes.

Suffix	Function	Meaning	Example
-dom	changes root or base word to noun	"state or condition"	*freedom*
-ly	changes root or base word to adverb or adjective	"in that way" (adverb) "like" (adjective)	*freely* (adverb) *friendly* (adjective)
-ment	changes root or base word to noun	"result or action"	*contentment*
-ish	changes root or base word to adjective or verb	"like" (adjective) "to make" (verb)	*childish* (adjective) *finish* (verb)
-en	changes root or base word to adjective or verb	"made of or like" (adjective) "to make" (verb)	*wooden* (adjective) *darken* (verb)
-er	changes root or base word to noun	"doer or native to"	*hunter*
-ate	changes root or base word to verb	"to form or become"	*nominate*
-ive	changes root or base word to adjective	"belonging to" or "having the quality of"	*creative*
-y	changes root or base word to noun or adjective	"state" (noun) "like" or "having"	*jealousy* (noun) *chilly* (adjective)

Apply the Standard

A. On the line following each sentence, write the part of speech and the meaning of each underlined word.

1. Bert Lahr is famous for playing the <u>Cowardly</u> Lion in the movie *The Wizard of Oz.*

Part of Speech: .... Meaning: ....

2. She took a nap because she felt <u>drowsy</u>.

Part of Speech: .... Meaning: ....

3. The performer <u>captivated</u> the audience with her beautiful voice.

Part of Speech: .... Meaning: ....

4. I was disappointed in the play because I thought the actors were <u>amateurish</u> in their performances.

Part of Speech: .... Meaning: ....

5. An encouraging speech might <u>hearten</u> the players before the challenging game.

Part of Speech: .... Meaning: ....

6. I will always <u>cherish</u> this beautiful card that you made for me.

Part of Speech: .... Meaning: ....

7. The edges of the flowers had a <u>bluish</u> tint.

Part of Speech: .... Meaning: ....

8. Practicing <u>preventive</u> medicine may help you to avoid sickness.

Part of Speech: .... Meaning: ....

B. Write the meaning of each word, using the meanings of the root or base word and the suffix, as well as the word's part of speech. Then use the word in a sentence that shows its meaning.

1. officialdom   Part of Speech: ....

Sentence: ....

2. wholly   Part of Speech: ....

Sentence: ....

3. enchantment   Part of Speech: ....

Sentence: ....

Language 4c

> **4c. Determine or clarify the meaning of unknown and multiple-meaning words and phrases based on** *grades 9–10 reading and content,* **choosing flexibly from a range of strategies.**
>
> • **Consult general and specialized reference materials (e.g., dictionaries, glossaries, thesauruses), both print and digital, to find the pronunciation of a word or determine or clarify its precise meaning, its part of speech, or its etymology.**

Explanation

A **dictionary** contains the definition, pronunciation, part of speech, and etymology of all words. Many words in the English language derive from Latin and Greek words.

A **thesaurus** provides **synonyms** for many words. When writing, use a thesaurus to find precise words that will help you to express the exact meaning that you want to get across to your audience.

Dictionaries and thesauruses are in your classroom or school library. You can also find them online. Refer to them when you need to clarify the meaning of an unknown word or one that has multiple meanings.

Examples

Notice what this **dictionary entry** reveals about the word *cohort.*

co • hort (kó-hort) **n.** [L *cohors,* enclosure, closed company, crowd] **1** an ancient Roman military unit of 300-600 men, part of a legion **2** a group or band, as of soldiers or workers **3** an associate or supporter [one of the senator's *cohorts*]

- A space or black dot inserted in the entry word indicates where the **syllables** break.

- Letters and symbols in parentheses show the word's **pronunciation.** Note the stress mark that indicates which syllable is stressed (CO hort).

- The **n.** tells the part of speech. *Cohort* is a noun. Other abbreviations used include **v.** (verb), **adj.** (adjective), and **adv.** (adverb).

- The word's **etymology**, or origin, then appears in brackets. *Cohort* comes from the Latin word *cohors*, which means "enclosure, closed company, or crowd."

- The word's definition follows. If there is more than one definition for the word, each is numbered. Sometimes a bracketed example appears to show the word's usage.

Now notice what this **thesaurus entry** for the word *cohort* offers.

cohort n. aide, ally, assistant, associate, companion, comrade, follower, partner, sidekick, supporter
Antonyms: enemy, opponent

- The part of speech follows the entry word.

- Synonyms are listed, followed by antonyms (if the word has antonyms; some do not). If the word has multiple meanings, they are listed separately and set off by numerals.

Name _____ Date _____ Assignment _____

Apply the Standard

Use the information in these dictionary and thesaurus entries to answer the questions.

Dictionary entry:

de • part (dē-pärt′) **v.** [L *dispartire,* to divide apart] **1** to go away; leave **2** to set out [Flight 12 *departs* at Gate A3.] **3** to die **4** to turn away from [to *depart* from the rules]

Thesaurus entry:

depart *v.*

1. beat it, cut and run, disappear, exit, go forth, hit the road, leave, part, retire, retreat, set off, start out, vacate, vanish, withdraw
Antonyms: arrive, come, continue on, enter, linger, remain, stay

2. abandon, desert, deviate, differ, discard, diverge from, forsake, reject, stray, turn aside, vary
Antonyms: continue, keep to, stay true to

3. cease to exist, die, decease, expire, pass away, perish, succumb
Antonyms: be born, begin, live

1. Which syllable in *depart* is the stressed syllable? ....

2. What part of speech is *depart?* ....

3. What language provided its etymology, and what did the original word mean? ....

4. Why are the second and fourth dictionary definitions followed by material in brackets? ....

5. Which dictionary definition (1, 2, 3, or 4) relates to the use of *depart* in each sentence below?

    a. When our cat *departed,* we buried her in the garden. ....

    b. Let's *depart* from tradition and serve fish instead of turkey on Thanksgiving. ....

    c. When my brother *departed* the house, I noticed that he forgot his keys. ....

6. Why does the thesaurus entry for *depart* contain three numbered sections? ....

7. Rewrite this sentence, using an appropriate **synonym** for *depart* found in the thesaurus. *I will depart from the pattern and make the birdhouse in my own way.* ....

8. Rewrite this sentence, using an appropriate **synonym** for *depart* found in the thesaurus. *I will depart for my interview promptly at two o'clock.* ....

Language 4d

4d. Determine or clarify the meaning of unknown and multiple-meaning words and phrases based on *grades 9-10 reading and content,* **choosing flexibly from a range of strategies.**

- **Verify the preliminary determination of the meaning of a word or phrase (e.g., by checking the inferred meaning in context or in a dictionary).**

Explanation

When you come to an **unknown word** in your reading, look for context clues to **determine its meaning**. Some clues might appear in nearby words or phrases or in the surrounding sentences. Others might be found in the unknown word's function in the sentence or in the overall meaning of the sentence or passage. Finally, you might find clues in the meaning of a word's root, prefix, or suffix. Always reread or read ahead to seek further context clues if the unknown word's meaning is still unclear. Then, **verify your preliminary determination** of the unfamiliar word's meaning by consulting a dictionary.

Examples

Clues in Nearby Words or Phrases. Examples of this type of context clue include the following.

> **Restatement or definition:** *The babysitter **coddled** the frightened child until he calmed down.*

(The clue suggests that *coddled* means "treated tenderly.")

> **Opposite or contrast:** *Has she thought through this plan, or is it merely a **caprice**?*

(The clues suggest that *caprice* means "a sudden, impulsive notion or action.")

> **Example:** *When not working, Mrs. Ramirez has two **avocations:** coaching soccer and baking bread.*

(The clues suggest that *avocation* means "hobby" or "work done for pleasure.")

Clues in the Word's Function in the Sentence. Use the word's function as a clue.

> *We couldn't sleep because of the noisy **caterwaul** of the neighbor's cats.*

(The clues suggest that *caterwaul* means "screeching or crying.")

Clues in the Overall Meaning of the Sentence or Passage. Reread a passage to clarify and then read ahead to seek further context clues.

> *As soon as we sat down, the waiter filled our **goblets** with ice water.*

(The overall meaning of the sentence suggests that *goblets* are glasses used for drinking.)

Clues in the Word's Root or Affixes. You know the meanings of many roots, prefixes, and suffixes. Use that knowledge to unlock the meaning of the unfamiliar word.

> *With years of experience in tight races, the candidate finally had an **uncontested** race.*

(Knowing that the prefix *-un* means *not* helps you to determine that *uncontested* means "not contested" or "not challenged.")

Name _____ Date _____ Assignment _____

Apply the Standard

A. Use context clues to find the meaning of the underlined word or phrase. Write its definition on the line.

1. Stand up tall, take a deep breath, and <u>assert</u> your opinions clearly and confidently.

....

2. Because lions are <u>predacious</u> animals, they hunt and kill zebras. ....

3. Mr. Long is a <u>congenial</u> host, always offering his guests hearty food and friendly conversation.

....

4. After the great victory, the team captain ran onto the field, <u>brandishing</u> the school banner.

....

5. Is that statement really true, or is it an unfair <u>prevarication</u>? ....

6. The <u>erudite</u> professor is famous for her fascinating and knowledgeable lectures.

....

7. I am trying to sharpen my writing skills, so I often <u>emulate</u> Mark Twain. ....

8. When I ride the crowded subway, I am often <u>jostled</u> by other passengers. ....

9. When handling a fragile glass vase, it is best to do so <u>gingerly</u>. ....

10. Please put the antique coins safely away in the metal <u>coffer</u>. ....

B. Use context clues, clues based on the word's function in the sentence, and clues based on prefixes, suffixes, or roots to define the underlined word. Write the definition on the line.

1. The punishment seemed <u>unjustified</u>. The man had done nothing wrong. ....

2. The <u>relentless</u> traffic noises, having gone on for several nights, made sleep impossible.

....

3. He did a <u>masterful</u> job of rearranging the furniture and changing the paint color to make the small

room seem larger. ....

4. After the crumbling palace was <u>restored</u>, it appeared as it did when new. ....

5. I prefer bright curtains printed with many colors rather than <u>monochromatic</u> ones.

....

Language 5a

5a. Demonstrate understanding of figurative language, word relationships, and nuances in word meanings.

- Interpret figures of speech (e.g., euphemism, oxymoron) in context and analyze their role in the text.

Figurative language is language that is used imaginatively rather than literally. It includes several different **figures of speech**, including **simile, metaphor, personification, symbol, paradox, euphemism,** and **oxymoron.**

To **interpret** figurative language, determine how it is used in **context** (the parts of a sentence or paragraph next to or surrounding the figurative language). The words surrounding figurative language will often serve as clues to the intended meaning. For example, consider the simile "like a flash of lightning" in this sentence: "When the race began, Carlos took off like a flash of lightning and led the other runners." If you aren't sure what the simile "like a flash of lightning" means or how it is being used in the sentence, look at the words surrounding it. You know that Carlos is in a race, where speed is key, and you know that he led the race after it began. Therefore, you can conclude that "like a flash of lightning" means something that happens very quickly.

Examples

- A **simile** compares two unlike things using *like, as, than,* or *resembles.*
  *The sun-baked pavement was **hotter than flames.***

- A **metaphor** compares two unlike things by stating that one thing *is* another.
  *His angry **words were a slap in my face.***

- **Personification** gives human characteristics to a nonhuman subject.
  Raindrops danced on the roof.

- A **symbol** is an object, a person, an animal, a place, or an image that represents something other than itself.
  *The **olive branch symbolizes peace.***

- A **paradox** is a statement or situation that seems contradictory but actually expresses a truth.
  *Socrates said, **"I know that I know nothing at all."***

- An **oxymoron** is similar to a paradox, although it is usually very brief—often just two words that seem to contradict each other.
  *an **honest thief***

- A **euphemism** is a word or phrase that is less direct but considered less offensive than another.
  a correctional facility (instead of "jail"); *departed this world* (instead of "died")

Name _____ Date _____ Assignment _____

Apply the Standard

A. Each sentence contains an underlined word or phrase. On the line preceding the sentence, identify the type of figurative language it represents. Write *simile, metaphor, personification, symbol, paradox, oxymoron,* or *euphemism.*

.... **1.** The secretary of state was eager to bring the <u>dove of peace</u> to the embattled nations.

.... **2.** He had a <u>numb feeling</u> in his right knee.

.... **3.** The sales manager told the sales staff to refer to used cars as "<u>pre-owned vehicles.</u>"

.... **4.** That wrinkled puppy is <u>so ugly that it is actually cute.</u>

.... **5.** The wind <u>whistled</u> through the trees.

.... **6.** Superman was once described as being able to fly <u>faster than a speeding bullet.</u>

.... **7.** Coming in the middle of my diet, the invitation to lunch was a <u>painful pleasure.</u>

.... **8.** <u>If you can't change the people around you, change the people around you.</u>

.... **9.** Tucked into their warm beds, the children were <u>as snug as birds in a nest.</u>

.....................................**10.** We will use most of the prize money to pay our bills, and the rest will be <u>gravy.</u>

B. Identify and interpret the underlined figures of speech. First, tell what type it is. Write *simile, metaphor, personification, symbol, paradox, oxymoron,* or *euphemism.* Then, interpret it by restating it in your own words.

> **Example:** Parting with her family was <u>sweet sorrow</u> for Marta.

> **Type:** oxymoron   **Interpretation:** Marta feels sad because she must leave her family, but also happiness in their presence.

1. <u>An angry storm</u> hit our town last night.

 Type: .... **Interpretation:** ....

2. Help yourself to Mom's <u>vegetarian meatballs.</u>

 Type: .... **Interpretation:** ....

3. The TV show was interrupted several times for "a <u>message from our sponsor.</u>"

 Type: .... **Interpretation:** ....

Language 5b

5b. Demonstrate understanding of figurative language, word relationships, and nuances in word meanings.

- **Analyze nuances in the meaning of words with similar denotations.**

Explanation

A word's **denotation** is its dictionary definition. Words sometimes have similar denotations, so you must **analyze nuances,** or slight variations, in meaning for a full understanding. To do this, use your prior knowledge (what you know from reading you have done and from life experience), a dictionary (to verify meaning), and context clues (the words surrounding the word you are analyzing) to understand a word's connotations—the ideas, images, and feelings that are associated with that word. A word's connotations might be positive, negative, or neutral. Knowing the connotation that an author intends is the key to understanding the differences in words with similar detonations.

Examples

This chart shows five words that share the **same denotation** but have **different connotations.**

Words whose common denotation is "talk"	Differing Connotations	Example Sentences
converse	calmly exchange views (neutral)	*Bill and I* converse *on the phone more often than face to face.*
discuss	constructively share ideas (positive)	*Let's* discuss *the pros and cons of this issue.*
chat	speak informally and pleasantly (positive)	*After lunch, we had a nice long* chat *about our hobbies.*
argue	forcefully disagree (negative)	*It's fine to disagree, but it makes me uncomfortable to* argue.
dispute	attack another's views aggressively (negative)	*I* dispute *your notion that the library must be closed.*

Name _____ Date _____ Assignment _____

Apply the Standard

A. Use prior knowledge, context clues, and a dictionary to tell whether the underlined word has a neutral, positive, or negative connotation. Circle your answer.

1. He was <u>new</u> at playing the trumpet.	neutral	positive	negative
2. He was <u>unpolished</u> at playing the trumpet.	neutral	positive	negative
3. The arrangement contained <u>fake</u> flowers.	neutral	positive	negative
4. The arrangement contained <u>synthetic</u> flowers.	neutral	positive	negative
5. The arrangement contained <u>phony</u> flowers.	neutral	positive	negative
6. He was <u>steadfast</u> in pursuit of his goals.	neutral	positive	negative
7. He was <u>stubborn</u> in pursuit of his goals.	neutral	positive	negative
8. She had a <u>clever</u> plan to present to the committee.	neutral	positive	negative
9. She had a <u>sly</u> plan to present to the committee.	neutral	positive	negative
10. She had a <u>brilliant</u> plan to present to the committee.	neutral	positive	negative

B. Each section contains a group of words. They have the same denotation but different connotations. On the line, write *neutral*, *positive*, or *negative* to identify the word's connotation. Then, use each word in a sentence that makes its connotation clear.

1. Denotation: inexpensive

   a. economical **Connotation:** ....

   Sentence: ....

   b. cheap **Connotation:** ....

   Sentence: ....

   c. bargain **Connotation:** ....

   Sentence: ....

2. Denotation: different

   a. odd **Connotation:** ....

   Sentence: ....

   b. rare **Connotation:** ....

   Sentence: ....

   c. one of a kind **Connotation:** ....

   Sentence: ....

For use with Language 5b

Language 6

> 6. Acquire and use accurately general academic and domain-specific words and phrases, sufficient for reading, writing, speaking, and listening at the college and career readiness level; demonstrate independence in gathering vocabulary knowledge when considering a word or phrase important to comprehension or expression.

Explanation

In each of your classes, you frequently use many **academic** and **domain-specific** vocabulary words and phrases.

- **Academic words** are those that you use every day to solve problems, discuss facts and opinions, and analyze literature.
  Examples include *context*, *perspective*, *speculate*, and *verify*.

- **Domain-specific words** are words that are specific to a course of study. In a science course, examples include *biology*, *molecule*, and *membrane*. In a social studies course, examples include *circumnavigate*, *commonwealth*, and *migration*.

Acquiring (understanding the definitions of) academic and domain-specific words and **using them accurately** will help you complete assignments and essay questions correctly and express your ideas clearly. When you encounter a word that you are unfamiliar with, use a dictionary and context clues (the words surrounding the word you are unfamiliar with) to define it. To reinforce your understanding, use the word in a sentence of your own creation.

Examples

In many of your courses, you are asked to complete tasks based on specific **academic words and phrases.** And, on many tests, you are asked to write essays that fulfill directions containing **academic words and phrases.** Here are examples:

*Use facts to **support your response** . . .*   ***Paraphrase** the poem . . .*

***Interpret and restate** the theme of . . .*   ***Summarize** the conflict . . .*

***Determine** the definition of . . .*   ***Build an effective argument** . . .*

In a literature and writing course, you use many **domain-specific words and phrases.**

Here are examples:

onomatopoeia	*tone*	*oral tradition*	*conflict*
resolution	*allusion*	*simile*	*mood*

Name _____ Date _____ Assignment _____

Apply the Standard

A. Match each domain-specific word with its definition. Write the letter of the definition on the line provided. Then, on a separate sheet, use the word in a sentence. If necessary, use a dictionary to help you define an unfamiliar word.

.... **1.** anecdote   **a.** a deliberate exaggeration

.... **2.** epic   **b.** a speech that a character delivers alone, expressing inner thoughts

.... **3.** image   **c.** a character who provides a contrast to another character

.... **4.** flashback   **d.** the pattern of beats, or stresses, in spoken or written language

.... **5.** parallelism   **e.** actions that took place before the current situation and actions unfold

.... **6.** soliloquy   **f.** a long narrative poem about the actions of heroes or gods

.... **7.** rhythm   **g.** a word or phrase that appeals to one or more of the senses

.... **8.** hyperbole   **h.** the repetition of a grammatical structure

.... **9.** exposition   **i.** a brief story about an interesting or amusing event

.... **10.** foil   **j.** the part of the plot that introduces the setting and characters

B. Answer each question about academic words and phrases. Underline each correct answer. If necessary, use a dictionary to help you define an unfamiliar word.

1. Something that is *ambiguous* has ....

     a. more than one meaning   **c.** both a denotation and a connotation

     b. a melancholy tone   **d.** language that appeals to the senses

2. To *articulate* means to ....

     a. participate in a debate   **c.** analyze the author's purpose for writing

     b. express ideas clearly   **d.** paraphrase the theme of a work

3. Things that are *credible* are ....

     a. believable   **c.** unlikely to produce results

     b. imaginary   **d.** difficult to support with facts

4. A *controversy* is a ....

     a. type of visual essay   **c.** rhymed pair of lines at the end of a poem

     b. defense of a point of view   **d.** discussion in which opposing ideas clash

Performance Tasks

Name _____ Date _____ Assignment _____

Performance Task 1A

Literature 1 Cite strong and thorough textual evidence to support analysis of what the text says explicitly as well as inferences drawn from the text.*

Task: Support Analysis of a Text

Write a response to literature in which you cite textual evidence to support your analysis of a literary text. Explain what the text says explicitly as well as any inferences you have drawn from the text as part of your response.

Tips for Success

Present a response to a literary selection you have read. In your response, include these elements:

- ✓ an analysis of the work's content

- ✓ a thesis statement that succinctly sums up your personal response to the literary work

- ✓ evidence from the text that explicitly supports the opinions you present

- ✓ inferences from the text that support the opinions presented in your response

- ✓ language that is formal and precise and that follows standard English

Rubric for Self-Assessment

Criteria for Success	not very				very
How effectively do you explain what the work was about?	1	2	3	4	5
How clear is your analysis and explanation of the text?	1	2	3	4	5
To what extent does the thesis explain your personal thoughts and feelings about the work?	1	2	3	4	5
How well do you support the thesis with explicit evidence from the text?	1	2	3	4	5
How well do you include inferences you made during reading to support your response?	1	2	3	4	5
How well do you use standard English?	1	2	3	4	5
To what extent do you use a formal style and appropriate tone for your audience?	1	2	3	4	5

*Other standards covered include: Writing 9a, Writing 10, Speaking 6, Language 6

For use with Literature 1

Name _____ Date _____ Assignment _____

Performance Task 1B

> **Speaking and Listening 1** Initiate and participate effectively in a range of collaborative discussions (one-on-one, in groups, and teacher-led) with diverse partners on grades 9-10 topics, texts, and issues, building on others' ideas and expressing their own clearly and persuasively.

Task: Discuss the Responses to a Text

Participate in a group discussion in which you explain your response to a literary text and respond thoughtfully to the points of view of others.

Tips for Success

Participate in a discussion about a response to a literary text. As a part of your participation in the discussion, include these elements:

- ✓ preparation by having read the literary text and thought through your personal response to it
- ✓ guidelines agreed upon by other members in the discussion for equal and full participation for each person
- ✓ prepare questions to evoke further discussion from participants and propel the discussion forward
- ✓ questions that will evoke further discussion from participants and propel the discussion forward in order to explore the work fully
- ✓ inferences from the text that support the different points of view presented
- ✓ summaries of different responses to the text

Rubric for Self-Assessment

Criteria for Discussion	not very				very
To what extent were the speakers prepared for the discussion?	1	2	3	4	5
How well had the participants thought through their responses to the text before the discussion started?	1	2	3	4	5
To what extent did the group establish guidelines for the discussion?	1	2	3	4	5
How well did the guidelines ensure that everyone would participate fully and equally?	1	2	3	4	5
How effectively did the discussion summarize the main perspectives of participants?	1	2	3	4	5
How well did the participants demonstrate politeness and respect to others in the group?	1	2	3	4	5

Name _____ Date _____ Assignment _____

Performance Task 2A

> **Literature 2 Determine a theme or central idea of a text and analyze in detail its development over the course of the text, including how it emerges and is shaped and refined by specific details; provide an objective summary of the text.***

Task: Identify Theme

Write an essay in which you discuss the theme of a literary text. In your essay, provide a brief, objective summary of the text and explain how the author uses the events, words, and images in the text to establish the theme.

Tips for Success

Write an essay identifying a theme, and explain how the theme is developed. As you write your essay, do the following:

- ✓ Take notes summarizing important events in the work and the characters' responses to the events.

- ✓ Look for patterns, or motifs, in the work, such as repeated phrases, images, or situations.

- ✓ Develop a clear, succinct statement of the work's theme.

- ✓ Use the information gathered in your notes to provide support for your analysis.

- ✓ Use language that is formal, precise, and follows the rules of standard English.

Rubric for Self-Assessment

Criteria for Success	not very					very
How effectively and clearly have you summarized the work?	1	2	3	4	5	6
How successfully do you find repeated patterns in the work?	1	2	3	4	5	6
How effectively do you develop a statement of the work's theme?	1	2	3	4	5	6
How successfully do you identify three or more key details used by the author to develop the theme?	1	2	3	4	5	6
To what extent do you use those details to support your analysis of the work?	1	2	3	4	5	6
How successful is your use of standard English?	1	2	3	4	5	6
How successful are you at using a formal style and creating an appropriate tone for your audience?	1	2	3	4	5	6

* Other standards covered include: Writing 2a, Writing 2b, Writing 2d, Writing 3e, Writing 4, Speaking 6, Language 3.

For use with Literature 2

Performance Task 2B

> **Speaking and Listening 4** Present information, findings, and supporting evidence clearly, concisely, and logically such that listeners can follow the line of reasoning, and the organization, development, substance, and style appropriate to purpose, audience, and task.

Task: Make a Presentation to a Small Group

Analyze a literary text and present your findings clearly and concisely to a group of peers. Choose an organization and style that suit your purpose, audience, and task.

Tips for Success

Present your analysis to a small group and listen closely as others present their analyses. Follow these tips for success:

✓ write an objective summary of the work before drafting your analysis

✓ use presentation guidelines agreed upon by group members

✓ present findings and supporting evidence in a format that suits your purpose and that will interest your audience of peers

✓ allow time for audience feedback in the form of questions or comments

✓ pay close attention to other members of the group as they make their presentations

Rubric for Self-Assessment

Criteria for Discussion	not very very
How successful were you in keeping your summary objective and concise?	1 2 3 4 5 6
How clear and well supported was your presentation?	1 2 3 4 5 6
Based on feedback from other members of the group, how effectively did you present your information?	1 2 3 4 5 6
How clearly and fully were you able to answer questions asked by other group members?	1 2 3 4 5 6
How successful were the guidelines agreed upon by the group?	1 2 3 4 5 6
How well were you able to follow and respond to the presentations of other group members?	1 2 3 4 5 6

For use with Speaking and Listening 4

Name _____ Date _____ Assignment _____

Performance Task 3A

Literature 3   Analyze how complex characters (e.g., those with multiple or conflicting motivations) develop over the course of a text, interact with other characters, and advance the plot or develop the theme.*

Task: Analyze Character

Write an analysis of a complex character from one of the literary selections you have read. Use evidence from the text to support your analysis.

Tips for Success

Write a character analysis based on a literary selection you have read. In your analysis, include these elements:

- ✓ a clear thesis statement that sums up your analysis of the character

- ✓ details from the text that show ways in which the character is complex, round, and dynamic, including what the character says about him- or herself

- ✓ details of how the character interacts with other characters and responds to events in the story

- ✓ evidence from the text that explicitly supports your analysis

- ✓ inferences from the text that support your analysis

- ✓ language that is formal, precise, and follows the rules of standard English

Rubric for Self-Assessment

Criteria for Success	not very				very	
How clear is your thesis statement?	1	2	3	4	5	6
How vividly and fully have you described the character?	1	2	3	4	5	6
How effectively were you in developing a statement of the work's theme?	1	2	3	4	5	6
How well have you explained the character's influence on other characters and events in the story?	1	2	3	4	5	6
How well have you supported your analysis with explicit evidence from the text?	1	2	3	4	5	6
To what extent have you supported inferences you have made?	1	2	3	4	5	6
How successfully have you used standard English and a formal style and appropriate tone for your audience?	1	2	3	4	5	6

* Other standards covered include: Writing 2, Writing 9, Writing 10, Speaking 6, Language 1, Language 6

Name _____ Date _____ Assignment _____

Performance Task 3B

Task: Discuss the Character Analyses

Participate in a group discussion in which you explain your character analysis and respond thoughtfully to others' viewpoints.

Tips for Success

Participate in a discussion about a character analysis. Follow these tips for success:

- ✓ take notes on your analysis of the character in order to clearly and persuasively present your ideas
- ✓ with group members, agree on guidelines for equal and full participation of each person
- ✓ prepare questions to evoke further discussion from participants and propel the discussion forward
- ✓ build on ideas of others during the discussion
- ✓ take notes on different points of view presented in the analyses
- ✓ summarize each group member's contribution to the discussion

Rubric for Self-Assessment

Criteria for Discussion	not very				very	
How clearly and persuasively did you present your ideas?	1	2	3	4	5	6
How successful was the group at establishing guidelines for the discussion, and how fully did everyone participate?	1	2	3	4	5	6
How successful were participants at asking thoughtful questions that helped explore the analyses presented?	1	2	3	4	5	6
How well did participants offer different perspectives on the characters and build on each other's ideas?	1	2	3	4	5	6
How well did the group summarize the main perspectives of participants?	1	2	3	4	5	6
How polite and respectful of other points of view were the participants?	1	2	3	4	5	6

For use with Speaking and Listening 1

Name _____ Date _____ Assignment _____

Performance Task 4A

> **Literature 4** Determine the meaning of words and phrases as they are used in the text, including figurative and connotative meanings; analyze the cumulative impact of specific word choices on meaning and tone (e.g., how the language evokes a sense of time and place; how it sets a formal or informal tone).*

Task: Analyze Language

Write a response to a literary selection in which you analyze the cumulative effect of the author's word choice on the overall tone of the selection. Support your conclusions with text evidence.

Tips for Success

In your response, include these elements:

- ✓ a clear thesis statement identifying the tone of the selection

- ✓ a description of the types of words and phrases used to describe people, places, or events in the selection

- ✓ a discussion of how the level of formality and language used in the selection help to establish its tone

- ✓ language that is formal, precise, and follows the rules of standard English

Rubric for Self-Assessment

Criteria for Success	not very					very
How clear is your thesis statement?	1	2	3	4	5	6
How well have you described the level of formality in the selection?	1	2	3	4	5	6
How well have you described the author's word choice and phrasing in the selection?	1	2	3	4	5	6
How clearly have you demonstrated a connection between the selection's level of formality and its tone?	1	2	3	4	5	6
How clearly have you demonstrated a connection between the selection's diction and its tone?	1	2	3	4	5	6
To what extent have you used evidence from the text to support your analysis?	1	2	3	4	5	6
How successful is your use of standard English?	1	2	3	4	5	6
How successfully have you used a formal style and created an appropriate tone for your audience?	1	2	3	4	5	6

* Other standards covered include: Writing 3, Writing 10, Speaking 6, Language 5, Language 5a, Language 5b

Performance Task 4B

Speaking and Listening 6   Adapt speech to a variety of contexts and tasks, demonstrating command of formal English when indicated or appropriate.

Task: Translating From Informal to Formal Style

Participate in an activity in which you tell a true story to a small group of classmates using informal language. Then "translate" your story into formal, expository English and share it with the group.

Tips for Success

Participate in an activity in which you tell a true story in two different styles, informal and formal. As part of your participation, include these elements:

✓ a true story that has a beginning, a middle, and an end

✓ informal language, for the first telling of the story

✓ formal language, for the second telling of the story

✓ guidelines agreed upon by group members for equal and full participation

✓ attention to other members of the group when they tell their stories

Rubric for Self-Assessment

Criteria for Discussion	not very					very
How successful were you in developing a true story to tell?	1	2	3	4	5	6
How well did you use informal language in telling your story?	1	2	3	4	5	6
How well did you use formal language in "translating" your story?	1	2	3	4	5	6
How successful was the group in establishing guidelines?	1	2	3	4	5	6
How successful was the group in listening to each story with respectful attention?	1	2	3	4	5	6

Performance Task 5A

> **Literature 5** Analyze how an author's choices concerning how to structure a text, order events within it (e.g., parallel plots), and manipulate time (e.g., pacing, flashbacks) create such effects as mystery, tension, or surprise.*

Task: Analyze Text Structure

Present a response to a literary selection you have read in which the author uses literary elements, such as foreshadowing, or presents events out of chronological order. Tell how those stylistic plot devices affected your response to the selection.

Tips for Success

Write an essay about the use of plot devices in a literary selection you have read. In your essay, include these elements:

✓ a thesis statement that succinctly sums up your ideas about the literary work

✓ an analysis of the work's plot and stylistic devices and how they affect the work as a whole

✓ evidence from the text that explicitly supports your analysis

✓ inferences from the text that support your analysis

✓ language that is formal, precise, and follows the rules of standard English

Rubric for Self-Assessment

Criteria for Success	not very					very
How clear is your thesis statement?	1	2	3	4	5	6
How thoroughly have you described the work's plot and stylistic devices?	1	2	3	4	5	6
How well have you supported your analysis with explicit evidence from the text?	1	2	3	4	5	6
How well have you supported your analysis with inferences made during reading?	1	2	3	4	5	6
How successful is your use of standard English?	1	2	3	4	5	6
How successfully have you used a formal style and created an appropriate tone for your audience?	1	2	3	4	5	6

* Other standards covered include: Writing 1a, Writing 1e, Writing 6, Writing 10, Speaking 5, Language 3

Name _____ Date _____ Assignment _____

Performance Task 5B

Speaking and Listening 5 Make strategic use of digital media (e.g., textual, graphical, audio, visual, and interactive elements) in presentations to enhance understanding of findings, reasoning, and evidence and to add interest.

Task: Adapt a Literary Selection

Participate in a group activity in which you work with others to adapt a literary selection into another medium, such as a comic book, a short animated or live-action film, or a radio-style drama.

Tips for Success

Participate in a group activity to adapt a literary work. Follow these tips for success:

✓ come to an agreement among group members about the literary selection and medium to which it will be adapted.

✓ formulate guidelines for equal and full participation in the activity, including assignment of tasks and responsibilities.

✓ prepare by reading the selected literary text and taking notes on characters, plot, and so on.

✓ practice and master the technology required for the adaptation.

Rubric for Self-Assessment

Criteria for Discussion	not very					very
How well did the guidelines ensure that everyone would participate fully and equally?	1	2	3	4	5	6
How well had the participants prepared for the activity?	1	2	3	4	5	6
How appropriate was the selected medium for presenting an adaptation of the literary work?	1	2	3	4	5	6
How well did the adaptation present the characters and plot devices of the original literary work?	1	2	3	4	5	6
How successful was the adaptation in retelling the original literary work?	1	2	3	4	5	6
How polite and respectful of each other were the group participants?	1	2	3	4	5	6

Name _____ Date _____ Assignment _____

Performance Task 6A

Literature 6   Analyze a particular point of view or cultural experience reflected in a work of literature from outside the United States, drawing on a wide reading of world literature.

Task: Write an Essay About A Character

Write an essay about one of the literary selections you have read that was written outside of the United States. Use the information from both the textbook and from outside resources to explain how the selection's cultural and historical context shapes the point of view of one or more of the characters in the story.

Tips for Success

Write an essay about a literary selection written outside the United States. In your essay, include these elements:

✓ a clear thesis statement that sums up your analysis of the character

✓ three or more carefully chosen and evaluated resources other than the textbook

✓ specific examples from the text that support your analysis of the character

✓ inferences from the text that support your analysis

✓ language that is formal, precise, and follows the rules of standard English

Rubric for Self-Assessment

Criteria for Success	not very					very
How successfully have you created a clear thesis statement?	1	2	3	4	5	6
How deeply have you explored the influence of cultural and historical context on the character's point of view?	1	2	3	4	5	6
How thoroughly have you explored resources other than the textbook to support your analysis?	1	2	3	4	5	6
How well have you supported your thesis with explicit evidence from the text?	1	2	3	4	5	6
How successfully have you included inferences you made during reading to support your analysis?	1	2	3	4	5	6
How successfully have you used standard English, a formal style, and an appropriate tone for your audience?	1	2	3	4	5	6

* Other standards covered include: Reading 3, Writing 7, Writing 8, Writing 9a, Language 3, Speaking and Listening 1, Speaking and Listening 3

For use with Literature 6

Performance Task 6B

> **Speaking and Listening 3** Evaluate a speaker's point of view, reasoning, and use of evidence and rhetoric, identifying any fallacious reasoning or exaggerated or distorted evidence.

Task: Evaluate a Speech

Review and critique a persuasive speech. Locate a speech online and watch it, taking notes as you watch. Then write a critique in which you evaluate the speaker's point of view and use of evidence and rhetoric. Point out any instances of faulty reasoning or weak and distorted evidence.

Tips for Success

As you prepare your critique of a persuasive speech, follow these tips for success:

✓ take notes about effective and ineffective aspects of the speech; use the pause and rewind features to allow yourself time to take notes and to review segments of the speech

✓ note ways in which the speaker uses vocal techniques and body language to emphasize key points

✓ prepare a written evaluation of the speech, and organize your main points logically

✓ provide specific details from the speech to support your evaluation

✓ language that is formal, precise, and follows the rules of standard English

Rubric for Self-Assessment

Criteria for Success	not very					very
How detailed are the notes you took while watching the speech?	1	2	3	4	5	6
How clearly have you noted the speaker's use of verbal and nonverbal techniques?	1	2	3	4	5	6
How successful is your analysis of the overall effectiveness of the speech?	1	2	3	4	5	6
How logically have you presented and supported your main points?	1	2	3	4	5	6
How successfully have you used standard English, a formal style, and an appropriate tone?	1	2	3	4	5	6

Performance Task 7B

> **Literature 7** Analyze the representation of a subject or a key scene in two different artistic mediums, including what is emphasized or absent in each treatment (e.g., Auden's "Musée des Beaux Arts" and Breughel's *Landscape with the Fall of Icarus*).*

Task: Compare and Contrast an Event or Scene in Two Artistic Mediums

Write an essay in which you compare and contrast the depiction of a single event or scene that is presented in two artistic mediums, such as print, photography, film, painting, and sculpture. Note elements that are present or absent from each depiction.

Tips for Success

Write an essay about a scene or event that presented in more than one medium. In your response, include these elements:

✓ a description of the scene or event being explored

✓ an analysis of the general similarities and differences of the two artistic mediums

✓ specific details that describe the different treatments of the event or scene

✓ a clear thesis statement that sums up the conclusions you have drawn

✓ specific evidence from both texts to support your thesis

✓ language that is formal, precise, and follows the rules of standard English

Rubric for Self-Assessment

Criteria for Success	not very					very
How well have you described the scene or event being explored?	1	2	3	4	5	6
How successful were you in creating one clear statement of the conclusions you have drawn?	1	2	3	4	5	6
How well have you explained the general possibilities and limitations of the two mediums you analyzed?	1	2	3	4	5	6
How well have you explained the specific differences in the way each medium represented the subject?	1	2	3	4	5	6
How well have you supported your conclusion with explicit evidence from both mediums?	1	2	3	4	5	6
How successful were you in using standard English?	1	2	3	4	5	6

* Other standards covered include: Writing 2a, Writing 2b, Writing 9a, Writing 10, Language 1b, Speaking and Listening 1b, Speaking and Listening 4, Speaking and Listening 5

Name _____ Date _____ Assignment _____

Performance Task 7B

> **Speaking and Listening 4** Present information, findings, and supporting
> evidence clearly, concisely, and logically such that listeners can follow the
> line of reasoning, and the organization, development, substance, and style are
> appropriate to purpose, audience, and task.

Task: Participate in a Small Group Presentation

Participate in a group activity in which you select a subject that is represented in more than one medium (for example, short story and film, painting and poem) and create a presentation for your classmates comparing and contrasting the two representations.

Tips for Success

Participate in a group presentation in which two artistic mediums are compared. Follow these tips for success:

✓ review both representations thoroughly and note your response to them

✓ develop guidelines with group members for equal and full participation for each person

✓ create a thesis statement that has been agreed to by all members of the team

✓ cite evidence from the works that supports the team's thesis

✓ develop presentation materials that help the audience to fully understand the subject presented

✓ create a tone that suits the presentation's material and your audience

Rubric for Self-Assessment

Criteria for Discussion	not very					very
How thoroughly did your group prepare for the presentation?	1	2	3	4	5	6
How well did the guidelines ensure that everyone would participate fully and equally?	1	2	3	4	5	6
How successful was the presentation team in developing a clear thesis statement?	1	2	3	4	5	6
How successful was the presentation team in using evidence from both works to support the thesis statement?	1	2	3	4	5	6
How successful was the team in producing materials that enhanced the presentation?	1	2	3	4	5	6
How successful was the team in using formal language and an appropriate tone?	1	2	3	4	5	6

Name _____ Date _____ Assignment _____

Performance Task 8

> **Literature 9 Analyze how an author draws on and transforms source material in a specific work (e.g., how Shakespeare treats a theme or topic from Ovid or the Bible or how a later author draws on a play by Shakespeare).***

Task: Write an Essay That Explores Source Material

Write an essay about a literary selection that draws on or transforms source material from another literary work. Analyze the changes that the author made to the characters, plot, or tone of the source material and the effect of that change.

Tips for Success

Write about a literary work that draws on another literary work and include these elements:

- ✓ a clear thesis statement that sums up your analysis
- ✓ a discussion of the characters, plot, or tone of the source material and how they have been adapted
- ✓ evidence from the text that explicitly supports your analysis
- ✓ inferences from the text that support your analysis
- ✓ an evaluation of the effectiveness of the adaptation
- ✓ language that is formal, precise, and follows the rules of standard English

Rubric for Self-Assessment

Criteria for Success	not very					very
How successful were you in creating one clear thesis statement?	1	2	3	4	5	6
How deeply have you discussed the characters, plot, or tone of the source material?	1	2	3	4	5	6
How well does your analysis address the transformation of the source material into the newer work?	1	2	3	4	5	6
How effectively have you used quotes, facts, or ideas from the texts to support your analysis?	1	2	3	4	5	6
How well have you supported your thesis with explicit evidence from the text?	1	2	3	4	5	6
How successful were you in including inferences made during reading to support your response?	1	2	3	4	5	6
How successful were you in using standard English, a formal style, and an appropriate tone for your audience?	1	2	3	4	5	6

* Other standards covered include: Reading 2, 3, or 5, Writing 9a, Writing 10, Speaking 6, Language 6.

For use with Literature 9

Performance Task 8B

Speaking and Listening 1 Initiate and participate effectively in a range of collaborative discussions (one-on-one, in groups, and teacher-led) with diverse partners on grades 9–10 topics, texts, and issues, building on others' ideas and expressing your own clearly and persuasively.

Task: Discuss the Essays

Participate in a group discussion in which group members share their essays about a literary text and the source material from which the author drew inspiration. Respond thoughtfully to the ideas of others and build upon their ideas in your discussion.

Tips for Success

Participate in a discussion about an essay on a literary text. Follow these tips for success:

- ✓ review the essay you wrote about a literary text and the ways in which the author adapted source material in its retelling
- ✓ with the group, develop discussion guidelines for equal and full participation for each person
- ✓ present your ideas clearly and simply when it is your turn to speak
- ✓ prepare questions that will evoke further discussion from participants and propel the discussion forward
- ✓ identify text passages that support the different points of view presented in the essays
- ✓ summarize the group's different responses to the text

Rubric for Self-Assessment

Criteria for Discussion	not very					very
How well had the participants prepared for the discussion?	1	2	3	4	5	6
How successful was the group in establishing guidelines for equal participation in the discussion?	1	2	3	4	5	6
How clearly did you express your ideas about the literary work and its source material?	1	2	3	4	5	6
How successful were participants in asking thoughtful questions that helped explore different points of view?	1	2	3	4	5	6
How well did participants offer different perspectives on the work?	1	2	3	4	5	6
How well did the discussion summarize the main perspectives of participants?	1	2	3	4	5	6

Name _____ Date _____ Assignment _____

Performance Task 9A

Literature 10 By the end of grade 9, read and comprehend literature, including stories, dramas, and poems, in the grades 9–10 text complexity band proficiently, with scaffolding as needed at the high end of the range.

Task: Respond to an Independent Reading

After doing independent reading, write an analysis of the text. Then, use textual evidence and inferences you have drawn during reading to support your analysis of it.

Tips for Success

Present a response to independent reading you have read outside of class. In your response, include these elements:

- ✓ a short, objective summary of the text
- ✓ an analysis of the content
- ✓ a thesis statement that clearly sums up your response to the text
- ✓ evidence from the text that explicitly supports the opinions you present
- ✓ inferences from the text that support your response
- ✓ language that is formal, precise, and follows the rules of standard English

Rubric for Self-Assessment

Criteria for Success	not very				very	
How clear and objective is your summary of the text?	1	2	3	4	5	6
How thoroughly have you analyzed the text's content?	1	2	3	4	5	6
How successfully have you created a clear thesis statement?	1	2	3	4	5	6
How well does your thesis explain your response to the work?	1	2	3	4	5	6
How well have you supported the thesis with explicit evidence from the text?	1	2	3	4	5	6
How successfully have you included inferences you made during reading to support your response?	1	2	3	4	5	6
How successfully have you used standard English, a formal style, and an appropriate tone for your audience?	1	2	3	4	5	6

* Other standards covered include: Reading 1, Writing 9a, Writing 10, Speaking 5, Speaking 6, Language 6.

For use with Literature 10

Name _____ Date _____ Assignment _____

Performance Task 9B

> **Speaking and Listening 5** Make strategic use of digital media (e.g., textual, graphical, audio, visual, and interactive elements) in presentations to enhance understanding of findings, reasoning, and evidence and to add interest.

Task: Make a Presentation to a Small Group

Create a presentation about a book you read independently by adapting an essay you wrote about it. Make use of digital media to illustrate your findings and reasoning and to add interest. Make your presentation to a small group of your classmates. Listen thoughtfully as other members of the group make their presentations.

Tips for Success

As your prepare for your presentation, follow these tips for success:

- ✓ carefully review your essay and adapt it from written to spoken language
- ✓ create presentation materials that are clear and engaging for your audience
- ✓ allow time for feedback from the audience in the form of questions or comments
- ✓ with group members, develop guidelines for presentations and discussions
- ✓ take notes as group members make their presentations and respond thoughtfully

Rubric for Self-Assessment

Criteria for Success	not very					very
How prepared were you to make your presentation?	1	2	3	4	5	6
How well did you use digital media to create presentation materials?	1	2	3	4	5	6
How clear and engaging were your presentation materials?	1	2	3	4	5	6
Based on feedback from your classmates, how well did you present your information?	1	2	3	4	5	6
How well were you able to answer questions asked by classmates?	1	2	3	4	5	6
How successful were the guidelines in ensuring that each presenter participated equally and fully?	1	2	3	4	5	6

For use with Speaking and Listening 5

Name _____ Date _____ Assignment _____

Performance Task 10A

Informational Text 1 Cite strong and thorough textual evidence to support analysis of what the text says explicitly as well as inferences drawn from the text.*

Task: Support Analysis of a Text

Write a response to an informational text you have read. As part of your response, identify the central idea of the text and the supporting details the author uses to support that idea.

Tips for Success

Present a response to an informational text you have read. In your response, include these elements:

- ✓ a clear, objective summary of the text
- ✓ a thesis statement that sums up your response to the text
- ✓ evidence from the text that explicitly supports your thesis
- ✓ inferences from the text that support your analysis
- ✓ language that is formal, precise, and follows the rules of standard English

Rubric for Self-Assessment

Criteria for Success	not very				very	
How clearly have you summarized the text?	1	2	3	4	5	6
How well have you analyzed the author's central idea and supporting details?	1	2	3	4	5	6
How successfully have you created one clear thesis statement?	1	2	3	4	5	6
How well have you used quotes, paraphrases, or facts from the text to support your analysis?	1	2	3	4	5	6
How successfully have you included inferences or conclusions you had drawn during reading?	1	2	3	4	5	6
How successfully have you used a formal style and an appropriate tone for your audience?	1	2	3	4	5	6

* Other standards covered include: Writing 9b, Writing 10, Language 6, Speaking 1, Speaking 6

For use with Informational Text 1

Name _____ Date _____ Assignment _____

Performance Task 10B

> **Speaking and Listening 1** Initiate and participate effectively in a range of
> collaborative discussions (one-on-one, in groups, and teacher-led) with diverse
> partners on grades 9–10 topics, texts, and issues, building on others' ideas and
> expressing your own clearly and persuasively.

Task: Discuss the Responses to a Text

Work one-on-one with a partner to explain your response to an informational text. Respond
thoughtfully to each other's point of view, and build on the ideas of your partner during the
discussion.

Tips for Success

Participate in a one-on-one discussion about a response to an informational text. Follow these tips
for success:

✓ read or re-read the informational text and take notes on your response to it

✓ with your partner, develop discussion guidelines for equal and full
   participation

✓ pose questions that will evoke further discussion from your partner

✓ find text passages that support the point of view presented by your partner

✓ summarize your partner's response to the text

Rubric for Self-Assessment

Criteria for Discussion	not very					very
How well had you and your partner prepared for the discussion?	1	2	3	4	5	6
How well did the guidelines ensure that both you and your partner participated fully and equally?	1	2	3	4	5	6
How successful were you in asking thoughtful questions that helped explore your partner's point of view?	1	2	3	4	5	6
How well did you and your partner build on each other's ideas?	1	2	3	4	5	6
How well did the discussion summarize your responses to the text?	1	2	3	4	5	6

Name _____ Date _____ Assignment _____

Performance Task 11A

> **Informational Text 2** Determine a central idea of a text and analyze its development over the course of the text, including how it emerges and is shaped and refined by specific details; provide an objective summary of the text.*

Task: Summarize an Informational Text

Write an objective summary of an informational text you have read, identifying the text's central idea and the key supporting details the author uses to support that idea.

Tips for Success

Write a summary of an informational text you have read. In your summary, include these elements:

✓ a clear statement of the text's central idea

✓ a narrative of how the text develops that idea, focusing on the details the author uses to make his or her point

✓ evidence from the text that explicitly supports your analysis

✓ inferences from the text that support your analysis

✓ language that is formal, precise, and follows the rules of standard English

Rubric for Self-Assessment

Criteria for Success	not very very
How clearly do you identify and express the central idea of the text?	1 2 3 4 5 6
How successfully do you identify the supporting details that shape the central idea?	1 2 3 4 5 6
How objective is your summary?	1 2 3 4 5 6
How well do you support your analysis with explicit evidence from the text?	1 2 3 4 5 6
How well do you support your analysis with inferences made during reading?	1 2 3 4 5 6
How successful is your use of standard English?	1 2 3 4 5 6
How successfully have you used a formal style and created an appropriate tone for your audience?	1 2 3 4 5 6

*Other standards covered include: Writing 2b, Writing 2e, Writing 10, Language 6, Speaking 4

For use with Informational Text 2

Name _____ Date _____ Assignment _____

Performance Task 11B

> **Speaking and Listening 6** Adapt speech to a variety of contexts and tasks, demonstrating command of formal English when indicated or appropriate.

Task: Present Your Summary

Present your summary to a small group of your classmates. Listen as they present their summaries. Give feedback on your classmates' summaries and welcome their feedback on yours.

Tips for Success

Present your summary of an informational text. As a part of your presentation, include these elements:

✓ prepare by thinking about how to adapt your written summary into a spoken presentation

✓ visual aids that will help your audience follow your presentation

✓ allow time for feedback from the audience in the form of questions or comments

✓ agreed upon guidelines with other members in the group for presentations

✓ pay attention to other members of the group as they present their summaries

Rubric for Self-Assessment

Criteria for Discussion	not very very
How prepared were you to make your presentation?	1 2 3 4 5 6
How successful were you in adapting your written summary into a spoken presentation?	1 2 3 4 5 6
How clear and helpful were your visual aids?	1 2 3 4 5 6
Based on feedback from other members of the group, how well did you present your information?	1 2 3 4 5 6
How helpful was your feedback to the questions and presentations given by your classmates?	1 2 3 4 5 6
How successful were the group guidelines in ensuring that each presenter was treated respectfully?	1 2 3 4 5 6

For use with Speaking and Listening 6

Name _____ Date _____ Assignment _____

Performance Task 12A

Informational Text 3 Analyze how the author unfolds an analysis or series of
ideas or events, including the order in which the points are made, how they are
introduced and developed, and the connections that are drawn between them.*

Task: Analyze an Informational Text

Write a short essay about an informational text you have read that uses such expository techniques
as description, comparison and contrast, or cause and effect. Identify the main idea and explain
how the author uses one or more expository techniques to present the details that support his or her
main point.

Tips for Success

Write a short essay about an informational text you have read. In your essay, include these
elements:

✓ an analysis of the text's main idea and the author's use of details

✓ a thesis statement that succinctly sums up your analysis

✓ an understanding of the expository technique or techniques that the author
uses to present his or her supporting details

✓ explicit evidence from the text to support your thesis

✓ language that is formal, precise, and follows the rules of standard English

Rubric for Self-Assessment

Criteria for Success	not very very
How well have you explained the text's main point and supporting ideas?	1 2 3 4 5 6
How well have you analyzed the technique or techniques that the author uses to present ideas or events?	1 2 3 4 5 6
How successfully have you created one clear thesis statement of your analysis of the work?	1 2 3 4 5 6
How well have you supported the thesis with explicit evidence from the text?	1 2 3 4 5 6
How successfully have you used standard English?	1 2 3 4 5 6
How successfully have you created a formal style and appropriate tone for your audience?	1 2 3 4 5 6

*Other standards covered include: Writing 9b, Writing 10, Language 6, Speaking 6

For use with Informational Text 3

Name _____ Date _____ Assignment _____

Performance Task 12B

> **Speaking and Listening 4** Present information, findings, and supporting
> evidence clearly, concisely, and logically such that listeners can follow the
> line of reasoning and the organization, development, substance, and style are
> appropriate to purpose, audience, and task.

Task: Create an Informational Presentation

Participate in a group activity in which you and a few of your classmates produce a short informational presentation for the class about a subject of your choice. In your presentation, use one or more expository techniques to present the details that support your main idea, such as description, comparison and contrast, or cause and effect in a clear and logical manner.

Tips for Success

Work as a team to create an informational oral presentation. As a part of your participation, include these elements:

✓ agreement among all members of the group about the topic and organization
for the presentation

✓ with group members, agree on guidelines for equal and full participation of
each person

✓ a main idea and strong, clear supporting evidence

✓ well-chosen visual aids or handouts that help your audience follow your
presentation

✓ a tone and level of formality appropriate for your subject and your audience

Rubric for Self-Assessment

Criteria for Discussion	not very				very	
How successful was the group in establishing guidelines for the activity?	1	2	3	4	5	6
How well did the guidelines ensure that everyone would participate fully and equally?	1	2	3	4	5	6
How effective was the group in creating a main idea for the presentation?	1	2	3	4	5	6
How successful was the group in developing strong supporting evidence for the group's main idea?	1	2	3	4	5	6
To what extent did the group choose a tone and level of formality appropriate for the audience and subject matter?	1	2	3	4	5	6

Name _____ Date _____ Assignment _____

Performance Task 13A

> **Informational Text 4** Determine the meaning of words and phrases as they are used in a text, including figurative, connotative, and technical meanings; analyze the cumulative impact of specific word choices on meaning and tone (e.g., how the language of a court opinion differs from that of a newspaper).*

Task: Analyze Tone and Language

Write a response to an informational text in which you identify the tone and describe how the words and phrases the author uses help to shape that tone.

Tips for Success

In your response, include these elements:

- ✓ a clear thesis statement identifying the tone of the selection

- ✓ a description of the types of words and phrases used to describe people, places, or events in the selection

- ✓ a discussion of how the level of formality and language used in the selection help to establish its tone

- ✓ language that is formal, precise, and follows the rules of standard English

Rubric for Self-Assessment

Criteria for Success	not very very
How well have you described the tone of the text?	1 2 3 4 5 6
How well have you analyzed the content of the text?	1 2 3 4 5 6
How clearly have you demonstrated a connection between the author's use of words and phrases and the overall tone?	1 2 3 4 5 6
How successfully have you explained how the author's use of language helps to create a tone for the text?	1 2 3 4 5 6
To what extent have you used evidence from the text to support your analysis?	1 2 3 4 5 6
How successful is your use of standard English?	1 2 3 4 5 6
How successfully have you used a formal style and created an appropriate tone for your audience?	1 2 3 4 5 6

*Other standards covered include: Writing 9b, Writing 10, Language 5a, Language 5b, Language 6, Speaking 6

For use with Informational Text 4

Name _____ Date _____ Assignment _____

Performance Task 13B

> **Speaking and Listening 1** Initiate and participate effectively in a range of collaborative discussions (one-on-one, in groups, and teacher-led) with diverse partners on *grades 9 topics, texts, and issues*, building on others' ideas and expressing their own clearly and persuasively.

Task: Discuss the Responses to a Text

Participate in a discussion with a partner in which you explain your response to the tone and word choice of an informational text. Then, discuss the topic with a larger group.

Tips for Success

Participate in a discussion about a response to an informational text. As a part of your participation in the discussion, include these elements:

- ✓ an analysis of its tone and use of language

- ✓ guidelines for equal and full participation in the activity, including assignment of tasks and responsibilities

- ✓ questions that will evoke further discussion from participants and propel the discussion forward in order to explore the work fully

- ✓ inferences from the text that support the different points of view

- ✓ summaries of different responses to the text

- ✓ language that is formal, precise, and follows the rules of standard English

Rubric for Self-Assessment

Criteria for Discussion	not very				very	
How well did the participants seem to know the informational text?	1	2	3	4	5	6
How well did the participants think through their analyses of the text's tone and language?	1	2	3	4	5	6
How successfully did the group establish guidelines for the discussion to ensure everyone participated equally?	1	2	3	4	5	6
How successfully did participants ask thoughtful questions that helped explore different points of view?	1	2	3	4	5	6
How well did the discussion summarize the main perspectives of participants?	1	2	3	4	5	6
How polite and respectful of each other were the group participants?	1	2	3	4	5	6
How successful was your use of standard English?	1	2	3	4	5	6

For use with Speaking and Listening 1

Name _____ Date _____ Assignment _____

Performance Task 14A

> **Informational Text 5 Analyze in detail how an author's ideas or claims are developed and refined by particular sentences, paragraphs, or larger portions of a text (e.g., a section or chapter).***

Task: Respond to an Informational Text

Present a response to an informational text you have read and found persuasive. Identify the part of the text that you feel is the most persuasive and explain why it was effective.

Tips for Success

Present a response to an informational text you have read, such as a speech or persuasive essay. In your response, include these elements:

✓ an analysis of the text's content

✓ a clear statement of what you feel is the most persuasive element of the text

✓ evidence from the text that explicitly illustrates your thesis

✓ inferences from the text that support the opinions presented in your response

✓ language that is formal, precise, and follows the rules of standard English

Rubric for Self-Assessment

Criteria for Success	not very			very		
How thoroughly have you analyzed the text's content?	1	2	3	4	5	6
How successfully have you identified the most persuasive element of the text?	1	2	3	4	5	6
How clearly has your response explained your personal reaction to the text?	1	2	3	4	5	6
How well have you supported the thesis with explicit evidence from the text?	1	2	3	4	5	6
How successfully have you included inferences you made during reading to support your response?	1	2	3	4	5	6
How successful is your use of standard English?	1	2	3	4	5	6
How successfully have you used a formal style and creating an appropriate tone for your audience?	1	2	3	4	5	6

*Other standards covered include: Writing 2b, Writing 9b, Writing 10, Language 6, Speaking 6

For use with Informational Text 5

Name _____ Date _____ Assignment _____

Performance Task 14B

Speaking and Listening 1 Initiate and participate effectively in a range of collaborative discussions (one-on-one, in groups, and teacher-led) with diverse partners on *grades 9–10 topics, texts, and issues,* building on others' ideas and expressing their own clearly and persuasively.

Task: Discuss the Responses to a Text

Participate in a discussion with a partner in which you explain your response to an informational text. Focus on the element of the text that you felt made it persuasive. Finally, discuss the topic with a larger group. Respond thoughtfully to the points of view of others.

Tips for Success

Participate in a discussion about a response to an informational text, such as a speech, review, or an editorial. As a part of your participation in the discussion, include these elements:

✓ prepare your personal response to the informational text and your reasons for finding it persuasive.

✓ with group members, agree on guidelines for equal and full participation of each person.

✓ prepare questions to evoke further discussion from participants and propel the discussion forward.

✓ build on ideas of others during the discussion.

✓ take notes on different points of view presented in the analyses.

✓ summarize each group member's contribution to the discussion.

Rubric for Self-Assessment

Criteria for Discussion	not very			very		
How thoroughly did each participant seem to know the informational text?	1	2	3	4	5	6
How successful was the group at establishing guidelines for the discussion, and how fully did everyone participate?	1	2	3	4	5	6
How successful were participants at asking thoughtful questions that helped explore the analyses presented?	1	2	3	4	5	6
How well did participants offer different perspectives on the text and build on each other's ideas?	1	2	3	4	5	6
How polite and respectful of other points of view were the participants?	1	2	3	4	5	6

Name _____ Date _____ Assignment _____

Performance Task 15A

> **Informational Text 6** Determine an author's point of view or purpose in a text and analyze how an author uses rhetoric to advance that point of view or purpose.*

Task: Respond to Rhetoric in a Text

Write a response to an informational text you have read in which the author uses rhetoric to make a point. As part of your response, identify the author's thesis and evaluate the rhetoric he or she uses to advance that idea.

Tips for Success

Present a response to an informational text you have read. In your response, include these elements:

- ✓ a clear thesis statement in which you sum up your analysis of the author's point of view or purpose in writing the text

- ✓ a discussion of how the author uses such persuasive techniques as parallelism, restatement, repetition, or analogy

- ✓ an explanation of how the author uses language and sentence structure to create his or her voice

- ✓ evidence from the text that supports and illustrates your analysis

- ✓ language that is formal, precise, and follows the rules of standard English

Rubric for Self-Assessment

Criteria for Success	not very					very
How well does your thesis explain your analysis of the author's point of view or purpose?	1	2	3	4	5	6
How well have you identified and explained the rhetorical techniques the author uses?	1	2	3	4	5	6
How well have you identified and explained the ways in which the author uses language and sentence structure to create a unique voice?	1	2	3	4	5	6
How well have you supported your analysis with evidence from the text?	1	2	3	4	5	6
How successfully have you used standard English?	1	2	3	4	5	6
How successfully have you used a formal style and created an appropriate tone for your audience?	1	2	3	4	5	6

*Other standards covered include: Writing 9b, Writing 10, Language 5, Language 5a, Language 5b, Language 6, Speaking 6

For use with Informational Text 6

Name _____ Date _____ Assignment _____

Performance Task 15B

Speaking and Listening 1 Initiate and participate effectively in a range of collaborative discussions (one-on-one, in groups, and teacher-led) with diverse partners on *grades 9–10 topics, texts, and issues*, building on others' ideas and expressing their own clearly and persuasively.

Task: Discuss the Responses to a Text

Participate in a group discussion in which you explain your response to an informational text and respond thoughtfully to the point of view of others.

Tips for Success

Participate in a discussion about a response to a literary text. As a part of your participation in the discussion, include these elements:

✓ preparation by having read the informational text and thought through your analysis of the author's rhetoric and point of view

✓ guidelines agreed upon by other members in the discussion for equal and full participation

✓ questions that will evoke further discussion from participants and propel the discussion forward in order to explore the work fully

✓ inferences from the text that support the different points of view presented in the responses

✓ summaries of different responses to the text

Rubric for Self-Assessment

Criteria for Discussion	not very					very
How well had the participants thought through their analyses of the text before the discussion started?	1	2	3	4	5	6
How successful was the group in establishing guidelines to ensure everyone would participate in the discussion?	1	2	3	4	5	6
How successful were participants in asking thoughtful questions that helped explore the different points of view presented?	1	2	3	4	5	6
How well did the discussion summarize the main perspectives of the participants?	1	2	3	4	5	6
How polite and respectful were the participants?	1	2	3	4	5	6

Name _____ Date _____ Assignment _____

Performance Task 16A

Informational Text 7 Analyze various accounts of a subject told in different mediums (e.g., a person's life story in both print and multimedia), determining which details are emphasized in each account.*

Task: Compare and Contrast

Write a short essay comparing and contrasting two different accounts of the same subject presented in different mediums. As part of your essay, explain which details are emphasized in each account.

Tips for Success

Write a short essay comparing two informational texts on the same subject and include these elements:

✓ an analysis of the general similarities and differences between the two accounts

✓ an analysis of the similarities and differences in the way the subject is presented in the two media

✓ a clear thesis statement that sums up the conclusions you have drawn

✓ specific evidence from both accounts to support your thesis

✓ language that is formal, precise, and follows the rules of standard English.

Rubric for Self-Assessment

Criteria for Success	not very					very
How successfully have you created one clear statement of the conclusions you have drawn from the two accounts?	1	2	3	4	5	6
How well have you explained the general possibilities and limitations of the two mediums you analyzed?	1	2	3	4	5	6
How well have you explained which specific details were emphasized in the two different works?	1	2	3	4	5	6
How well have you supported your conclusion with explicit evidence from both works?	1	2	3	4	5	6
How have you included inferences you made during reading/ viewing to support your conclusions?	1	2	3	4	5	6
How successfully have you used a formal style, creating an appropriate tone for your audience, and used standard English?	1	2	3	4	5	6

*Other standards covered include: Writing 9b, Writing 10, Language 6, Speaking 6

Name _____ Date _____ Assignment _____

Performance Task 16B

> **Speaking and Listening 2** Integrate multiple sources of information presented in diverse media or formats (e.g., visually, quantitatively, orally) evaluating the credibility and accuracy of each source.

Task: Create a Comparison Chart

Participate in a group activity in which you create a chart or presentation that graphically represents the differences between two works that are in different media but are about the same subject. As you create the chart, try to think about the difference the medium makes when presenting information.

Tips for Success

Discuss as a group the two works and create a chart or presentation as the final product. As a part of your participation in the activity, include these elements:

✓ preparation by having read both works and thought through the similarities and differences between them

✓ analysis about why different details would be emphasized in different media

✓ guidelines agreed upon by the group for equal and full participation of each person

✓ careful thought and group discussion about what type of visual medium the team will need to represent the differences between the works

✓ a clear, easy-to-read chart or presentation as a final product

Rubric for Self-Assessment

Criteria for Discussion	not very					very
How well had the participants thought through the differences between the accounts in the two mediums before the discussion started?	1	2	3	4	5	6
How successful was the group in establishing guidelines for creating the chart or presentation?	1	2	3	4	5	6
How well did the guidelines ensure that everyone would participate fully and equally?	1	2	3	4	5	6
How successful were you in showing the differences and similarities of the details emphasized between the media?	1	2	3	4	5	6
How clear and readable was the final product?	1	2	3	4	5	6

For use with Speaking and Listening 2

Name _____ Date _____ Assignment _____

Performance Task 17A

> **Informational Text 8 Delineate and evaluate the argument and specific claims in a text, assessing whether the reasoning is valid and the evidence is relevant and sufficient; identify false statements and fallacious reasoning.***

Task: Evaluate an Argument

Write a short essay about an informational text you have read that presents an argument. As part of your response, analyze the author's argument and evaluate its reasoning and credibility.

Tips for Success

Write a short essay about an informational text you have read and analyze its argument. In your essay, include these elements:

- ✓ a clear thesis statement in which you sum up your analysis of the author's argument and credibility
- ✓ a discussion of whether the argument was clear, logical, and reasoned
- ✓ an explanation of whether or not the evidence presented was credible and comprehensive
- ✓ evidence from the text that supports and illustrates your analysis
- ✓ language that is formal, precise, and follows the rules of standard English

Rubric for Self-Assessment

Criteria for Success	not very					very
How well have you analyzed the reasoning and argument of the text?	1	2	3	4	5	6
How well does your thesis explain your analysis of the author's argument?	1	2	3	4	5	6
To what extent have you explained whether the argument was logical and well-reasoned?	1	2	3	4	5	6
How well have you identified and evaluated the evidence the author uses to support the argument?	1	2	3	4	5	6
How well have you used evidence from the text to support and illustrate your thesis?	1	2	3	4	5	6
How successfully have you used standard English?	1	2	3	4	5	6
How successfully have you used a formal style, creating an appropriate tone for your audience, and used standard English?	1	2	3	4	5	6

*Other standards covered include: Writing 9b, Writing 10, Language 6, Speaking 2, Speaking 3, Speaking 6

For use with Informational Text 8

Name _____ Date _____ Assignment _____

Performance Task 17B

Speaking and Listening 3 Evaluate a speaker's point of view, reasoning, and use of evidence and rhetoric, identifying any fallacious reasoning or exaggerated or distorted evidence.

Task: Evaluate Essays

Work with a partner to review and critique a short essay in which you analyze the reasoning and argument of an informational work. Read your essays aloud to each other and evaluate both how well you analyzed the text and the author's credibility.

Tips for Success

Participate in a partner activity where you critique an essay about the argument and reasoning in an informational text. As a part of your participation in the discussion, include these elements:

- ✓ preparation by having read the informational text and thought through your own analysis of it

- ✓ thoughtful attention to your partner's essay

- ✓ guidelines agreed upon by you and your partner for critiques

- ✓ questions that will evoke further discussion from your partner to explore the work fully

- ✓ a written outline of your evaluation of your partner's essay to supplement your verbal critique

Rubric for Self-Assessment

Criteria for Discussion	not very					very
How successful were you in evaluating whether your partner created one clear statement of his or her analysis of the text?	1	2	3	4	5	6
How well were you able to evaluate whether your partner's evaluation of the author was credible?	1	2	3	4	5	6
How successful were you in determining if the argument in your partner's essay was logical and well-reasoned?	1	2	3	4	5	6
How well could you determine if your partner was able to identify and evaluate the evidence the author uses to support the argument?	1	2	3	4	5	6
How well did your partner use quotes, facts, or ideas from the text to support and illustrate his or her thesis?	1	2	3	4	5	6
How successful was your partner in using standard English?	1	2	3	4	5	6

Name _____ Date _____ Assignment _____

Performance Task 18A

> **Informational Text 9** Analyze seminal U.S. documents of historical and literary significance (e.g., Washington's Farewell Address, the Gettysburg Address, Roosevelt's Four Freedoms speech, King's "Letter from Birmingham Jail"), including how they address related themes and concepts.*

Task: Analyze a Speech

Write a response to a speech that is significant in U.S. history. For your response, analyze the main theme or purpose of the speech and explain what images and details the speaker uses to convey that theme.

Tips for Success

Write a response to a speech you have read or heard. In your response, include these elements:

- ✓ an analysis of the speech's main idea and the details the speaker uses to support that idea

- ✓ an explanation of the rhetoric, figurative language, and expository techniques used to present the supporting details of the speech

- ✓ a thesis statement that succinctly sums up your analysis

- ✓ explicit evidence from the text to support your thesis

- ✓ language that is formal, precise, and follows the rules of standard English

Rubric for Self-Assessment

Criteria for Success	not very very
How well have you explained the text's main theme and supporting ideas?	1 2 3 4 5 6
How well have you analyzed the technique or techniques that the author uses to present the supporting details?	1 2 3 4 5 6
How successfully have you created one clear thesis statement of your analysis of the work?	1 2 3 4 5 6
How well have you explained the significance of the work?	1 2 3 4 5 6
How well have you supported the thesis with explicit evidence from the text?	1 2 3 4 5 6
How successfully have you used a formal style, creating an appropriate tone for your audience, and used standard English?	1 2 3 4 5 6

*Other standards covered include: Writing 7, Writing 9b, Writing 10, Speaking 6, Language 6

For use with Informational Text 9

Name _____ Date _____ Assignment _____

Performance Task 18B

> **Speaking and Listening 4** Present information, findings, and supporting evidence clearly, concisely, and logically such that listeners can follow the line of reasoning and the organization, development, substance, and style are appropriate to purpose, audience, and task.

Task: Give a Group Presentation

Participate in a group activity in which you do further research on the historical context and significance of a speech and create a group presentation that you give to the class.

Tips for Success

Participate in a group activity to create a group presentation. As a part of your participation in the activity, include these elements:

✓ further research on a speech or document, using credible, well-chosen sources

✓ guidelines agreed upon by other members of the group for equal and full participation

✓ clear point of view, organization, and line of reasoning for the presentation that have been agreed to by all members of the team

✓ tone that is appropriate for the presentation's subject and for your audience

Rubric for Self-Assessment

Criteria for Discussion	not very					very
How successful was the group in finding information about the history, context, and significance of the speech?	1	2	3	4	5	6
How well did the guidelines ensure that everyone would participate fully and equally?	1	2	3	4	5	6
How successful was the presentation team in organizing the information into a clear line of reasoning and point of view?	1	2	3	4	5	6
How successful was the presentation team in organizing the information to support one clear point of view?	1	2	3	4	5	6
How successful was the team in using formal language and an appropriate tone?	1	2	3	4	5	6

Name _____ Date _____ Assignment _____

Performance Task 19A

> **Informational Text 10** By the end of grade 9, read and comprehend literary
> nonfiction, in the grades 9–10 text complexity band proficiently, with scaffolding
> as needed at the high end of the range.

Task: Respond to an Independent Reading

Read a book of literary nonfiction listed for your class as independent reading. Then write a response to the book using textual evidence and inferences you have drawn from the text to support your analysis of it.

Tips for Success

Present a response to a work of literary nonfiction you have read outside of class. In your response, include these elements:

- ✓ a short summary of the work and an analysis of its contents
- ✓ a thesis statement that succinctly sums up your personal response to the work
- ✓ evidence from the text that explicitly supports the opinions you present
- ✓ inferences from the text that support the opinions presented in your response
- ✓ language that is formal, precise, and follows the rules of standard English

Rubric for Self-Assessment

Criteria for Success	not very					very
How well have you summarized the book and analyze its content?	1	2	3	4	5	6
How successfully have you created one clear statement of your response to the work?	1	2	3	4	5	6
How well does the thesis explain your feelings about the work?	1	2	3	4	5	6
How well have you included at least three or more quotes, facts, or ideas from the text to support your analysis?	1	2	3	4	5	6
How well have you supported the thesis with text evidence?	1	2	3	4	5	6
How successfully have you included inferences you made during reading to support your response?	1	2	3	4	5	6
How successfully have you used a formal style, creating an appropriate tone for your audience, and used standard English?	1	2	3	4	5	6

* Other standards covered include: Reading 1, Writing 9a, Writing 10, Speaking 5, Speaking 6, Language 6.

For use with Informational Text 10

Name _____ Date _____ Assignment _____

Performance Task 19B

> **Speaking and Listening 5** Make strategic use of digital media (e.g., textual, graphical, audio, visual, and interactive elements) in presentations to enhance understanding of findings, reasoning, and evidence and to add interest.

Task: Make a Presentation to a Small Group

Create a short presentation about a book you read, making use of digital media to illustrate your points. Make your presentation to a small group of your classmates. Listen thoughtfully as other members of the group make their presentations.

Tips for Success

Make a presentation to a small group about a book you have read and listen as others make their presentations. As a part of your participation, include these elements:

- ✓ preparation by having carefully reviewed your book and thought about ways to present it
- ✓ guidelines agreed upon by other members in the group for equal participation in the presentation
- ✓ presentation materials that are clear and engaging for your audience
- ✓ time allowed for feedback from the audience in the form of questions or comments
- ✓ attention to other members of the group as they make their presentations

Rubric for Self-Assessment

Criteria for Discussion	not very				very	
How prepared were you to make your presentation?	1	2	3	4	5	6
How successful was the group in establising guidelines for equal participation in the presentation?	1	2	3	4	5	6
How effective was the digital media used to create the presentation?	1	2	3	4	5	6
How clear and engaging were your presentation materials?	1	2	3	4	5	6
Based on feedback from your classmates, how well did you present your information?	1	2	3	4	5	6
How well did you listen to presentations by other groups?	1	2	3	4	5	6
How successful were the guidelines in ensuring that each presenter was treated respectfully?	1	2	3	4	5	6